Eco-Homiletics and the Craft of Narrative Preaching

Eco-Homiletics and the Craft of Narrative Preaching

T. Nzanthung Ngullie

Christian World Imprints

First Published in 2021 by

Christian World Imprints
Christian Publishing & Books from India
C-3, Wazirpur Industrial Area
Delhi-110052
cwidelhi2017@gmail.com
www.ChristianWorldImprints.com
Phone: +91 11 41526079

ISBN: 978-93-5148-447-9 (HB)
ISBN: 978-93-5148-448-6 (PB)

Printed in India.

Contents

Acknowledgements

At the outset, I give all glory and honour and thank the Almighty God for facilitating me to accomplish this humble project. Part of the book is an extract from my D.Th dissertation submitted to Senate of Serampore College (University). I thank the department of research/SATHRI, Senate of Serampore College (University) for granting me the opportunity to do my doctoral study program directly under SATHRI. I express my gratitude to the Principal, Tamilnadu Theological Seminary Arasaradi, Madurai for providing me the required family accommodation to do my residential doctoral studies in the campus. I sincerely thank the Library staff at Tamilnadu Theological Seminary, Madurai for their delightful cordiality and the valuable assistance given to me. I truly value their friendship and help.

I am extremely indebted to my mentor Rev. Dr. A. Alfred Stephen, Professor of Homiletics, Tamilnadu Theological Seminary Arasaradi, Madurai for transmuting to me his wealth of intellectual resources throughout my research work. I remain grateful to him for his ever willing heart to accommodate me in his intellectual journey; his spirit of excitement to share his resourceful insights without any reservation to me; his patience for bearing with my limitations and making every possible effort in shaping me to become a better human being at higher intellectual level.

I would like to mention in particular the Lotha Baptist Churches Association for their constant support and encouragement. I sincerely acknowledge the immense support and inexpressible help extended to me by my family members and relatives. I thank my loving parents, Thungbenshan Ngullie and Ntseno Ngullie, my brothers and sisters, my sister –in- laws and my brother- in-laws for their unceasing prayer support. I am ever grateful to my dear wife Nsungbeni N. Ngullie for shouldering untold pain and difficulties, for gracefully shouldering the responsibilities on my behalf, for sacrificing her precious time and opportunities, for her valuable words of encouragement and untiring support and for standing by me through the thin and thick stages of my hectic work. Finally, I thank my children for their cheerful companion and for being the source of my inspiration and delight. I dedicated this book to my wife, my sons Orhumthung and Fuchumo and my daughter Ekirhoni.

Preface

The pulpit can no longer deny or ignore its deepest responsibility of responding to the social realities of the human society. Pulpit must respond to the challenges of our time by concentrating on inventing and discovering homiletic theories and methodologies with the changes of time and space. In this book, I have argued against the traditional Christian understanding of human dominance over the natural world. Human beings are assumed in the Christian tradition to be isolated from the natural world especially through the misinterpretation of the word 'dominion' in the book of Genesis (cf. Gen.1:28). Perhaps this aspect of misinterpretation is explicitly explained in the first chapter of the book. I have approach ecology from a broader perspective of the whole *oikos* or the household of God. The arguments presented are not only for the survival of human beings and the future human generations but also for the myriad of other earthly creatures that co-exist with each other and the human beings on the planet earth. In a way, the book seeks to uncover the theological foundation for a proper relationship between God, humanity and the cosmos. I assume that it is possible to combine the environmental concern and an understanding of God, thus the word eco-theology was used. The book seeks to go beyond surface-level literature review and has sought to bring more theological discourses especially on the main tenets of faith.

Some of the books extensively have dwelled on eco-liberation and I consider those as very resourceful materials. Yet none of the books have specifically address issue on eco-homiletics. For instance, the work of Sigurd Bergmann marked a significant importance in the field of eco-liberation issues in the modern era. Bergmann in his book on *Creation set Free: The Spirit as Liberator of Nature* exemplified the survey of the historical initiatives toward an ecological theology and exposes Gregory of Nazianus' Trinitarian theology in the light of the historical initiatives. Bergmann then correlated the interpretation of Gregory into dialogue with the ecological theology of John Cobb, Jurgen Moltman, Christian Links, Gerhard Liedke, Salie McFague and Rosemary Ruether. Bergmann in his book tried to bridge the social movement of the Latin American liberation theology and the understanding of the Early Church and the Orthodox Church on the doctrine of physical redemption. All in all, Bergmann concern is on cosmology and soteriology. For him, redemption encompasses the whole cosmos and not only human salvation and thus he portrays that it is the Trinitarian Spirit that creates, liberates and redeems life.[1]

Jurgen Moltman famous work on *God on Creation: An Ecological Doctrine of Creation* also project pneumatology and ecology. He attributes the work of creation to the Trinitarian God and argues that God through His Spirit 'dwells in his creation as a whole and in every individual created being.'[2]

One of the well-known liberation theologian Brazilian Leonardo Boff, in his book *Ecology and Liberation: A New Paradigm* was more concern in doing ecology in terms of relations, interaction and dialogue of all the creatures. For him, relationship is central and nothing exists outside relationships. Boff then using this model of relationship reflected on human social structures and institutions. He critiques capitalism and power and opine for a participation

[1] For detail study see Sigurd Bergmann, *Creation Set Free: The Spirit as Liberator of Nature* (Grand Rapids: William B. Eerdmans Publishing Company, 2005). See also Travis E. Ables on the Review of Bergmann's *Creation Set Free: The Spirit as Liberator of Nature*, in the Journal for Cultural and Religious Theory vol. 8 no. 3 http://www.jcrt.org/archives/08.3/Ables.pdf (September 3, 2014).

[2] Jürgen Moltmann, *God in Creation: An Ecological Doctrine of Creation* (London: SCM Press Ltd, 1985), xii.

in ecological and theologically liberated life as God is present with the creation in mystery.[3] Boff extended his argument on liberation of the whole creation in his book *Cry of the Earth, Cry of the Poor.* He related the cry of the oppressed with the cry of the earth. The earth cries for liberation in the hand of the powerful exploits classes and few affluent and powerful countries. Boff show how human beings who are called to be the guardian angel of the cosmos can commit homicide and ethnocide as well as biocide and geocide.[4] Boff anticipates for a society of integration and harmony instead of dominance and division. He further challenges to perceive oneself as part of a cosmic community.

The purpose of this book is rather different from these scholarly works. The aim is to offer as resource book that seeks to evaluate the seriousness of the Biblical eco-theology. The book seeks for an active theological construction and move towards constructing the sermons on ecology. In a sermon construction, theological reflection plays a very important role and hence more active theological construction is sought.

The book has four elaborative chapters. The first chapter deals with the ecological crisis and the Biblical perspective on ecology. The beginning of ecological consciousness especially by Christianity was indicated briefly and the basic contemporary issues on ecology were discussed. The chapter raise environmental crisis and problem to set the stage for deeper theological discussion. Issues such as climate change were also included in the discussion. Such discussion was presented with the intention to give a flavour of the issues and problems for those who are new to the subject. On the other hand, the discussion might appear to be very basic yet they are the basis for which the contemporary ecological discourses emerged. In the Biblical perspective on ecology, I have rather limited the study by discussing some of the major ecological themes from the Bible. Theological dialogue on the main tenets of Christian faith

---

[3] Leonardo Boff, *Ecology and Liberation: A New Paradigm* (New York: Orbis Books, 1995), 32-36.

[4] Leonardo Boff, *Cry of the Earth, Cry of the Poor* (New York: Orbis Books,1997), xi.

such as eco- Christology, eco-eschatology, etc., were all deliberated elaborately in the chapter.

A thoroughly all-round, satisfying, well-proportioned and a comprehensive history of preaching have not yet been sufficiently written. I do not limit the valuable resources available on the history of preaching and I am indebted to those authors for their contributions. Indeed I have referred to the books that are available for supplementing my arguments. Nevertheless, it was a challenging task for me to concretely and systematically write about homiletic methodologies throughout the centuries. The second chapter of the book discloses about the historical, theological and homiletic developments throughout the ages.

The third chapter presents the various homiletical theories in the recent homiletic academia. The influence and relationship of the Aristotelian rhetoric with homiletics was also briefly discussed. In the fourth chapter, I have move towards explaining the narrative method for preaching on ecology.

My intention is to open up the field of eco-homiletics so that others will be encouraged to venture and produce more literatures to enhance eco-homiletics. I hope that the book will encourage the readers to engage in active reflection and positive action.

Chapter 1

The Environmental Problem and Crisis Biblical Perspectives on Ecology

1. Etymology and Definition

In 1859, St. Hilaire Isodore Geoffory, a French Zoologist suggested the word 'ethology' for the study of the relationship between organisms and their environment. In the same way in 1894, British Naturalist, St. George Jakson Mivart also used the word 'hexicology' for the study of the same.[5] However, the word ecology was first generated in 1866 by Darwinian Ernst Haeckel a German biologist, from the Greek word *oikos* which means 'house,' referring literally to the house of all living creatures on the earth and their relations and interdependence. The understanding on ecology was later widened by a geographer Eugenius Warming who published writings on plant ecology in 1895. Later, in 1928 Walter Johnson first established the co-relation between the meaning of ecology and economy.[6] The

[5] H. M. Saxena, *Enviromental Studies* (Jaipur: Rawat Publications, 2006), 6.

[6] Anna Bramwell, *Ecology in the 20th Century A History* (London: Yale University Press, 1992), 41.

term 'ecology' etymologically means "the study of the conditions and relations that make up habitat (the house) of each and every person and, indeed, organism in nature."[7] Ecology was first understood as subheading in the study of biology by Ernst Haeckel, yet the understanding spread deep and wide. Eventually, ecology became an important subject of study for the whole cosmos.[8] The study of ecology encompasses four areas namely atmosphere, hydrosphere, lithosphere and the biosphere.[9]

Odum defines ecology "as the study of the relations of organisms or groups of organisms to their environment, or the science of the interrelations between living organisms and their environment"[10] Ecology in a nutshell can be referred to the study of the connections and intimacy between the living organism and the environment in which they lives.[11] The important thing in ecology is not a simple study of the life and existence of different plants and species but it is the study of the relationship, interconnections and interdependencies between the living organisms.

---

[7] Sebastain. Kochupurackal, *Eco-Mission: A Paradigm Shift in Missiology* (Bangalore: Asian Trading Corporation, 2007), 60.

[8] Leonardo Boff, *Cry of the Earth, Cry of the Poor* (New York: Orbis Books, 1997), 2.

[9] David L. Gosling, *Religion and Ecology in India and Southeast Asia* (London: Routledge, 2001), 5. The atmosphere is the body of air which surrounds our planet. Most of our atmosphere is located close to the earth's surface where it is most dense. The air of our planet is 79% nitrogen and just under 21% oxygen; the small amount remaining is composed of carbon dioxide and other gasses. The lithosphere is the solid, rocky crust covering entire planet. This crust is inorganic and is composed of minerals. It covers the entire surface of the earth from the top of Mount Everest to the bottom of the Mariana Trench. The hydrosphere is composed of all of the water on or near the earth. This includes the oceans, rivers, lakes, and even the moisture in the air. Ninety-seven per cent of the earth's water is in the oceans. The remaining three per cent is fresh water; three-quarters of the fresh water is solid and exists in ice sheets. The biosphere is composed of all living organisms. Plants, animals, and one-celled organisms are all part of the biosphere. *http://www.geography. about.com.* (August 13, 2016).

[10] H. M. Saxena, *Enviromental Studies* (Jaipur: Rawat Publications, 2006), 7.

[11] Kochupurackal, *Eco-Mission*..., 60.

In the 1860s for Haeckel initially ecology was a branch of biology, yet today the understanding and definition of ecology has also broaden along with the changes of time. Ecology has become an important subject of discussion for the global community because it has threatened the survival of human communities, nature (living and non-living) and the entire ecosystem; it includes the rich, the poor, and the marginalized. Therefore, as suggested by Brazilian liberation theologian Leonardo Boff, the definition of ecology on the independence and interaction has to be extended from nature to culture and society inculcating such as human ecology, social ecology[12] and others.[13] Ecology helps human community to understand how every organism both living and non-living interact with each other. The important concept in the study of ecology today is the interrelatedness and interdependence of all the creation.

2. The Origin and History of Ecological Development

The origin and history of ecological consciousness is not very well developed and as such not much is known about its proper beginning. Ecology became a major importance of subject only after the amalgamation of the science and technology by the Western Europeans and the North Americans. Even though the concept and the word ecology appeared in English literature only in 1866, the crisis on environmental pollution can be trace back to the 13th century. In fact as early as 1285, London had a pollution problem from the burning of the soft coal.[14] Lynn White, Jr. in a critic to ecological crisis states that, "When the first cannons were fired, in the early 14th century, they affected ecology by sending workers scrambling to the forests and mountains for more potash, sulphur, iron ore, and charcoal, with some resulting erosion and deforestation."[15] Eventually by the end of the 15th century the European world with

---

[12] I will further discuss the social ecology in detail in the later part of the writings.

[13] Leonardo Boff, *Ecology and Liberation: A New Paradigm* (Maryknoll: Orbis Books, 1995), 9.

[14] Lynn White, Jr., "The Historical Roots of Our Ecological Crisis," http://www.siena.edu/ellard/historical_roots_of_our_ecologic.htm. (November 13, 2015)

[15] White, Jr., "The Historical Roots of Our Ecological...

their technological superiority were able to establish their dominance to the rest of the world through conquering and colonizing.[16]

Until the year 1972, the matter of discussion on ecology was confined within the periphery of biological scientific discipline. The awareness of ecological crisis came into urgent consciousness in 1972, in the report of a widely known Club of Rome[17] called *The Limits to Growth.*[18] The *Limits to Growth* examined major trends on the increasing industrialization, population growth, prevalent malnutrition, exhaustion of renewable resources and decaying environment. The findings call for a radical reform in the existing policies on growth and development and work towards creating a state of global equilibrium.[19] By the middle of the 1980's ideas of addressing the ecological issues became dominant. The ecological imbalance is a result of human greed and wants. Boff citing Gandhi said, "The earth is sufficient for everyone's needs but not for everyone's greed."[20] Almost all the cultures and customs know the value of nature and the role of biodiversity in human societies. Yet because of the greed for power and dominance, the common understanding on the importance of nature cannot be made more realistic.[21] According to the United Nations Department of Economic and social affairs in 2010, the world population was 6.919 billion. Later the United States Census Bureau estimated in March 2012 that the world's population is more than 7 billion and at this rate, the world population is expected to cross 9 billion by 2050. The global human population growth is around 75 million annually which is 1.1% growth per year.[22] On the other hand the food production rate

---

[16] White, Jr., "The Historical Roots of Our Ecological...

[17] A club of more or less prominent figures from business, policy-making, and science.

[18] Leonardo Boff, *Cry of the Earth...*, 105.

[19] Maarten A. Hajer, *The Politics of Environmental Discourse: Ecological Modernization and the Policy Process* (Oxford: Clarendon Press, 2000), 80.

[20] Boff, *Cry of the Earth...*, 3.

[21] Anup Shah, "Environmental issues," http://www.globalissues.org/issue/168/environmental-issues. (November 16, 2015).

[22] "World Population," http://www.en.wikipedia.org/wiki/Population_growth (November 16, 2015).

is 0.9 % -1.6% and by current production rate, the food production rate will not meet the human's need by 2050.[23]

2.1. Eco-Theology: A Glimpse of Development Throughout the Ages in the Church's History

2.1.1. The Early Church Fathers

The early Christian communities might not have dealt extensively in relation to nature, human and God. However, the writer wants to re-visit the theology of Trinitarian interpretation by some of the early church theologians where they have linked their interpretation of Trinity to the development of eco-theology. The term such as eco-theology were not formulated as such yet a deep sense of ecological understanding were reflected in their theology of creation. The epoch of the early Christian church was a period of serious thinking and formulation of various theologies. The early Church fathers had a logical and serious theology on creation. This logical interpretation on creation has been a source for drawing inspiration for the modern theological community and also an interesting area of research as well. By the beginning of the third century, in the text of *The Apostolic Tradition of Hippolytus,* the early Christians were encouraged to pray along with the celestial body like the stars, the natural creation like the forests and the waters.[24] In the second half of the fourth century three prominent theologian of Cappadocia, Basil of Caesarea (ca.330-379), Gregory of Nyssa (ca.330-395), and Gregory of Nazianzus (ca.330-389) developed theology of the Holy Spirit and the Trinity. It was in the context of high imperial taxation especially on land, unjust dissemination of land and unjust social order the Cappadocian fathers wrote their creation theology. They explained the Triune God as united, equal and they are in profound communion (*koinonia)* with each other. The Trinity is always in relationship

[23] "Current global food production trajectory won't meet 2050 needs," http://www.sciencedaily.com/releases/2013/06/130619195135.htm (November 13, 2015).

[24] Celia Deane – Drummond, *Eco – Theology* (London: Darton, Longman and Todd Ltd, 2008), 58.

and thus the Cappadocian theologians assumed God as Persons-in-Communion, a being of relations.[25] The Cappadocian explains creation theology as the expansion of the Trinity or the Divine Community. The communion (*koinonia*) is thus extended to all the creatures and the purpose of the perfect unity of the Godhead is to let the entire cosmos participate in the perfect community of the Triune God.[26] Gregory of Nyssa in his interpretation on the Trinity in relation to creation takes Psalm 33:6[27] as the point of reference. For them everything is created through the Son because Jesus Christ who is the eternal *logos* where everything is preceded from the word.[28] Another early Church theologian whose work and interpretation of the Godhead Trinity includes love and care for the other creation is Augustine (354-430). Augustine did not teach on the intrinsic relationship of the natural world and human beings but advocated community of goods. The earth's resources belong to everyone and one must be responsible enough to use diligently and preserve for the future generations.[29]

One of the major developments of the early church fathers on Christian faith was the formulation of the Nicene Creed. The Creed acknowledges the Father, Son as well as the Holy Spirit as the Creator of all life; it refers to the creation of biological life. Thus, for the early Church fathers creation is a holistic activity of the Trinitarian God where the Father creates through the Son in the power of the Holy Spirit.[30]

---

[25] Denis Edwards, Ecology at the Heart of Faith (Maryknoll: Orbis Books, 2008), 68-69.

[26] Sigurd Bergmann, Creation Set Free: The Spirit as Liberator of Nature, translated by Douglas Stott (Grand Rapids: William B. Eerdmans Publishing Company, 2005), 83-84.

[27] By the word of the Lord the heavens were made, and all their host by the breath of his mouth. See The Holy Bible, NRSV (Grand Rapids: Zondervan, 1989), 441.

[28] Per Larsson, "Your Will be Done on Earth..." *Ecological Theology for Asia: An Ecumenical Textbook for Theological Schools* (Hong Kong: Clear-Cut Publishing & Printing Co., 2004), 60.

[29] Hart, "Catholocism," *The Oxford Handbook..., 68.*

[30] Larsson, "Your Will be Done on Earth..." *Ecological Theology for Asia...*, 63.

2.1.2. The Middle Ages

In the beginning of the Middle Ages theologians like Maximus the Confessor (580-662 A.D) further developed theology relating human beings as part of the entire creation of God. The grace of God is extended to the human beings and the whole creation alike.[31] Maximus theology of creation proposes that the whole universe is originated with God out of His loving kindness. In his creation theology Maximus located human beings at the centre of creation and considers humans as priestly mediators between God and creation. However, he rejects the attitude of anthropocentrism and proposes theocentricism. He further explains that created beings are interrelated to each other.[32] In his notion of the natural world as expression of *logos* and *logoi,* Maximus stress on the notion that the logoi or God's words as transcendent yet immanent in other words the *logoi* are pre-existent but manifested in the natural order.[33]

One of the most prominent personality in relation to the love of all creation was Francis of Assisi (1182-1226) who considers all creation either living or non-living as brother or sister. He lived his life exhibiting a deep sense of kinship with all the creation. Francis deepest concern and love for the entire creation was expressed in his best-known work 'Canticle of Brother Sun' or 'Canticle of Creation' or 'Canticle of All Creatures.'[34] In the 13th century Thomas Aquinas (1225 – 1274) followed the path and interpretation of St. Augustine.

---

[31] Larsson, "Your Will be Done on Earth…" *Ecological Theology for Asia…*, 63.

[32] Radu Bordeianu, "Maximus And Ecology: The Relevance of Maximus The Confessor's Theology of Creation For The Present Ecological Crisis," http://www.duq.edu/documents/theology/_pdf/faculty.../art-mordeianu-max.pd. (December 05, 2015).

[33] Deane – Drummond, *Eco – Theology* …, 61.

[34] Most High, all-powerful, and all good Lord, praise, glory, honor, and blessing are yours.

To you alone, Most High, they belong, although no one is worthy to say your name.

Praise be my Lord, with all your creatures, especially my lord Brother Sun,
Through whom you give us day and light.
Beautifully he shines with great splendour: Most High, he bears your likeness.
Praise be my Lord, by Sister Moon and Stars: in the heavens you made them bright and precious and beautiful.

For him, God is understood as a vibrant self-communicator who relates with His creations.[35]

2.1.3. Reformatory Age

Martin Luther thought on eco-theology are explicitly visible in his explanation of the beginning section of the Apostle's Creed. For Luther creation are in the truest sense the revelations of God. In the creation, human beings are to live as co-workers of God. Creation is a continued process and human beings are to become an agent in participating in the 'renewing and development work of God'[36] on creation. Luther "depicts God as being with all creatures, flowing, and pouring into them, filling all things....When I truly grasp the significance of the incarnation of the Son of God in this world all creatures will appear a hundred times more beautiful to me than before."[37]

John Calvin theology on nature some how goes deeper than Martin Luther. For Luther the Word of God directly speaks to us while for Calvin the Word of God is a lens through which one can seek and understand God. John Calvin understands creation as 'the theatre of God's glory'[38] where one can contemplate God in and

---

Praise be my Lord, by Brother wind, and air and cloud and calm and all weather through which you sustain your creatures.

Praise be my Lord, by Sister Water, who is so helpful and humble and precious and pure.

Praise be my Lord, by Brother Fire, through whom you brighten the night: who is beautiful and playful and sinuous and strong.

Praise be my Lord, by our Sister Mother Earth, who sustains us and guides us, and provides varies fruits with colourful flowers and herbs.

Praise and blessed be you, my Lord, and gratitude and service be given to you with great humility.

See Hart, "Catholocism," *The Oxford Handbook...*, 69-70.

[35] Edwards, *Ecology At The Heart of Faith...*, 70.

[36] Larsson, "Your Will be Done on Earth..." *Ecological Theology for Asia...*, 69.

[37] H. Paul Santmire and John B. Cobb Jr., "The World of Nature According to the Protestant Tradition," *The Oxford Handbook of Religion and Ecology*, ed., Roger S. Gottlieb (New York: Oxford University Press, 2006), 119.

[38] Santmire and John B. Cobb Jr., "The World of Nature According to the Protestant..., 121.

through these creations, the God who is invisible. The beauties of nature are in fact the manifestation and revelation of God's invisible image and His glory. H. Paul Santmire and John B. Cobb Jr., citing Calvin's interpretation on the theology of nature shows:[39]

> In grasses, trees, and fruits, apart from their various uses, there is the beauty of appearance and pleasantness of odor. For if this were [was] not true, the prophet would not have reckoned them among the benefits of God, "that wine gladdens the heart of man and oil makes his face to shine...." Has the Lord clothed the flower with the great beauty that greets our eyes, the sweetness of smell that is wafted upon our nostrils, and yet will it be unlawful for our eyes to be affected by that beauty or our sense of smell by the sweetness of that odor? What? Did he not endow gold and silver, ivory and marble, with a loveliness that renders them more precious than other metals or stones? Did he not, in short, render many things attractive to us from their necessary use?

2.2. India's Ecological History

The Indian environmental degradation can be trace back to the British colonial history in India.[40] Aruna Gnanadason while citing Gadgil and Guha explains that, "World ecology has been profoundly altered by Western capitalism, in whose dynamic expansion other ecosystems were disrupted, first through trade and later by colonialism. Not only did such interventions virtually reshape the social, ecological and demographic characteristics of the habitats they intruded upon, they also ensured the ensuing changes that primarily benefit Europe."[41] The industrial revolution in Europe has wide consequences in the ecological state in India.

---

[39] Santmire and John B. Cobb Jr., "The World of Nature According to the Protestant..., 121-122.

[40] Aruna Gnanadason, "Women, Patriarchy and Creation: Insights from Eco-Feminism," *Green Theology*, ed., Wati Longchar (Kolkata: SCEPTRE, 2014), 85.

[41] Gnanadason, *Green Theology*..., 85.

For instance natural resources were made to view only as objects or commodities for making profits. Thus, wood which normally served in domestic fuel and shelter were transformed into paper and were burnt as fuel for various mechanical transport systems. On the other hand, the British colonial government acquired legal license by the Indian Forest Act of 1865 and 1878 respectively and manipulated the Indian 'reserved forests.' The British colonial government devastated the remote tense forest regions particularly the trees such as teak, *sal* and cedar. The Indian forests were replaced by species of trees which has commercial values and as such varieties of tree species were eventually uprooted and vanished. For instance, the Himalayas had trees species of conifers and others which are useful for sieving and regulating rainwater. But, the rest of the trees were replaced with conifers which had commercial value.[42] It is recorded that during the First World War (1914-1919) 1.7 million cubic feet of timber was exported to Britain and in the Second World War (1939-1945), 909,000 tons of timber had been supplied to the British defence department. This supply of timber was carried out at the range of severe deforestation in India which was done forcefully without any concern for communities whose livelihood was depended on the forest. The indigenous people's rights were ignored and their customary law which governs the use of forest were forcefully neglected.[43] When the British colonized India in the late eighteenth and early nineteenth century, India was in a position of substantial surplus agricultural product. However, the agricultural products was reduced to a large extend by 1920. With the increase of population serious deficit was developed. Also as mentioned in the above lines the Indian forest and resources had been seriously exhausted by the two World Wars. So, when the British colonial system left India in 1947, India was at a low point in terms of resources and agricultural production.[44] By large the European industrial energy system was responsible for the early

[42] Gosling, *Religion and Ecology in India…*, 35.

[43] Gnanadason, *Green Theology…*, 85

[44] Madhav Gadgil and Ramachandra Guha, *Ecology and Equity: The Use and Abuse of Nature in Contemporary India* (New Delhi: Penguin Books, 1995), 12-13.

large scale deforestation in India.[45] After the Independent India, unfortunately the government rejected Mahatma Gandhi's ideology and followed the model of 'forestry for industry' and continued to import trees. This was done to sustain the development model of the country yet sadly it resulted in the destruction of nature and the natural resources.[46] The Independence the Prime Minister Jawaharlal Nehru followed the capitalistic development model considering the dams as the modern temples of the nation. As cited by P. R. Trivedi and Gurdeep Raj, on the event of commissioning Nagarjuna Sagar project in Andhra Pradesh one of the local farmers expresses his lament to the then Prime Minister Jawaharlal Nehru as "You lighted a lamp in our homes, little knowing that his children were soon to suffer from a disease called Knock-knee; the disease had been traced to a change in the fluoride content of the fields that came to be irrigated soon afterwards.[47] India by 1970s had begun to have established environmental organizations to combat destruction of the environment. Most of the environmental movements are centred on the protection of forest and waters. The movements opposed deforestation from commercial logging and construction of the big dams. One of such movements on deforestation was the Chipok movement in 1973, at the central Himalayas where the movement successfully stopped the commercial timber logging. The other movement is the well Narmada Bachao Andolan, a movement that protest against the building of a big dam project. This project would displace and relocate more than 100000 people especially the tribal.[48]

Today survey shows that India today has become one of the leading highly polluted nations in the world. *The Hindu* (Madurai) newspaper on April 7, 2015 reported that the survey of the Environmental Preference Index in 2014 has ranked India 174 out

---

[45] Gosling, *Religion and Ecology in India…*, 36.

[46] Gnanadason, *Green Theology…*, 86.

[47] R. R. Trivedi and Gurdeep Raj, eds., *Environmental Ecology* (New Delhi: Akashdeep Publishing House,1992), 191.

[48] Knut A. Jacobsen, "India," *The Encyclopedia of Religion and Nature,* Bron R. Taylor et al. (London: Thoemmes Continuum, 2005), 826-827.

of 178 countries for air quality. It is also reported that the survey of World Health Organization on 1,600 cities in the world confirms Delhi as the world's most polluted capital. Another survey of WHO in 2014 found that out of the world's 20 most polluted cities, 13 cities are identified in India.[49]

3. Ecology in Dialogue with Religion

What is religion? How does one defines religion? Religion can be understood in one's personal conviction or acceptance of God or it might be a matter of faith that connects a person to God. I will like to put forth the definition of the holiness Dalai Lama on religion.[50] On the question on what is the best religion? He answered, "The best religion is that one that gets you closest to God. It is that makes you a better person." He was asked again what is that makes me better? He replied, "Whatever makes you more compassionate, more sensible, more detached, more loving, more humanitarian, more responsible, more ethical."[51] Perhaps the answers of Dalai Lama ushers insightful reflection on human beings relationship to the natures. A more directional definition in relation between religion and ecology is noted in the writings of Sarkar as he cites C. A. Caulson book on *Science and Christian belief.* He defines religion as, "the total response of a man [human] to all his [their] environment."[52] It is a definite truth that world of religions have been active in formulating views on human relationships to nature. As such critically reviewing the world religious view especially on ecological issues and concerns is vital so as to propose a substantial solution for the alarming ecological crisis today. With the limitation of space, I will not be able to deal extensively with all the religious traditions more so this is also not the main focus of the chapter.

---

[49] *The Hindu* (Madurai) April 7, 2015. 1.

[50] It was said on the occasion of a personal interview to the holiness Dalai Lama by Leonardo Boff, a Latin American Liberation theologian in March 2012.

[51] Leonardo Boff, "The Dalai Lama on Religion," *Meetings Rivers: Reflections On Culture, Religion And Ecology*, ed., Siddhartha (Bangalore: A Meeting Rivers Publication, 2014), 15.

[52] R. L. Sarkar, *The Bible, Ecology and Environment* (Delhi: ISPCK, 2000), 74.

I herewith outlines in a nutshell how ecological concerns are deeply embedded in each religious tradition. For human beings our religion shapes and directs the most part of our perceptions and perspectives. Our religious beliefs system, rituals, practices and moral teachings controls us with the way we relate ourselves to the surroundings and the earth.[53] Perhaps human beings were created by God to live in relation with the natural surroundings and to depend on the nature for food, water, air and other needs. Religious teaching always does include values on nature and concern on humans' relationship and attitude towards nature. The Bible does have concrete teaching on ecology; human interdependence and relationship to nature. For the indigenous religion the earth and the natural world cannot be separated from their religious beliefs and practices since they are so closely embedded to the natural world. Daoism include humans and part of nature, Hinduism considers the entire cosmos as God and Buddhism equality of all – human and the natural world alike. Thus, ecology and religion are always in dialogue with each other. It is important here to review the ecological concerns expressed by four world religions during the World Wildlife Federation's Twenty-fifth Anniversary celebration in Assisi Italy. From Buddhism Lungrig Nomgayal expresses that Buddhism is a religion known for its propagation on love, compassionate and non-violence. Thus, Buddhism is also committed towards healthy relationship with the environment that surrounds. Just as human kind inherits the undeniable right to live so also the other species have the right for survival. Karan Singh representing Hinduism enlightened that the Hindu scriptures such as the Vedas, Upanishads, the Puranas and others have explicit teaching on reverence for each life and the web of relationship between natures, animals and humanity. Hinduism upholds the earth as mother and the entire creation as children. The Muslims believe in unity, trusteeship and accountability as put forward by Abdullah Omar Nassef. He further affirms that the Quran teaches

---

[53] Roger S. Gottlieb, "Introduction: Religion and Ecology-What is the Connection and Why Does it Matter?" *The Oxford Handbook of Religion and Ecology*, ed., Roger S. Gottlieb (New York: Oxford University Press, 2006), 3.

and encourages living a life of charity. For a Muslim if one plants a tree where human beings, animals and birds can depend on it, they regard it as charity. Earth is to be taken care as good stewards of God. Arthur Hertzberg opined that Judaism teaches that man was accorded dominion over nature but were commanded to exercise justice and compassion for all creation.[54] Roger S. Gottlieb citing Bartholomew, a spiritual leader of an orthodox Christians stated that, "To commit a crime against the natural world is a sin... to cause species to become extinct and to destroy the biological diversity of God's creation... to degrade the integrity of the earth by causing changes in its climate, stripping the Earth of its natural forests, or destroying its wetlands...to contaminate the Earth's waters, its air, and its life with poisonous substances – these are sins."[55] Religious consciousness for the environmental sacredness cannot assure success over the ecological crisis yet it perhaps can help in sustaining the future of the global community. Religion and ecology recognises the commonality as both the subject deals with God's creation and their relations. As such it can fuse together in developing a model that can work together towards addressing ecological agendas in a deeper interrelated ways and means.[56]

4. Causes of Ecological Crisis

4.1. Population and Consumption

Population growth perhaps is one of the many factors behind the ecological crisis in the world as the earth resources and energy is increasingly become insufficient to meet the needs of the global growing population. Celia Deane-Drummond citing one of the writers in the 1960s Paul Ehrlich on human population writes that population growth can be compared to a bomb that will very soon inflict devastation on the existence and survival of human beings on

---

[54] Nancy G.Wright and Donald Kill, *Ecological Healing: A Christian Vision* (Maryknoll: Orbis Books, 1993), 136-138.

[55] Gottlieb, "Introduction: Religion and Ecology..., 13.

[56] R. L. Sarkar, *The Bible, Ecology and Environment* (Delhi: ISPCK, 2000), 72.

the earth.[57] The world Global issues statistics shows that each year nearly half i.e., 45% of deaths in children under five are caused by poor nutrition.[58] Every day more than 805 million people continue to struggle with hunger and 1.2 billion people still live in extreme poverty line. Every year more than 2.6 million children die in the world as a result of hunger related causes.[59] Exactly today record shows that human population is growing very rapidly and becoming as one of the agents for environmental degradation. The human population in the world today is more than 7 billion and the birth rate is increasing along with the ticking of the clock in the global world. Most of the countries in the world are trying way and means to decline the birth rate and stabilized the population growth. Yet this process has not declined much in the population growth. The ecological global network reported (2011 estimate) that there are four birth each second and nearly two people dies each second. Each minutes 250 birth takes place and 105 people die each minute, in one hour there are 15,000 births and 6,316 people dies each hour, there are 360,000 births per day while 151,600 people die each day. In a year the birth rate is 131.4 million while the death rate is 55.3 million.[60] Historical survey on population reveals that in the year 1650 human population was 0.5 billion with the growth rate of 0.3 per year. Eventually by the year 1900 the world's population increased to 1.6 billion with the growth rate of 0.5 per year. After seventy years in 1970 the world population increased to 3.6 billion with 2.1 growth rate per year. By 1991, the human population exceeded 5 billion to be specific 5.4 billion and by 2010 the human population has already exceeded 7 billion.[61] The United Nations has projected that by the current population growth the world human

---

[57] Deane – Drummond, *Eco – Theology* ..., 1.

[58] Anup Shah "Today, Around 21,000 Children Died Around the World," http://www.globalissues.org›Issues›Articles (November 16, 2015).

[59] "About Global Hunger," http://www.bread.org›About Hunger (November 13, 2015).

[60] "Birth *and Death Rates,"* http:/www.ecology.com/birth-death-rates/ (November 13, 2015).

[61] Ramprasad Sengupta, *Ecology and Economics: An Approaches to Sustainable Development* (New Delhi: Oxford University Press, 2009), 101.

population will certainly reach 9 billion by 2050.[62] However, in spite of the recent precautions and measures to stabilize the global population growth, one does not notice in quick decline because of the phenomenon of demographic momentum.[63]

The increase in population may not directly lead to environmental problem and crisis yet it definitely locates a liability to the earth's ecosystem. The migration of certain groups of people from rural areas to densely populated urban cities could perhaps demonstrate practices of ecological destructive cycles. For instance in search for alternative living poor people's migration to the urban cities increases the slum areas on the land, forest are burned or cut down, and the soils are used exhaustively until it cannot be used further.[64] As the population increases consumption on the energy sources and even the natural resources will escalation. However it is observed that the rate of consumption is extremely high in the rich countries then the developing and the underdeveloped countries. This is criticised not only for the amount of ecological degradation but also for the injustice as rightly observed by James B. Martin-Schramm and Robert L. Stivers.[65] The World Resource Institute report on the survey of emissions from 1850 to 2007 shows that USA 28.8%, China 9.0%, Russia 8.0%, Germany 6.9% and U.K. 5.8%. India emission percentage is only 2.44%. Now comparatively the population of the USA is only one fourth of the population of India but the emission percentage is incomparable higher than India. This is what injustice is about in relation to global warming and climate change. The effect of climate change cause by the rich developed countries have to be bore by a poor slum dwellers and

---

[62] James B. Martin-Schramm and Robert L. Stivers, *Christian Environmental Ethics: A Case Method Approach* (Maryknoll: Orbis Books, 2003), 11.

[63] Demographic momentum is such that you can't simply change something overnight. Whatever goal you might set, you have to start doing something about it about a generation ahead of time. http://www.encyclo.co.uk/meaning-of-Demographic%20momentum.

[64] Martin-Schramm and Robert L. Stivers, *Christian Environmental Ethics*..., 11.

[65] Martin-Schramm and Robert L. Stivers, *Christian Environmental Ethics*..., 12.

people in the streets who neither knows nor use any scientific tools that contributes to global warming.

The world in spite of the huge production still could not eradicate hunger and poverty because of the system of distribution. Survey on food grain production shows that food grain production fall to a minim level from 1869 million tons in 1999 to 1840 million tons in 2000. However the production steadily increased and in 2005 the food grain production was measured to 2015 million tons. It is disheartening to notice that more than four million people live on less than 2 dollars a day while 20% of the world population is consuming the earth's resources and energy. By 2032 it is projected that 50% of the world population will face fresh water crisis as to the existing 40%. In the world it is estimated that every year more than 3.4 million people die of water related diseases which is mostly to do with the inadequate sanitation. The use of fossil fuel has increased to three and half times more than that of 1950 reaching to 3.8 billion tons (83.3 million barrels) a day. According to the survey in 2005, the largest consumer of fossil fuel is USA at 20.8 million barrels a day, the second is Europe with 15.6 million barrel a day, China 6.6 barrels a day and Japan 5.4 million barrels a day.[66]

The visible alternative solution to protect the environmental degradation is to adopt production and consumption which will have less effect on the global ecosystem. But, the solution is made vulnerable with the question whether if it will be sufficient or not[67] with such system of control protection and also consumption. Even if the production may increase unless the production is equally distributed through proper system, the global community will have to wrestle with the environmental issues.

4.2. Mechanical and Technological Developments

The major cause of ecological destruction can be trace back to the invention of machineries. The technological advancement has used

---

[66] Celia Deane – Drummond, *Eco – Theology* (London: Darton, Longman and Todd Ltd, 2008), 4.

[67] Martin-Schramm and Robert L. Stivers, *Christian Environmental Ethics*..., 12.

nature in the selfish interest of humanity. Heavy machineries were invented, tested and used at the expense of nature. The world has used these inventions to destroy tones of forest trees, lands and polluted the ecosystem. The invention of nuclear weapons which is so destructive is destroying the nature at rapid pace. Rapid industrialization, urbanization, use of automobiles, etc. also has aggravated the pain of nature. Military activities have been considered as one of the biggest threat to our environment. For instance in the American-Vietnam war it is recorded that forests suffered irreparable damage because of the dumping of twenty-five million gallons of defoliants and toxins. As a result of the American's military bombings the Vietnamese lost twenty-five million acres of farm land. After the war farmers have turned to the use of heavy pesticide for increasing their production. Now, more than eighty million people continue to suffer because the bombing in the forest have lost the fertility of the soil which ultimately affected in the agricultural production.[68] James B. Martin-Schramm and Robert L. Stivers have made a comparative explanation of how technology and machines serves humanity at the expense of ecological degradation:[69]

> 1) Increased access to multiple levels of experience, yet the dominance of narrow technical reason; 2) greater wealth, yet greater inequality; 3) more freedom, yet increased and more concentrated control and manipulation; 4) more variety, yet the cutting off of traditional choices; 5) more frequent interaction, yet the neglect of community and the increase power of impersonal bureaucracies; 6) greater potential to improve the well-being of all people, yet control by small groups pursuing narrow interest; 7) greater control of nature, yet the degradation of ecosystems; 8) the promise of mastery, yet the feeling that things are out of control; and 9) unlimited power,

---

[68] Heather Fisher Lindsay, "Balancing Community Needs Against Individual Desires," www.law.fsu.edu/journals/landuse/vol102/lindsay.html (December 06, 2015).

[69] Martin-Schramm and Robert L. Stivers, *Christian Environmental Ethics...*, 13.

for example, nuclear power, yet the possibility of total destruction.

4.3. Patriarchal and Hierarchical Model

Hierarchical and patriarchal form of social structure put few males at the apex of the pyramid. This model clearly serves few powerful group of people sanction authority and the claim of superiority for themselves. The world of scientific management sadly justifies indirectly hierarchal domination. The philosophy of hierarchy and patriarchy sees the natural world from pure anthropocentric view and assault the natural resources to their interest and benefits.[70] The hierarchical system of social structure in human society perhaps creates imbalance within the society which in fact leads to the notion of dominion over the natural world of creation. The system of man having dominion over women and children in the family has indeed even extended to the dominion over nature. The eco-feminist strongly argue that man in their dominion nature have destroyed and subdued nature for the self-interest. The patriarchal and hierarchical structures viewed animals as valuable to be hunted and nature to be oppressed and exploited. Patriarchy is shown in the sense of dominion and superiority. Patriarchal and hierarchical structures allow man to perceive that they have control over the nature and web of life and so can exploit creation in any manner they wanted to use. Therefore, the patriarchal and hierarchal model encompasses attitudes of anthropocentricism, dualistic ideology and dominion philosophy. Richard Young argues that nature does have rights and that is the reason human kinds have moral responsibilities towards nature.[71] The contemporary ecological argument is more concern on the rights of natures and animals and pressing towards an egalitarian lifestyle of all God creation. Animals as God's creatures have their God given rights so also the natural life.

---

[70] Martin-Schramm and Robert L. Stivers, *Christian Environmental Ethics…*, 19.

[71] Richard A.Young, *Healing the Earth: A Theocentric Perspective on Environmental Problems and their Solutions* (USA: Broadman & Holman Publishers, 1994), 121.

4.4. Irresponsible Economic Developments

The prevailing culture of unlimited economic growth and the market policies which are committed to commodity accumulation and consumption can be seen as another dimension of factors that has resulted in ecological crisis.[72] The economic capitalist system has indeed endangered the human existence on the earth, the nature and the earth's resources because the system has put the resources into the disposal of the greedy who amass wealth and mammon at the expense of nature. The rise of capitalism has further put forward a threat to the values and rights of land by projecting land as a commodity which is meant for and source of making financial profit. The business policies and market system of rapid competition focused towards meeting the luxurious need and demands of the customers without realizing the long-term threat and exhaustion of natural resources has to be taken seriously and viewed critically. The model of economic growth and expansion by the affluent economists and the developed counties at the expense of ecological destruction has to be questioned and the world needs to adopt sustainability policies from saving the planet earth.[73] The policy of capitalism allows the managers to acquire the earth's resources and in turn produce as waste products for the ecosystem. The policy of aggressive search for profit and maximum benefits in the capitalists world view leads to the exploitation of the earth and pollution of the ecosystem. For instance, the present economic growth in the capitalistic world overlooks the amount of toxic waste produced and the discharge of carbon dioxide gas but fully concentrates on the measure of income. The hunger for economic power and political power in order to gain dominance in the global arena has also resulted in the environmental degradation.

Development philosophy is always in line with capitalists' worldview and as such some people are very critical about development. For Sarkar development should and must always

[72] Randy Hayes, "The Root Causes of Social and Ecological Crisis," http://www.ecowatch.com/2011/11/.../the-root-causes-of-social-and-ecological-crisis. (December 9, 2015).

[73] Rongsen, *Development and…*, 53.

be rejected not necessarily because it is Western but it is harmful economically, politically, socially and also ecologically.[74] On the other hand some people justify the position of development citing the positive changes brought about by development in the human society. Robert Royal was of the view that development has benefited humanity enormously and so humanity must acknowledge science and technology. He further insists that science and technology should continue with more ecological conscious programs.[75] In the contemporary approach to ecology and economy, the global community has come to a proposal for certain limits and condition to the economic development policies. In other world economic development can take place with conscious effort to the ecological problems. The term for this integrated development policy is 'sustainable development.' Sustainability can be understood in terms of adopting a lifestyle and habits within the limits of the earth's resources. In the other sense of interpretation sustainability is implementation of judicially using the earth resources looking beyond the present for future generations. Biologist and an ecologist Celia Deane – Drummond is quite suspicious about achieving sustainability with the present trend of market economy. With reference to the carbon emission limit, leading economist country like USA could not agree to the Kyoto agreement[76] even though it is reported in *The Hindu* (Madurai) newspaper on Nov. 13, 2014 that the two nations China and U.S have agreed to limit the emission of Greenhouse gases on a time table. In 2012 China was producing highest greenhouse gases, 8547 million metric tonnes, the U.S 5270 million metric tonnes, India 1830 million metric tonnes, Russia 1781 million metric tonnes and Japan 1259 million Metric tonnes.[77] Deane – Drummond further suggested John Cobb idea of building

---

[74] Saral Sarkar, *Eco-Socialism or Eco-Capitalism? A Critical Analysis of Humanity's Fundamental Choices* (London: Zed Books, 1999), 239.

[75] Robert Royal, *The Virgin and the Dynamos: Use and Abuse of Religion in Environmental Debate* (Michigan: Ethic and Public Policy Center & W. B. Eerdmans, 1999), 15.

[76] Deane – Drummond, *Eco – Theology…*, 20.

[77] "China-U.S deal on emission cuts," *The Hindu* (Madurai), 13th November 2014, 1.

up the small self-sufficient regions in terms of basic human needs or survival needs through the process of economic decentralization.[78] Ramprasad Sengupta, a professor of economics has outlined some concerns for sustainable development:[79]

a) dematerialization of economic process;
b) decarbonization of energy;
c) increase substitution of non-renewable resources by renewables;
d) recycling of waste by converting it into a manmade resource;
e) non-recyclable waste treatment before disposal;
f) enhancement of primary productivity of biospheric space in ecosystems;
g) facilitation of the redistribution process of income by increasing the productivity of wage goods and creating more employment opportunities.

5. The Ecological Crisis

God created human beings to be a part of the many species that inhabits the earth and live on the earth making and extending their relationship to their environment with the living as well as non-living organisms. Yet, this relationship between human kind and the natural world has distorted because of human kind's greed which is driven by the spirit of individualism. With the development of science and technology human kind has manipulated the nature and her resources and has turned them into products for consumption and luxurious living. This has inflicted pain on the other species in the world because of the global human community is experiencing severe ecological crisis. The fresh air we breathe is already polluted, the water we use now contains high amount of toxins, chemicals and other dangerous bacteria, the green grass lands are mostly being replaced by the dumping of waste products and the tropical forests which are much in need for human survival and rainfall were

---

78 Deane – Drummond, *Eco – Theology*..., 21.

79 Sengupta, *Ecology and Economics: An Approaches* ..., 225.

destroying. The life and existence of the global community now is threatened with what is called drastic and severe climate change. The destruction on ecology is greater today than the years earlier because of the new trends of scientific development and the excessive use of those developments for human easy lifestyle and benefits.

5.1. Climate Change

World is experiencing an uneven change in the climate and weather within a period of short time. The main reason for the global warming is the result of greenhouse effect. The earth is surrounded by a layer of natural gases which act like a greenhouse. The "sunlight enters the atmosphere unimpeded. About one-third is absorbed and heats the earth. The earth radiates infra-red energy back into the atmosphere. This is absorbed by the gases. About 30 per cent escapes back into space. Some heat is then sent back to earth by the greenhouse gases, which act as a blanket keeping the heat in."[80]

It is reported in The Hindu (Madurai) newspaper on Nov. 13, 2014 that while discussing on the issue of how to combat climate change, the two nations China and U.S have agreed to limit the emission of Greenhouse gases on a time table. In 2012 China was producing highest greenhouse gases, 8547 million metric tonnes, the U.S 5270 million metric tonnes, India 1830 million metric tonnes, Russia 1781 million metric tonnes and Japan 1259 million Metric tonnes.[81] The effect of the global warming may result in the rise of the sea level, which is caused by the melting of polar ice and glaciers. Some Island nations will experience sever lose. Because of the rapid climate change there will be loss of species as well as trees and plants. There will be very little rain fall and the tropical countries will experience devastating storms and hurricanes. The climate will become hotter for human beings to survive.[82] The burning of coal, fuel wood or petroleum produce contain sulphur and nitrogen.

---

[80] R. L. Sarkar, *The Bible, Ecology and Environment* (Delhi: ISPCK, 2000), 252-253.

[81] "China-U.S deal on emission cuts," *The Hindu* (Madurai), 13th November 2014, 1.

[82] Sarkar, *The Bible, Ecology...*, 258-260.

These two elements are highly soluble in water, so when it rain, these oxides react with large quantities of water vapour in the atmosphere and produce sulphuric acid, sulphurous acid, nitric acid and nitrous acid. These acid returns to the earth surface along with the rain which is called 'Acid Rain.' These acids are highly concentrated and dangerous as they can destroy life. They ruin forests as they fall on the trees and plants, kill fish if the precipitation[83] falls on the water and thus destroy the fertility of the soil.[84]

Climate change is one of the most impending ecological threats to the livelihood of global community in the planet earth. The consciousness on climate change goes back to 1958, when scientist begin to observe the emission of carbon dioxide gas and initiated to analyse to work on the possibility of excessive emission of greenhouse gases and increase in temperatures. However, it was only in 1975 the term climate change was coined to describe about the global warming. The United Nations Second Assessment Report (1995) of the Intergovernmental Panel on Climate Change (IPCC) pointed out that there is certain tangible evidence of human activities on global climate. In 2007, in its third report the IPCC more specifically reported that research and survey for the past 50 years confirms human influence to the global warming. Finally the IPCC in its fourth report in 2007 declared that global warming as the result of human activities.[85]

---

[83] A precipitate is an insoluble solid that emerges from a liquid solution. The emergence of the insoluble solid from solution is called precipitation. Often the precipitate emerges as a suspension. Precipitates can form when two soluble salts react in solution to form one or more insoluble products - as discussed in the famous example below. The insoluble product separates from the liquid and is called a precipitate.

Precipitates can also form when the temperature of a solution is lowered. The lower temperature reduces the solubility of a salt, resulting in its precipitation as a solid.

[84] Kochupurackal, *Eco-Mission...*, 81-82.

[85] George Zachariah, *Gospel in a Groaning World: Climate Injustice and Public Witness* (Tiruvalla: Christian Sahitya Samithi & NCCI, 2012), 18.

Climate Change is basically the variability and inconsistency in the atmospheric movements such as the global temperature, rainfall, unpredictable seasons and other climatic systems. Perhaps more explanation on the definition of climate change categorically will help in deeper understanding and identify climate change as the consequences of human insensitive and irresponsible activities. George Zachariah, an associate professor of theology and ethics who has done extensive writings on ecology has defined climate change, "as the fluctuations in temperature, precipitation, and other climatic systems of the earth."[86] He further citing the United Nations Framework Convention on Climate Change (UNFCCC) definition on climate change stated that climate change is "a change of climate which is attributed directly or indirectly to human activity that alters the composition of the global atmosphere and which is in addition to natural climate variability observed over comparable time periods."[87] For Daniel Anand Raj A, Olaganathan S, and Duraipandi P, "Climate Change is not just change in weather, it refers to seasonal changes over a long period of time. These climate patterns play a fundamental role of shaping natural ecosystems, human economies and cultures that depend on them."[88]

The main causes of global warming are gases like Carbon Dioxide, Chlorofluorocarbons, Methane and Nitrous Oxide. It is said that an ordinary cow produces about 73,000 litres of methane gas every year. Much of the waste we create daily also produces methane gas and passed into the atmosphere. The gas from coal mines and natural gas – exploitation sources produces major source of methane. The CFCs (Cloroflurocarbons) gas which is exclusively an industrial product affects the greenhouse. The use of anti-perspirant, a paint spray, an insect killer or air freshener cause the earth to become warmer. Carbon Dioxide which is produced by burning of forest, fuel wood, charcoal, etc., profoundly affects the greenhouse. The

---

[86] Zachariah, *Gospel in a Groaning World: Climate…*, 19.

[87] Zachariah, *Gospel in a Groaning World: Climate…*, 19.

[88] Daniel Anand Raj A, Olaganathan S, and Duraipandi P, *Perceived Impact of Climate Change in Agriculture: From a Livelihood Perspective* (Madurai: Palmyrah Workers Development Society, 2012), 12.

nitrous oxide gas which emits from vehicle exhausts also affects the green house. The safety limit of the global atmospheric concentration on carbon dioxide gas is 350ppm but survey from 1988 show the increase in the atmospheric carbon dioxide gas rapidly. During the pre-industrial period the atmospheric level of carbon dioxide was 280ppm. However, in 2005 the atmospheric level of carbon dioxide gas was 379ppm[89] which exceeded already the safety limit and in February 2012, the atmospheric level of carbon dioxide was increased to 393.65ppm.[90] The twentieth century has exhibited rapid and drastic increase in the emission of the greenhouse gases and if the global world continues at the present rate of emission then as per the study shown by the US Climate Change Science program, the world will experience faster level of climate change in the coming 100 years than what the world has experienced for the past 10000 years ago.[91] This is so alarming and disturbing to notice the facts and figures for the global warming and the future to which the twenty first century world is moving to. Some ecologists like James Lovelock the proponent of Gaia Hypothesis expresses the view that population growth and climate change are two sides of the same coin. However, evidences and survey shows that climate change is the result of human activities. One of the core issues pertaining global warming is because of climate injustice. Rich nations, powerful nations, industrialised nations by large produces the atmospheric polluting gases which primarily causes global warming. However, the poorer nations which contribute least to global warming become the worst victims of climate change.

---

[89] James B. Martin-Schramm, 'Human Rights and Climate Change," *God, Creation and Climate Change: Spiritual and Ethical Perspectives,* ed., Karen L.Bloomquist (Geneva: Lutheran University Press, 2009), 34.

[90] Zachariah, *Gospel in a Groaning World: Climate...,* 20.

[91] US Climate Change Science Program, The effects of Climate Change on Agriculture, Land Resources, Water Resources, and Biodiversity, http://www.climatescience.gov/Library/sap/sap4-3/public-review-draft/sap4-3prd-all.pdf. (November 07, 2015).

The result of global warming has increased heat in the world leading to the annihilation of human lives. It is recorded that in Europe alone the number of deaths as a result of extreme heat went above 50,000 in 2005[92] and in India the CNN on May 27, 2015 reported that the heat wave within one week's time had claimed more than 1,100 lives in India. Andhra Pradesh as reported by authorities bears the worst affected State with number of death to 852 followed by Telangana with 266 dead's.[93] This if followed by severe floods and droughts making the survival option even more difficult. The increase in the melting of permanent ice and glaciers has led to enormous threats to people living in low-lying islands and coastal communities. Glaciers in Alaska and neighbouring Canada which are more than 13% of the mountain glaciers on earth have thinned at the rapid pace of 50-100 meters at the lower elevations and about 18 meters at the higher elevations. In South America, the Quelccava glacier in Peru retreated 32 times faster and in Argentina, glaciers in the Patagonian ice fields have receded 1.5 kilometers since 1990. In Africa, Mount Kilamanjaro's ice fields have disappeared at least 80% since 1912 and the Mount Kenya's ice cap has reduced around 40% since the 1960s. The glacier of the Himalayas which is the largest ice glaciers outside the polar caps is disappearing faster than any in the world. Report suggests that at this rate the Himalayas glaciers will be melted completely by 2035. The permanent sea ice like the Arctic Ocean is shrinking by the size of Netherlands every year. The Center for Atmospheric Research predicts the Arctic as ice free ocean by 2040. With the increase of temperature the Antarctic have melted large ice shelves.[94] It is also a threat to different species of animals, fish and birds. Climate change will adversely affect agricultural, forest, human settlements, water and so on. Yet, the most severely affected will be agriculture especially in the production of rice. This will paralyse the food production rate for the poor section of

---

[92] Zachariah, *Gospel in a Groaning World: Climate...* 24.

[93] "Heat wave kills more than 1,100 in India – CNN.com," http://www.cnn.com/2015/05/25/asia/india-heatwave-deaths/ (November 20, 2015).

[94] Water Encyclopaedia, "Global Warming ad Glaciers," http://www.waterencyclopedia.com/Ge-Hy/Global-Warming-and-Glaciers.html#ixzz3lKaYytxB. (November 18, 2015).

communities in the developing countries. So, where do the global world go from here? The world surely is in need of a drastic paradigm shift in our attitudes and actions for building a new sustainable global community. The post-modern world must strive for using maximum solar and wind energies and reduce the uses of fossil fuels to a minimum.

5.2. Pollution of Land, Air and Water

After the World War II, pollution became a popular issue due to the emitting of radioactive from the atomic warfare and testing.[95]

5.2.1. Land Pollution

The major cause of land pollution comes from industries such as paper mills, oil refineries, power and heating plants, chemicals and fertilizer manufactures, iron and steel plants, plastic and rubber producing factories and others.[96] The household garbage dumped areas pollutes the environment and produces a harmful toxic waste where the chemicals can cause cancer. The land is not only destroyed by the pollution load upon but it is also destroyed by the use of chemical fertilizers, pesticides, insecticides, etc.[97] It is estimated that because of soil – degradation annually 6-7 million hectares of agricultural land usually suffer loss and soil erosion causes 23 billion tonnes loss of soil every year.[98] With the present rate of land degradation around the globe 35% of the earth surface is predicted to turn into a desert land making it possible to sustain species which can adapt to the condition of desert land. The Mesopotamian land which is situated between the two great rivers Tigris and Euphrates was one of the most fertile land some 400 years ago but today it has turned into a desert land because of poor irrigation and excessive of the land. It is surveyed that top soil takes 200 years to 1, 20,000 years

---

[95] "Pollution," http://www.en.wikipedia.org/wiki/Pollution (November 16, 2015).

[96] Sebastain Kochupurackal, *Eco-Mission: A Paradigm Shift in Missiology* (Bangalore: Asian Trading Corporation, 2007), 83.

[97] M. Rongsen, *Development and Ecology* (Delhi: ISPCK, 1999), 47.

[98] Kochupurackal, *Eco-Mission…*, 83.

to form and develop but it can be lost quickly within a period of a month.[99] In India calculation from 1947 – 1994, 80 million hectares of land have been degraded by means of soil erosion (162.4 million hectares), water logging (11.6 million hectares) and salinity (10.1 million hectares).[100] Land degradation is caused by large because of human activities. It is caused because of soil erosion, over use of the land, salinity, land pollution, water logging and mining and quarrying.

5.2.2. Water Pollution

Water Pollution is a major problem for the world today. It is observed to be the leading cause of diseases and death. In India it is estimated that 580 people die of water pollution related illness every day. The underdeveloped, developing and developed countries continue to struggle with the water pollution in the world. In the recent national report on water quality, in United States 45% of stream miles, 47% of lake acres and 32% of bay were classified are polluted.[101] The Ganges is the largest river in India with an extraordinary religious importance for Hindus. It is situated along the banks of one of the world's oldest cities like the Varanasi and Patna. It provides water to about 40% of India's population across 11 states, serving an estimated population of 500 million people or more. Today, it is considered to be one of the most polluted rivers in the world.[102] The Ganges River Pollution is now at such a high level that the amount of toxins, chemicals and other dangerous bacteria found in the river are now almost 3000 times over the limit suggested by the WHO as 'safe.[103]

---

[99] Celia Deane-Drummond, *A Handbook in Theology and Ecology* (London: SCM Press Ltd, 1996), 6.

[100] Sengupta, *Ecology and Economics: An Approaches to…*, 140.

[101] "Water Pollution," http://www.en.wikipedia.org/wiki/Pollution. (Nov. 16, 2015)

[102] "Pollution of the Ganges," http://www. en.wikipedia.org/wiki/Pollution_of_the_Ganges (November 16, 2015).

[103] "Ganges River Pollution," http://www.all-about-india.com/Ganges-River-Pollution.html (November 16, 2015).

5.2.3. Air Pollution

Air Pollution is the introduction of particulates, biological molecules, or other harmful materials into the Earth's atmosphere which can cause disease, death to humans, damage to other living organisms such as food crops, or the natural or built environment. It affects adversely the eco-system of the earth. The air pollutant substance can be solid particles, liquid droplets, or gases which are produced either by manmade activities or natural. The primary pollutants of air pollution can be from the ash from a volcano, carbon monoxide gas from motor vehicle exhaust and sulphur dioxide release from the factories. When these gases interact and react with each other in the natural air pollution occurs.[104]

5.3. Deforestation

The tropical forests occupy on 6% of the land mass yet it is said to be the home of all plants and 70% of animals in the world. This valuable forest which is a shelter for most of the plants and animals in the world is being destroyed at an alarming rate of 11 million hectares per year.[105] The world's rainforests could completely vanish in a hundred years at the current rate of deforestation.[106] According to the United Nations Framework Convention on Climate Change (UNFCCC), the major part of deforestation is due to agriculture. It is observed that sustenance farming causes 48% of deforestation, commercial agriculture causes 32% of deforestation. Logging is responsible for 14% of deforestation while fuel wood cause 5% of deforestation. The degradation of forest ecosystems can also be seen in the economic incentive which appears forest exchange more profitable than forest conservation.[107] Deforestation affects the climate adversely; it affects supply of water resources, it leads to

---

[104] "Air Pollution," http://www. en.wikipedia.org/wiki/Pollution. (Nov. 16, 2015).

[105] Rongsen, *Development and…*, 48-49.

[106] "Deforestation," http://www.livescience.com/27692-deforestation.html. (November 18, 2015).

[107] "Deforestation," http://www.en.wikipedia.org/wiki/Deforestation. (Nov. 18, 2015).

soil erosion and over all destruction of biodiversity.[108] The writing of P. J. Sanjeeva Raj explains that in India deforestation has vastly affected and deprived the livelihood of the poor. Fishermen are forced into want of logs for their fishing purpose, basket weavers were left with no or less bamboo in the forest, Apple – growers are faced with the scantily of wood from the forest for packing and transporting the product. Deforestation has not only led to the extinction of species and loss of wild life but it has also led to the loss of the tribal ancient habitats, native food and herbal medicines.[109] In 1989 Ulrich Duchrow and Gerhard Liedke in their research on the destruction of the forest around the globe have shown that in East and West Africa 72% of the forests are already destroyed, in Central Africa 45% of forests are lost, in Latin America 37% of the forests have disappeared, South Asia 63% of the forests are destroyed and South East Asia have lost already 38% of their forests. On average there was a total 42% loss of forests area.[110] Recently in 2010, the World Preservation Foundation website survey shows the top seven countries on deforestation where each of the countries have around a total of 60% on deforestation. The countries are Brazil in Latin America, Canada and the United States in North America, Indonesia and China in Asia, Russia in Europe and the Democratic Republic of Congo in Africa. It is also alarming to notice the data compiled by the World Resources Institute that the global world has already lost 80% of the forests area[111] and with the present trends of ecological destruction the remaining 20% of forests will soon be stripped leaving the global community to a grave danger of life existence. The lethal force of deforestation is

---

[108] J. Pramananda Das, "Earth Needs Shepherds: Ecological and Theological Issues in our Context," *Green Theology*, ed., Wati Longchar (Kolkata: SCEPTRE, 2014), 262.

[109] P. J. Sanjeeva Raj, "Ecological Predicaments of the Humankind," *Ecology A Theological Response*, ed.,Andreas Nehring (Madras: The Grukul Summer Institute, 1993), 32.

[110] Ulrich Duchrow and Gerhard Liedke, *Shalom: Biblical Perspectives On Creation, Justice & Peace* (Geneva: WCC Publications, 1989), 17.

[111] "Deforestation Statistics," http://www.worldpreservationfoundation.org/blog/news/deforestation-statistics. (November 18, 2015).

leading to the enormous loss of animals, plants and other living organism. Biological studies reveals that so far only a segment of around 1% around the global plant species have been identified for their potential value towards humankind and in the current rate of deforestation many of the plant species will extinct before their potential values can be identified.

6. Environmental Justice

According to Robert Melchior Figueroa, "Environmental justice refers to a broad range of issues that combine values of social justice with environmental values and practices. Environmental justice pertains when the cause of social injustices are [is] mediated by environmental conditions, or the environmental burdens that threaten human health are bound by social injustices of marginalization, exploitation, discrimination, racism, sexism, and various forms of imperialism."[112] The concept of environmental justice came into active movement in North America in the 1980 upon the realization that there are disproportionate number of environmental problems inflicted to communities located in low income neighbourhood and minority communities as a result of industries, power plants and waste disposals. It is a concept which strives primarily towards ensuring healthy environment for all color, nationality, gender, age, income and so on. In other words it is a movement for fair distribution of environmental burdens to all the people despite their backgrounds.[113] Environmental justice is a part of environmentalism which is aimed at equal dissemination of the environmental hazard and also benefit.[114] Environmental justice is mostly concern with the harm inflicted upon the physical health. Environment justice is closely related to market economy

[112] Robert Melchior Figueroa, "Environmental Justice and Environmental Racism," *The Encyclopedia of Religion and Nature,* Bron R. Taylor et. al. (London: Thoemmes Continuum, 2005), 608.

[113] Rebecca Gillaspy, http://www.study.com/.../what-is-environmental-justice-definition-principles-exampl... (November 24, 2015).

[114] Manning Marable, "Environmental Justice: The Power of Making Connections," *Theology For Earth Community*: A Field Guide ed., Dieter T. Hessel (Maryknoll: Orbis Books, 1996), 155.

even if comparative study shows the economic justice is about the distribution of monetary goods while environmental justice is about the amount of distribution of harm.[115] As mentioned above environmental justice grew out of the comprehension on the harm inflicted to the poorer section of communities or nation from the affluent dominant political economy. The concern of environmental justice movement is not only with the environmental problem caused by anthropocentricism but it is instituted broadly to counter the separation of environmental issues from social justice. Environmental justice for many communities is about protecting their religious, environmental, economic and social values which cannot be separated. For instance, the struggle of the Chiapas indigenous people in Mexico is about their land right and sustainable agriculture. In India, it is the protection of the sacred groves from industrialization and population growth. In San Jose, Philippines environmental justice is the struggles of the farmers against hostile biochemical farming and the uses of genetically altered seeds of the American biotechnologies replacing their traditional farming seeds.[116] However, Celia Deane – Drummond in her quest for formulating intermediate mediating strategies has indicated that the low income or minority communities are also accountable to higher ratio of pollutant. For instance, it includes the introductions of carbon sink crops in the poorer nations which ultimately relocating other native crops or the mandatory implementation of these method without proper consultation.[117]

7. The Ecumenical Responses

The Ecological crisis is no longer a concern for a particular nation or religion of individual. It is a serious universal concern because it is a threat to the cosmos. Church can no longer sit as an isolated body or distinct organization from the secular world, rather uniting with the rest of the world the church must be serious enough and willing to approach the various factors that are challenging to the good creation

---

[115] Deane – Drummond, *Eco – Theology...*, 27.

[116] Melchior Figueroa, "Environmental Justice..., 610.

[117] Deane – Drummond, *Eco – Theology...*, 27.

of God. The World Council of Churches has realized this seriously and has responded to the challenges and has worked closely with the United Nations, World Wild Fund and World health Organization and others to protect and save the beautiful planet earth. Christian theologians Protestants, Orthodox and the Roman Catholics have responded adequately to the ever mounting environmental crisis so far even though there seems to have distinction in their position and approaches.

Wati Longchar opined that Christian theology of creation shares some part for the ecological destruction because of its uncritical and partial interpretation of the Bible. He further identified four theological factors that have indirectly influenced the thinking and attitude of the people towards the creation of God. The first is the hierarchical perception of explaining God's creation that human has the superior status among the creation and they have the ultimate right over other creation. The second is the anthropocentric view of creation; human alone are created in the image of God and have the right to subdue the earth in their inherent right. The other creation exists for the benefit of human kind. The third is the dualistic view of creation; the created world is purely material and evil whereas God is absolutely different form the sinful created nature. The fourth factor is the teaching on heaven and hell as different units. The end of the world is at hand and all the material world will be destroyed and only saved human souls will live eternally. The ecumenical theologians have made serious attempts to rectify this hierarchical, anthropocentric, dualistic and androcentric view by demonstrating human creation as interrelated, interdependent and co-partners in this planet earth. Countering these misconceptions Wati Longchar further suggested four steps of ecumenical response. The first is the non-dualistic view of life. Re-imagining the concept of God and understanding God as lover of the world who is interested in saving the entire cosmos which is sick. The second view is the 'Inter-connectedness of life.' It is to build a concrete connected view of intrinsic relationship between God, humanity and creation. The other suggestion is the sacramental view. Because God entered into a total communion with all the creation through Jesus Christ and the Holy Spirit, the celebration of Eucharist is for the salvation of the Whole creation.[118] Thus "...the Eucharist bread and wine symbolize the universe, the whole created order. Creation is also called to share in the life and glory of the creator."[119] His fourth response was the WCC program on Justice, Peace and Integrity of Creation-a call for the unity beyond the four walls of the church.[120]

The ecumenical movement begin their quest and agendas on environmental concerns from the 1970s, in response to the United Nations conference on 'Environment and Development' at Stockholm in 1972. The World Council of Churches after its Nairobi Assembly 1975 initiated a study of a Just Participatory and Sustainable Society (JPSS). The JPSS study was an eye opener for an ecumenical world to respect the rights of the creation. The issue on the relationship between technology and nature was the focus of the WCC 1979 conference where the theme was on 'Faith, Science and the Future.' A serious agenda for addressing theologically and programmatically the ecological and environmental issues was recognized clearly in the WCC's Sixth Assembly, Vancouver 1983. In this assembly the WCC constituted a program on the Justice, peace and the integrity of creation (JPIC).[121] Human has no right to exploit and oppress creation. Creation has inborn values and right to live. Hence, respecting the integrity of the whole inhabited earth and stimulating awareness on maintaining ecological balanced community on the earth is vital.[122] Justice, Peace and Integrity of Creation were also the main theme for the WCC, during their Vancouver Assembly 1983. Wati summaries the purpose of the theme as.[123]

---

[118] Wati Longchar, "Ecumenical Responses to Ecological Crisis: A Critique from the Indigenous Peoples' Perspective," *Green Theology*, ed., Wati Longchar (Kolkata: SCEPTRE, 2014), 239-246.

[119] Longchar, *Green Theology...*, 246.

[120] Longchar, *Green Theology...*, 247.

[121] Sarkar, *The Bible, Ecology...*, 269-272.

[122] Wati Longchar, "Ecumenical Response to Ecological Crisis: A Critique from the Indigenous Peoples' Perspective," *Green Theology*, ed., Wati Longchar (Kolkata: SCEPTRE, 2014), 250.

[123] Longchar, *Green Theology ...*, 247.

> The first concern was to show that justice, peace and integrity of creation are essentially one whole; they are inseparable and indivisible. The second concern was to articulate theologically our understanding of human predicament and spell out our specific Christian responsibility. And the third concern was to respond to the central question of the modern ecumenical movement, that is, the unity of the church. Theologically it was a radical shift from the earlier assumption. The theological emphasis is now on the unity of the whole world, not only the church and humanity.

The WCC in its seventh assembly (Canberra 1991) continued their theological discussion on creation on the theme 'Come, Holy Spirit – Renew the whole Creation.' The WCC made an important participation in the United Nation Conference for Environment and Development (UNCED), the Earth Summit at Rio de Janeiro in June 1992. The WCC broadcasted the message of their consultation through a booklet entitled '*Searching for the New Heavens and the New Earth.*'[124]

The Rio Earth summit was organized by the United Nations Conference on Environment and Development (UNCED) at Rio de Janeiro in June 03-14, 1992. Representatives of 178 nations attended the summit and apart from the government delegates, over 1400 NGOs participated. The World Council of Churches was a major part of the summit. The Earth Summit offered a world of challenges to the churches and ecumenical body to consider deeply and seriously the pathos of Christ in the contemporary exploitation, destruction and turmoil of the earth. The churches and the ecumenical body are to discern this suffering and joined the outstretched arms of Christ the redeemer to bring healing and life.[125] The Rio Earth Summit, along with the WCC's continues effort on Justice, peace and Integrity of Creation has called upon the Ecumenical Movement to offer spiritual response to the crisis

---

[124] Sarkar, *The Bible, Ecology…*, 272-274.

[125] Wesley Granberg-Michaelson, *Redeeming the Creation, The Rio Earth Summit: Challenges for the Churches* (Geneva: WCC Publications,1992), x-xiv.

of environment and development. It was a central calling for the church to develop a 'spirituality of creation,' so that the Church participates with our hearts and our totality with God's redeeming love for the earth and the humanity.[126]

8. Contemporary Ecological Philosophies and Concepts

8.1. Population Ecology

P. H. Collin defines Population ecology as the study of the various aspects for determining the rich multi-diverse population of species and the variations in the population of the species.[127] It is concerned with the intra-relation and interrelation within the individual species or between the other species. The species interact and relates with each other through the process of symbiosis where equal benefit takes place between two species. For example, a bird finding its food at the back of a cow while they graze. This mutual relation also takes place among various plants and animals. The algae functions in giving oxygen to the animals and other aquatic species while in turn the animals' produces carbon dioxide and nitrogen to the plants. The other example can be referred to cross-pollination of flowers by insects and birds. The species also interacts through a process called commensalism. Here, the process of interaction is centred on food. In the interaction, at least one species derives benefits while the others are neither benefited nor harmed. Parasitism is another area where in two individual species interacts. The parasite derives benefits at the expense of the host. Another dimension where the species interact is in competition. This interaction occurs between two or more organisms especially in regards to food, space and shelter. Competition takes place when the materials needed for the animals are not supplied adequately and sufficiently. In this process of interaction the weaker organisms mostly becomes victims and it often results in death.[128] There are perhaps other processes of interactions which I did not mention in

---

[126] Granberg-Michaelson, *Redeeming the Creation…*, 36-39.

[127] P. H. Collin, *Dictionary of Environment & Ecology*, Fifth Edition (London: Bloomsbury Publishing Plc, 2004), 168.

[128] Trivedi and Gurdeep Raj, eds., *Environmental Ecology …*, 99-103.

the above list of interaction and relations. The growth and limit of the various species depends upon temperature, light, nutrients and other factors that are essential for the growth and development of an organism. The condition of the entire ecosystems depends upon the size of the population of the various species. The growth and expansion of the species population is absolutely measured by the birth rate, death rate and the amount of migration that takes place in the population of species. The population growth potential of the various species is determined through pre-reproductive, reproductive and post-reproductive. These stages indicate the ratio of growth or reduction or regular state of the species.[129] The most concrete aspects that limit population growth among the species are food and water, light, space, predators,[130] diseases and parasitism.[131]

8.2. Social Ecology

The term 'social ecology' was first coined by American ecologist, E. A. Gutkind in 1954. Social ecology articulates the present ecological crisis from the view point of the difference in the social set up. It denounces dominion and hierarchy and strives towards democracy, community and co-operation. Social ecology works for the enhancement of the principle of unity in diversity. Perhaps it is also concern with the transformation of society so as to bring about a change in our relationship with the natural world. The social ecology in its effort to liberate human and nature from exploitation and dominion do extents their recognition towards the poor and the oppressed in the society.[132]

In the epoch of ecological crisis, it is very critical to define and understand what nature means. Most truly human definition and ethical response towards nature eventually decides whether if human society will endorse nurturing natural world or create a world which is uninhabitable for the multifaceted forms of

[129] Sengupta, *Ecology and Economics* ..., 91-95.

[130] Animals that naturally prey on others.

[131] Kirti Agarwal, *Population Ecology* (Delhi: Pacific Publication, 2010), 26-27.

[132] Sarkar, *The Bible, Ecology* ..., 65-66.

life including even humanity. Defining nature is a complex issue because it can vary from person to person according to each philosophy of understanding on nature. As Murray Bookchin opines whatever may be the case and whatever nature may mean, it is vital to define nature in a way that humanity also fits into it. Bookchin further states that unless we define nature including humanity, we will have no proper ethical direction in doing ecological problems.[133] Bookchin argument of creating ecological society is worth mentioning here:[134]

> To say that nature belongs in humanity just as humanity belongs in nature is to express a highly reciprocal and complementary relationship between the two instead of one structured around subordination and domination. Neither society nor nature dissolves into the other. Rather, social ecology tries to recover the distinctive attributes of both in a continuum that gives rise to a substantive ethics, wedding the social to the ecological without denying the integrity of each....If we are to create a truly rational and ecological society, we must nourish the insights provided by reason to create a sense of a shared humanity that is bound neither by gendered outlooks nor by beliefs in deities – all of which, ironically, are merely anthropomorphic projections of our own beings and sensibilities-and we must commit ourselves to a belief in the potentialities of humanity to foresee and understand, to be the embodiment of mind.

8.3. Deep Ecology

The word 'deep ecology' and 'shallow ecology' was first used in 1973 by Norwegian philosopher Arne Naess to study the location and place of humanity on the earth household. The proponents of deep ecology are called deep since they perceive beyond the

---

133 Murray Bookchin, *The Philosophy of Social Ecology*: Essay on Dialectical Naturalism (New Delhi: Rawat Publications, 1996), 3.

134 Bookchin, *The Philosophy of Social Ecology...*, 92.

surface level of the ecological problem to the root causes of the crisis.[135] Deep ecology like the social ecology is radical ecologist because their argument is based on holism where the essence is interrelatedness and interconnectedness.[136] Naess based his philosophical ecological argument on the norm of self-realization; a realization of the intrinsic interconnectedness of humanity and other the creations. George Sessions while articulating Naess' paper on deep ecology has explained Naess position on his conviction on deep ecological philosophy for enhancing deep ecology movement. He advocates simple life and oppose consumerism; efforts must be made to fulfil important need rather than one's desires. We are to live in nature promoting community rather than individualistic society and appreciating the ethnic and cultural diversity. Naess further goes on elaborating the need of appreciating all forms of life and non-violent action oriented lifestyle.[137] Deep ecology deals with the relationship and interdependence of all forms of life from micro-organism to macro- organism to human species. The survival of the human species largely depends upon the harmony of all life on the planet and keeping a balance interrelationship with the other organisms.[138] It challenges materialism, militarism, human dominion over the natural world, industrialism and so on. Anything that devalues the intrinsic values of the nature is critically observed. The philosophy of deep ecology entails that humanity has no right to destroy and reduce the richness and diversity of all forms of life in the planet earth. They observed that the present status of human interference with the non-human world is excessive and unlimited as such economic, technology and ideological policies need to be changed.[139] Unlike other philosophies, deep ecology argues and goes beyond biocentrism that it is not enough

---

[135] Sarkar, *The Bible, Ecology* …, 64.

[136] Sarkar, *The Bible,Ecology* …, 68.

[137] George Sessions, "Deep Ecology as WorldView," *World Views and Ecology*: Religion, Philosophy and the Environment, ed., Mary Evelyn Tucker and John A. Grim (Maryknoll: Orbis Books, 1994), 213.

[138] Sebastian Kochupurackal, *Eco-Mission: A Paradigm Shift in Missiology* (Bangalore: Asian Trading Corporation, 2007), 68.

[139] Sarkar, *The Bible, Ecology* …, 64.

to extend the same value given to humanity to the other creatures. It is not the extension of value but has to do with the interrelation and interconnectedness of all the creatures. They argue that there is neither internal cosmos nor external cosmos. There is only one cosmos where all lives are included.[140]

8.4. Shallow Ecology

Shallow ecology elevates humans higher and superior than the other creation. In a way shallow ecology shares the ideas and values of anthropocentricism. They follow the philosophy of conservationists and preservationists. Conservationists' commitment towards nature is based on the utility for human use and not on intrinsic value. Conservationists stress on the scientific management and rely on the proper use of technology. They are confident that meticulous use of scientific technology within the periphery will enhance the use of resources without damaging the limits of the ecosystem. They strive for controlling nature yet rationally, efficiently and with proper care.[141] The preservationists observe nature from the view point of preservation as a result of harm from human activities. In other words, they challenge the conservationist philosophy of anthropocentricism and utilitarianism and advocates biocentrism especially with regard to species and ecosystem. Their commitment towards environment can be articulated in terms of moral responsibility; all the species must be protected from extinction. The preservationists advocate holistic and communitarian while being critical towards the scientific technology for the very fact of their historical role technology has played in the environmental degradation. [142]

8.5. Eco-Feminism

Eco-feminism is concern with the environmental degradation that affects the role of women in the society. They are in fact radical

---

[140] Celia Deane-Drummond, *A Handbook in Theology and Ecology* (London: SCM Press Ltd, 1996), 82.

[141] Martin-Schramm and Robert L. Stivers, *Christian Environmental Ethics…*, 25.

[142] Martin-Schramm and Robert L. Stivers, *Christian Environmental Ethics…*, 27-28.

ecologists yet promote non-violent change. Eco-feminist is in solidarity with the nature as victims from exploitation, oppression and manipulation especially through domination, patriarchal and hierarchal systems. They argue that assault on the nature is purely from androcentric ideology and not from anthropocentricism. As such environmental problem is deeply rooted in the social, cultural and political institutions. Thus, eco-feminism gives a new dimension of approaching the environmental crisis and has ushered in regenerating new definition with human relationship to nature. The relationship encompasses a just relationship without any discrimination on gender, color and species. As a matter of fact, their approach is holistic and perceives all life on earth as interrelated. Eco-feminism identifies themselves with nature in two dimensions – from their biological uniformity of reproduction and nurturing and as the victims of androcentric philosophy. Therefore, the core issue and agenda behind the eco-feminist movement is liberation of both the nature and women.

Eco-feminism is oriented towards the ideology of praxis. Dean-Drummond and others have described eco-feminism as the 'third wave of feminism.'[143] Heather Eaton compares eco-feminism as a juncture of multiple roadways and a place of convergence for various activists, environmentalists and feminists.[144] In the development of eco-feminism, Dean – Drummond has pointed out that some eco-feminists have lost their confidence to draw inspiration from the Scriptures because of the number of instances where women are portrayed very negatively in the biblical account. Yet many have echoed the concept of eco-feminism spirituality in spite of the difference in their opinions. Dean-Drummond further suggested Susan Griffin book on *Woman and Nature: Roaring Inside Her* as instrumental in imparting awareness in influencing eco-feminist theology. In her book, Griffin ushered a close affinity between humanity and nature in poetic language. Perhaps such developments and ideas have served to influence eco-feminist

[143] Deane – Drummond, *Eco – Theology…*,146.

[144] Heather Eaton, *Introducing Ecofeminist Theology* (London: Continuum, 2005), 3.

theologians to formulate spirituality that participates in other Christian theologies.[145]

8.6. Gaia Hypothesis

The Gaia hypothesis[146] is a development brought about in the interface between science, religion and spirituality. It was propounded by a British scientist, James Lovelock in the early 1970s. The Gaia is a metaphor used for the living Earth. Lovelock in his research and exploration for the existence of life on the planet Mars comprehended that there is an enormous difference of the atmospheric encircling a life sustaining planet and dead planet. Lovelock discovered that the earth possesses 'life' which has been instrumental in constantly maintaining the temperature and gaseous composition of the earth and also adapts to the environmental conditions. The name *Gaia* was suggested by his friend William Golding in his hypothesis on the life bearing earth. *Gaia* is an ancient Greek goddess of the earth. The noticeable difference of Lovelock theory and other scientific accepted theories was on his idea that the planet earth is alive in spite of the traditional norm which envisages that it is dead and inactive. The living organisms called the *biota* and the non-livings such as the atmosphere functions a single unit. Each function and role are inevitable important for the *Gaia.* The Gaia has her own life sustaining function and as such interference to the work and function of *Gaia* through human irresponsible intervention might cause an unbearable consequential response.[147] For Lovelock the *Gaia* has the potentiality to reconstitute and darn herself and perceive that the entire *Gaia* is a 'delicately tuned interacting system.' The atmosphere forms part and parcel of that interacting system as it is generated and sustained by the life processes within the *Gaia.*[148] One of the major criticisms of Lovelock hypothesis from ecologists was in his theory of homeostatic regulation of the

---

145 Deane – Drummond, *Eco – Theology...*,147.

146 The Gaia hypothesis is now called as Gaia theory.

147 Deane-Drummond, *A Handbook in Theology and Ecology...*, 98-100.

148 Sarkar, *The Bible, Ecology ...*, 83.

Gaia. *Gaia* hypothesis proves that the earth has enough capacity within itself to handle and bear the assault as it has been adapting to the circumstantial changes over the past millions of years. The *Gaia* might take a new adaption process for her life sustaining process; only humankinds, flora and fauna might have to bear the consequences.

9. Biblical Perspective on Ecology

There are different approaches and understanding on ecology as some have already been discussed but here I would like to go deeper into the biblical eco-theology and take an overview on the biblical teachings concerning ecology and unveil the biblical foundation in dealing with the issues on ecology. Biblical perspective on ecology is such a vast area to cover and at no point I will be able to do justice in this limited discussion to produce a detail study on the subject. Therefore, the discussion will be limited to a brief general understanding of the Biblical perspectives and concentrates more on elaborate discussion on some of the ecological themes in the Bible.

The Bible as a whole takes the good purpose of God for the whole creation very seriously. The Biblical writers portrayed the very presence of God in nature through their writings. The declaration of God as 'good' in His whole creation explicitly exhibits that all creation is intrinsically valued by God. In fact the first name of the human being Adam which is in Hebrew word *adam* means '*dirt.*' As such human kinds are of the land and closely connected to the soil. So, the question of human superiority does not arise.[149] The Old Testament consistently affirms that God is the owner of the earth and all its resources. The opening chapter of Genesis is now universally recognized as the chapter to portray the absolute sovereignty of God over the created universe- living and non-living. The book of Leviticus (Lev. 25) further reaffirms how the Israelites were to be responsible in caring and protecting

---

[149] Mark Bredin, *The Ecology of the New Testament*: Creation, Re-creation and the Environment (Colorado Spring: Biblica Publishing, 2010), 16.

the Promised Land especially in the principles of Sabbath[150] and Jubilee. In Deut. 11:12-15 caring for the creation is elaborated in terms of human stewardship. The wisdom literature has explicitly expounded to God's care and concern towards all creatures. The psalmist was very particular in Psalms 24 in reaffirming the belongingness of the earth to the Creator. Human beings are entrusted with greater responsibility to care and protect the cosmos against the threat from chaotic forces. For instance Psalm 24:1 -2 "The earth is the Lord's and all that is in it, the world and those who live in it; for he has founded it on the seas and established it on the rivers."[151] Here proper exegesis will discover that commentators have noticed the Hebrew word for sea (*yam*) and river (*nahar)* are words attributed to the names of the chaotic gods of the ancient Near East. If the whole creation is not given the right care and love as they deserve, and if we continue to distort them, then creation will return to the primeval chaotic condition. In the New Testament teachings, care for the whole creation is reaffirmed in the Gospels and the Pauline writings. Jesus reaffirms the continued care for the creation in Matt. 6:28-30 when he invited the audience to consider the beauty of the lilies of the field. He clearly mentioned about his provisions for his creation in Luke 12:6-8. Jesus' teaching in Luke 12:6-7 implicitly declares that God's fatherly care reaches even to the smallest of the creation. It is explicitly defined in the writings of Paul to the Romans 8:18-23, the future hope of the reign of God's justice and righteousness for all creation. Paul emphasise that the greed and dominance of the human being have left the natural order ill and in pain. Paul envisages that the reconciliation, redemption and the covenant of God was for the whole creation, human beings and non-human beings. Thus, the non-human part of creation should also share in the glorious freedom of God.[152] Paul also further explains the ecological concern in Colossians

---

[150] It will be further discussed below under the principle of Sabbath.

[151] The Holy Bible, NRSV (Grand Rapids: Zondervan, 1989), 436.

[152] R. L. Sarkar, *The Bible, Ecology and Environment* (Delhi: ISPCK, 2000), 98.

1:15-20[153] when he says that, "He is the image of the invisible God, the first born of all creation: for in him all things in heaven and on earth were created, things visible and invisible, whether thrones or dominions or rulers or powers – all things have been created through him and for him...and through him God was pleased to reconcile to himself all things, whether on earth or in heaven by making peace through the blood of his cross."[154] Paul's teaching elaborates that Jesus Christ is the core basis for the unity and purpose of the whole universe. Therefore, the entire Bible teaches that human beings are to be servants, brothers and sisters of the whole cosmos. Human beings are united to nature in origin and thus we are to see the entire creation as brothers/sisters. Humans are also in a sense servants of all creation in taking care of their well-being and act like trustees.

One of the distinctive features of biblical affirmation on the value of creation which often is left unnoticed is the responses of the creation to the Creator God for the blessings in the form of creation's praise. References of the creation's praise are found explicitly in the Old Testament as well as in the New Testament – Isa.42:10; Psm. 19:1-4; 69:34; 96:11-12; 98:7-8; 103: 22; 150:6; Phil.2:10; Rev. 5:13. Some of these passages contain the acknowledgment from the creations for being who they are and some of the passages have salvific themes where the non – human creation participates with the human beings in praising God. The other area of biblical account is the participatory occasion of the earth in the act of creation as found in Genesis 1:11 and 24. The expression of the earth giving forth plants and the earthly animals depicts the involvement of the non-human creatures in the work of creation in obedience to the divine command.[155] Ultimately, it resonates that from the very beginning of the Divine creation non-human life was also involved. For Robert Murray the Noahic covenant (Genesis 9:8-17) was a cosmic covenant

---

[153] I will discuss this in detail in Eco-Christology in the next area of discussion.

[154] The Holy Bible, NRSV ..., 956.

[155] Deane – Drummond, *Eco – Theology...*, 86.

that established a realistic account of relationship between humans and non-human creatures.[156]

10. Ecology and Christian Doctrines

To consider all the Christian doctrinal themes may not be possible in this brief discussion owing to the limitation of space. I will confine here to the discussion which I feel it's important as Christian response towards global ecological problem takes into serious reflection from our faith praxis perspective. Thus, consideration on ecology in relation to Christology, Pneumatology, Theodicy and Eschatology will be the main focus in this section. Substantial discussion on these theocentric biblical doctrines will lay a sound theological foundation for the ecumenical community to respond adequately to the contemporary ecological crisis. In the discussion I prefer to use the prefix 'eco' to describe the relation of ecology to the doctrinal themes that will be discussed hereafter.

10.1. Eco-Christology

The topic on ecology has been a prominent theme of discussion or most deliberated issues in the contemporary theological fraternity yet it is noticed that sufficient writings and arguments have not been produced in its relationship with Christology. The very fact that Jesus Christ is the foundation of Christian faith, beliefs and practices, challenged the ecumenical community to deeply consider seriously the doctrine of Christology and engaged it with the ecological concerns. Unless this relationship is developed, discussion on ecology will simply become a shallow deliberation on the reference to God as the Creator and superficial affirmation of God's sovereignty. In order to make ecology deeply rooted in Christian faith and practices thereby respond to the present ecological problems it is crucial to relate the Christological significance to ecology. A concrete and sound relationship between ecology and Christology must be at the centre of Christian ecological theology.

---

[156] Robert Murray, *The Cosmic Covenant* (London: Sheed and Ward, 1992), 34.

For the discussion on eco-Christology, I begin by venturing into the priestly writing of Genesis, the Garden of Eden where human beings were attributed as the *imago Dei* (Gen. 1:26-27). Jürgen Moltmann argues that the *imago Dei* attributed to human beings have not been justified vividly in the Biblical tradition except on the priestly writing of Genesis (Gen. 1:26, 27, 5:1,9:6) and sporadic references in the wisdom tradition (Psl. 8:5). Further this traditional concept was not developed explicitly in the New Testament writings either. Moltmann explains that "Christ is 'the image of God' through whom everything is created (Col. 1:15ff, Heb. 1:3). Consequently, as a Son of God, he [He] is also the 'first-born' to whom believers 'are to become like in form (Rom. 8:29). The *imago Christi* is an *imago Dei* mediated through Christ."[157] Therefore, for him, human beings are rather created 'to be His image' and the full image of God, the true image is completed only in Christ (2 Cor. 4:4, 6; Rom.1:23). It is at this point, I would argue that since Christ bears the true and complete image of God, He bears in Him, God's care and responsibility towards the entire creation-humans and non-humans. Larry L. Rasmussen, professor of social ethics also shares the same Christological understand with Moltmann. For him, Christ bore the full image of God as the cross was an indirect manifestation of God. God exposed Himself through the cross; in Jesus, God was made poor and abused. God identifies Himself with the weak, the poor, the oppressed, the rejected, the wretched, the broken, the sufferings and the pains. And sure enough, with the turmoil of creation, sufferings of the nature and the earth God is affected. Thus, Larry L. Rasmussen expresses the *imago Dei* as practicing a godly lifestyle towards one another and to the other creatures. It is also to share in the responsibility with God to love and care the earth.[158] The other writer who shares the same Christological concept with Moltmann is Denis Edwards. In his expression on *imago Dei*, he affirms that

---

[157] Jürgen Moltmann, *God in Creation*: *An Ecological Doctrine of Creation* translated by Margaret Kohl (London: SCM Press Ltd.,1985), 218.

[158] Larry L. Rasmussen, *Earth Community, Earth Ethics* (Maryknoll: Orbis Books, 1996), 280.

Jesus Christ is the full image of God and the whole creations are the self-expression of God, i.e., imaging God.[159] Deane – Drummond pointed out that Christ had existed in relationship with all the created things in the logos (John 1:1-5). But, it is only after His incarnation, the unity and oneness of Christ with all the flesh was realized and the kinship type of relationship was established with all the creation – humans and non-humans.[160] Niels Gregersen, a Danish theologian called this 'word made flesh' in John's account as a deep incarnation. He affirms that "in Christ, God enters into biological life in a new way and is now with evolving creation in a radically new way."[161] I will further discuss the Eco-Christology with particular reference to Philippians 2:6-11 and Colossians 1:15-20.

10.1.1. Kenotic Christology: Philippians 2:6-11

Kenosis talks about God's incarnation. God in His attempt to identify Himself with His creation took the full form of humanity through Jesus Christ. Kenosis is about a generous self-giving, an emptying of self or a self-giving out of sheer love for the whole creation. In this regard S. Bulgakov argues that the primary purpose of incarnation is God's love for the whole creation rather than his simple response to human sinfulness.[162] Kenotic Christology therefore, needs to be understood from the perspective of the existence of all the creation and not just humans alone. Here I would like to put forth a discussion on the atonement in relation to the non-humans as this holistic understanding on atonement is vital and necessary for understanding the work of redemption[163]

---

[159] Denis Edwards, *Ecology at the Heart of Faith: The Change of Heart that Leads to a New Way of Living on Earth* (Maryknoll: Orbis Books, 2008), 14.

[160] Deane – Drummond, *Eco – Theology…*, 100.

[161] Niels Henrik Gregersen, "The Cross of Christ in an Evolutionary World," *Dialog: A Journal of Theology*, 40/3 (2001): 205.

[162] Sergii Bulgakov's work are significant in his books, *The Bride of the Lamb* (Grand Rapids: Eerdmans, 2002), *The Lamb of God* (Grand Rapids: Eerdmans, 2008).

[163] I will deal more on the redemption aspect in the later discussion on eco-theodicy and eco-eschatology.

on the humans and the non-humans. Moltmann has explicitly pointed out that, "If Christ is the first-born from the dead, then he cannot be merely 'the new Adam' of a new humanity. He must also be understood as the first-born of the whole creation."[164] Here the concern is what kind of atonement theory is most applicable to consider for the non-human world; since there could be very little sense of conceptualizing the 'godlessness' of the non-human world. It is important at this point to bring out the discussion of Deane-Drummond on Moltmann's account of the atonement. He has coined the word 'suffering'[165] as a metaphor for the atonement. He perceives that Christ suffering must be interpreted in the light of His resurrection. The resurrection of Christ from the dead offers new avenues of hope to all the creaturely beings, not only for the human beings alone.[166]

10.1.2. The Cosmic Christology: Col. 1:15-20

The world is in need of peace and justice for the survival of the human beings as well as the non - human beings. There can be peace only when there is justice and vice versa and this peace and justice can be realized only in the state of complete equilibrium. It can be established only when the structural violence towards the nature and other creaturely beings are broken down. The apostle

---

[164] Jürgen Moltmann, *The Way of Jesus Christ: Christology in Messianic Dimensions* (Minneapolis: Fortress Press, 1993), 278-279.

[165] Moltmann has discussed that 'sufferings, affliction, reproach and shame of Christ are words used in the New Testament particularly by Paul in his description on "i) the personal suffering of Jesus from Gethsemane to Golgatha, ii) the sufferings of the apostle who proclaims the gospel of Christ, is therefore persecuted and has to suffer iii) the sufferings of Israel, the prophets and John the Baptist and iv) the sufferings of the whole groaning creation in this present time." So the sufferings of Christ are not confined to Jesus alone. Christ suffering is not his own personal suffering but they are apocalyptic sufferings which He suffered for the whole world. They are not fortuitous suffering but they are necessary, they are not fruitless sufferings but fruitful sufferings. See more in Jürgen Moltmann, *The Way of Jesus Christ: Christology in Messianic Dimensions* (Minneapolis: Fortress Press,1993).

[166] Deane-Drummond has discussed this in her book on *Christ and Evolution: Wonder and Wisdom* (Minneapolis: Fortress Press,2009). See also Jürgen Moltmann, *Theology of Hope* (London: SCM Press Ltd,1967).

Paul has developed this vision of cosmic peace through the cosmic Christology in the epistle to the Colossians. Paul unlike his other epistles where he expounded mostly on the salvation through Christ has addressed in this particular passage in Colossians because of the need of the context to affirm Christ's cosmic significance. Paul stresses that Christ is the agent of the cosmic peace because he has reconciled everything in heaven and on earth to God. Through the blood of the cross, Christ has brought forth peace not only to human beings but also to the whole creation. The passage can be viewed having two sections – the whole creation was made through Jesus Christ and it is through Christ all things were reconciled to God. In the words of Moltmann, Christ has "reconciled through his death and gathered up into the peace of the new community of creation.... Mutual destruction is replaced by a community of peace in which all created beings are there for one another, with one another and in one another, and through the interchange of their energies keep one another in life, for one another and together."[167] Paul explains that in his relation to the cosmos, Christ is the first born over all the creation, which means Christ was from the beginning, before all the creation. Christ is the unifying principle to God and sustainer of all the creation.[168] Michael Trainor claims that "What creation is about is revealed in him, in his relationship to God. In Jesus the cosmos is taken to a new height; it is sanctified and revelatory of God's own being."[169] Everything in the cosmos is created in Christ and is reconciled in Him. So, the death and resurrection of Christ have ushered a new beginning of transformed life in the form of new creation for the whole creation. Vincent Rossi an Eastern Orthodox theologian interpreted the hymn in Colossians in terms of the Logos. He attributed the reconciliation in the passage to the source that was from the beginning, the Logos. He then relates it to the epistle of

---

[167] Moltmann, *The Way of Jesus Christ...*, 255.

[168] Curtis Vaughan, "Colossians," *The Expositor's Bible Commentary*, vol. 11, Frank E. Gaebelein et al. (Grand Rapids: Zondervan Publishing House,1978), 182.

[169] Michael Trainor, "Celebrating Diversity: The Hymn to Christ in a letter from Ancient Colossae (Col. 1:15-20)," *Biodiversity and Ecology as Interdisciplinary Challenge*, ed., Denis Edwards and M. Worthing (Adelaide: ATF, 2004), 70.

Philippians 2:10[170] and draws the conclusion that reconciliation with the Logos reinstates order and harmony in the cosmos.[171]

10.2. Eco-Pneumatology

Eco-Pneumatology is another area of discussion that is very crucial in Christian theological reflection. Perhaps it is appropriate to point out that the role and place of the Spirit in the field of ecology needs elaborative discussion so as to bring about fruitful deliberations and locate the place and role of the Spirit for ecological reflections. The task is also difficult at the same because the working of the Holy Spirit is solely perceived in His involvement for human community. The task is challenging yet deliberations and arguments on the involvement of the Spirit beyond human community to the non-human communities needs to be implicitly articulated so as to establish a concrete foundation in the Christian responses to ecological problems today. The biblical reference to the work of the Spirit amongst the creation was visible from the Genesis account-Genesis 1:2 speaks of the involvement of the Spirit in dispelling the formless void and deep waters. In Genesis 2:7, the Spirit is witnessed as a life giving agent to God's creation. This life giving role of the spirit is further substantiated in the wisdom literatures in Psalm 104:29-30 and Job 33:4.

God breathed out His *Ruach* or *Pneuma* and through the Spirit relates and worked among not only with the humans but also with the non-human world. The Spirit has it role not only in the Creation account but also in the work of redemption. As Deane - Drummond pointed that the Spirit was at work with the Father in the creation and was at work with the Son in the redemption.[172] For clearer understanding and reflection in relation to the role of the Spirit to the whole creation, I wishes here to bring forth the doctrine of trinity and discuss the various arguments advocated by scholars on Eco-Pneumatology. The work of a Cappodician theologian,

---

170 *The Holy Bible,* NRSV..., 954.

171 V. Rossi, "Christian Ecology is Cosmic Christology," *Epiphany,* 8 (1988), 54.

172 Deane – Drummond, *Eco – Theology...,*132.

Gregory of Naziansus on the role of the Spirit to the whole creation reviewed by Sigurd Bergmann[173] is worth mentioning here. Gregory of Naziansus in his interpretation on the doctrine of Trinity explains that creation was an expansion of the divine communion[174] so as to allow the world of creation to participate in the sociality of God. Naziansus claims that it is the Spirit that guides, sanctifies, creates and confers life. He further expresses that the Spirit is also active in the work of liberation – humans and the natural world. Bergmann in his work also pointed out that the Work of the Spirit cannot be confined only as a mediator between God and the world but the Spirit is in Triune God who plays the role to liberate creation. Moltmann in his work on the Trinitarian doctrine of creation emphasises that the Spirit was the agent and efficacious power of the Creator. The Creator breathed forth the Spirit and indwells Himself in His creation. As such through the Spirit, God the Creator preserves His creation and participates in the future of the creation. The theory of *Kenosis* the self-emptying, self-giving plays an important role in Moltmann's Eco-Pneumatology. Through this theory he understands that the Spirit is identified with the sufferings of the creation – humans and the creaturely beings. Thus, through the Spirit, the Creator God suffers with the sufferings of the humans and the other creaturely beings.[175] In the Trinitarian concept of creation, Moltmann attributes the Father to the creating origin in creation, the Son to the shaping origin and the Spirit to the life-giving origin. For Moltmann theological consideration on the Spirit must begin with the work of the Spirit in the community of the Church. Firstly, the Spirit is active in the faith conviction of a person (2 Cor. 5:17); secondly in breaking down the natural and social barriers in a community (Gal. 3:28); thirdly in bestowing spiritual gifts to the individuals (1 Cor. 12) and fourthly all these experiences of the Spirit's presence points towards the future hope which include the whole cosmos. The working of the Spirit in the

---

[173] See Bergmann, *Creation Set Free*: The Spirit as Liberator of Nature…

[174] It has already been explained in detail under the sub-heading the early Church fathers.

[175] Moltmann, *God in Creation* …, 96-97.

Church enables leads to discover the role of the Spirit in natures. He affirms that firstly the Spirit is the source of creativity of all matter and life. It is the Spirit who operates in opening possibilities for new creation. Secondly, it is the Spirit that creates interactions, harmony, cooperation and community. Thirdly, all the creation in the Spirit is directed towards the common eschatology. Therefore, Moltmann, "perceives in the Holy Spirit himself 'an inexpressible sighing' (Rom. 8:26). So, what believers experience and perceive in the Holy Spirit reveals the structure of the Spirit of creation, the human spirit, and the Spirit in the whole non-human creation; because it is to this that their experience corresponds. What believers experience in the Holy Spirit leads them into solidarity with all other created things."[176] Mark I. Wallace, professor of Christian Ethics also argues in some sense in line with Moltmann's view. He expresses that the Spirit needs to be radically identifies with all forms of life. For him it is the Spirit that indwells and sustains all forms of life; as the Spirit is the inner and unseen power within the creation. Wallace was more affirmative in developing earth spirituality that projects all forms of life as interdependent even including the divine life. As such for him, ecocide is not only death for the nature but it brings sufferings to the Spirit and ultimately decimates the image of God.[177] I feels that, discussion on Eco-Pneumatology should not push us to pantheism but Eco-Pneumatology show be view more from the Trinitarian concept along with Jürgen Moltmann. While acknowledging the indwelling of the Spirit in all forms of life, I would also agree with Deane-Drummond that the Spirit is expressed differently among the varieties of creatures at different levels. However, this conviction should not erect barriers among the creaturely beings; there must be greater mutual respect of the differences of each creature.

---

[176] Moltmann, *God in Creation* ..., 101.

[177] Mark I. Wallace, *Fragments of the Spirit: Nature, Violence and the Renewal of Creation* (Harrisburg: Trinity Press International, 2002), 143.

10.3. Eco-Theodicy[178]

New World Encyclopaedia has defined theodicy as, "a specific branch of theology and philosophy, which attempts to solve the Problem of Evil—the problem that arises when trying to reconcile the observed existence of evil in the world with the assumption of the existence of a God who is fully good (or benevolent) and who is also all-powerful (omnipotent)."[179]

Traditionally suffering or evil in its comprehensive understanding consists of natural evil and moral evil. Natural evil arises out of suffering and pain through natural causes such as an earthquake. It also includes the biophysical evil, a suffering caused to the non-human world caused by non-human agents. Moral evils are sufferings generated and inflicted to self and extents to other as well through human intervention particularly with the choice and exercise of free will. Celia Dean-Drummond has added another classification of evil which she term it anthropogenic evil. The evil and sufferings that arises out of growth in human population, industrialization, urbanization and rapid economic growth in the form of chemicals waste adversely affecting climate change.[180] I forth eco-theodicy here to reflect on extending the understanding of evil and suffering beyond human society and perceive theodicy from holistic approach. With the contemporary ecological ill which is becoming more visible day by day, humanity needs to confess the guilt of anthropogenic evil inflicted upon the natural world. There might have existed different levels of arguments on eco-theodicy yet at this juncture it is vital to retrospect if the traditional understanding on theodicies in relation to human beings are completely sufficient enough to meet the sufferings visible in the non-human sphere or in the present context, do we need any further thinking of non-human sufferings?[181] The issue on eco-theodicy has not been dealt with in detail by scholars; I

---

[178] I have borrowed this term from Celia Dean-Drummond from her book on *Eco-Theology.*

[179] http://www.newworldencyclopedia.org/entry/Theodicy (December 6, 2015).

[180] Deane – Drummond, *Eco – Theology…,* 116.

[181] Deane – Drummond, *Eco – Theology…,* 118.

noticed that Dean-Drummond has brought out this new avenue of discussion on eco-theodicy in the face of the contemporary ecological ill and sufferings. Thus much of the reflection here will be pointed out from Dean – Drummond's work and reflection.

Different dimensions of arguments have developed in regards to the problem of evil or suffering. With the limitation of space I do not envisages to produce a detail explanation. But, a brief discussion is vital for deeper understanding on evil and good. There is the process argument which considers that the overall process is good and suffering which is directed towards achieving this good can be recognized as part of the process. The next is the possibility arguments where argument is centred on the good that arises comprises the possibility of the presence of evil. It is best understood from the perspectives of the free will defence. Unlike the Genesis account of human fall because of the choice of free will, the possibility philosophy argues that the existence of free will does not necessarily mean the existence of evil. Rather human can choose good not necessarily evil in their free will. Ontological philosophers argue that the existence of good is intrinsically attached to the experience of suffering or evil. Another form of argument is the unreality argument which was developed by Thomas Aquinas. They perceive that evil is illusory at the same time unreal.[182] For the philosophy of Mystery argument, understanding God from the apophatic tradition is essential; the working of God is unknown and beyond comprehension. Dean–Drummond citing Denis Edwards argues that, "suffering does not find any kind of full explanation in the Christian tradition, but is understood as a critical memory that calls for liberating and healing praxis and that opens in hope to a future in God; God is not subject to our limited human concepts but confronts us as incomprehensible and uncontrollable Mystery."[183] In the ethical arguments, it is proposed that humanity needs to be bro-active by choice in countering evil and intervene in protection of the species. It further proposes that humanity cannot

---

[182] Deane – Drummond, *Eco – Theology...*,118-122.

[183] Deane – Drummond, *Eco – Theology...*,123.

act only as the priest of creation but also can be co-redeemer in 'saving those lives that otherwise would be lost.'[184]

The above forms of arguments on theodicy have their own limitations and Dean–Drummond has suggested a synthesis of extracting the positive arguments in each theodicy that will work towards deeper and meaningful eco-theodicy. She further more suggested that one model of reflecting on the synthesis is through 'shadow sophia.'[185] In her description of shadow sophia, she explain that;[186]

> Shadow sophia offers an account of evil that takes up, then, the different dimensions of theodicy, and gives them appropriate expression in both the non-human world and human worlds....I suggest that here is its particular strength, for it reminds us of the limitations of all types of theodicy, and seeks to offer a synthetic account of what evil might entail, while remaining qualified as to precisely what it represents – shadow sophia, like wisdom more

---

[184] Deane – Drummond, *Eco – Theology...*,125.

[185] Dean –Drummond has borrowed this logical and philosophical term from Russian writer, Sergius Bulgakov. Bulgakov expresses Shadow Sophia as the dark possibility of evil in the world. He speaks of evil as a shadow and illusion because evil for him is associated with misdirected freedom. In Bulgakov's view, after the fall of humanity, the beauty of nature is arrested by the darkness existing in the creaturely Sophia. "The beauty of nature has no moral attributes; it is neither good nor evil in the sense of moral decision making. However, following the fall, humanity begins to direct undo attention to beauty in the created world, so that it becomes the object of human possession and thereby an occasion for sin. In this sense, it is impossible for the Holy Spirit to enkindle the universal spiritual transformation of creation until the parousia, but in the meantime, the Holy Spirits as the 'natural grace of creation' working towards the sophianizing of the created world, when creaturely Sophia will be united with the divine Sophia and God will be all in all."

I understood the term 'Shadow Sophia' as the dark side of evil which has cast over the natural world. In other words it is the expression of the suffering present in the natural world, non-humans. see Celia Deane-Drummond, *Christ and Evolution*: Wonder and Wisdom (Minneapolis: Fortress Press, 2009), 185-187, S. Bulgakov, *The Bride and the Lamb* (Grand Rapids: Eerdmans Press, 2002), C. Graves, *The Holy Spirit in the Theology of Sergius Bulgakov* (Geneva:WCC, 1972), 233-234.

[186] Deane – Drummond, *Eco – Theology...*,127.

generally, is deliberately elusive as far as clear definition is concern – for it cannot be tied down to one particular form of reasoning.

The role of shadow Sophia and the existence of the evil remains mysterious as it is beyond human comprehension to understand the wisdom of God. It is at this point words are limited for any deeper theological explanation and human language are abridged to stillness. The explanation of shadow sophia needs also to take into consideration the Christological dimension as Christ atoning and reconciliation work towards the cosmos finds its expression in shadow sophia. As such, in as much the Christian community shares in the suffering of Christ, it also embraces the suffering that is embedded in the shadow sophia[187] and takes the form of what has been discussed above – the co-redeemer. The cross and resurrection of Jesus Christ have shown us the way of love. In His redemption the distress and agony of the whole creation was embraced with His love. It is not through human's progressive intervention in the non-human world that they become co-redeemers but only through their sharing in Christ self-emptying sacrifice on the cross. Therefore, perhaps the most fitting way of 'being with Jesus'[188] is to walk, to reach out to the place of sufferings and finding God's love and power amidst the sufferings and pains.

10.4. Eco-Eschatology

It is clear enough that the future of global community – human and other species are in danger as a result of human activities and industrial development. The issue on eco-eschatology has not been deliberated extensively in the Bible and as such dealing with the issues is difficult at the same time sensitive. Much cautious approach needs to be improvised as one deal with the subject on eco-eschatology. On the other hand, with the alarming threat to the natural world in the post–modern world, it becomes vital to place the position of the future of the nature. Eschatology is mostly understood rather narrowly concerning the doctrine of the last thing or of the end. This traditional

[187] Deane – Drummond, *Eco – Theology...*,128.

[188] I means loving Jesus and making allegiance to follow His precepts.

understanding towards eschatology has been critically evaluated by modern scholars for making the concept too narrow. Yet, with the changes of time and context, eschatological understanding needs to go beyond human world of existence and view holistically; the expression should also find its place in the natural world of creation. Modern theologians have expressed and defined the new kingdom of God in terms of realised eschatology which can be experienced now through the participation of the Holy Spirit. One of the theologians who have written extensively on creation and the future of creation is Jurgen Moltmann. Moltmann in his '*Theology of Hope*' affirmed that the traditional understanding on eschatology "were like a loosely attached appendix that wandered off into obscure irrelevancies."[189] For Moltmann, the restricted understanding of eschatology only to the doctrine of the end does not denote any relation to the cross and resurrection of Jesus Christ,[190] Since Christ coming has ushered a new beginning for all the creation through His redemptive work. For him Christian eschatology must extend towards cosmic eschatology. Perhaps, God would be contradicting to himself if the redemption is not extended to everything He created. Thus, for him "eschatology means the doctrine of the Christian hope, which embraces both the object hoped for and also the hope inspired by it. From first to last, and not merely in the epilogue, Christianity is eschatology, is hope, forward looking and forward moving, and therefore also revolutionizing and transforming the present.... Eschatology should not be its end, but its beginning."[191] Moltmann is of the view that in the eschatology, rather than the restoration of the creation new creation-new heaven and new earth, will take place where God himself will dwell universally.[192] In fact the future hope directs to the theology that in the consummation, the whole creation will take

---

[189] Jurgen Moltman, *Theology of Hope*: *On the Ground and the Implications of a Christian Eschatology* (London: SCM Press Ltd., 1977), 15.

[190] Moltman, *Theology of Hope...*, 15.

[191] Moltman, *Theology of Hope...*, 16.

[192] Jurgen Moltman, *The Future of Creation* (London: SCM Press Ltd, 1979), 125.

the divine image and transformed into the *imago die.*[193] Moltmann interprets the apocalyptic book of Revelation 21:4[194] as a visualisation of positive reality in anticipation and a creation of classless society.[195] Moltmann total concept of eschatology and ecology can be cogently summed up in the following words,[196]

> This earth, with its world of the living, is the real and sensorily experienceable promise of the new earth, as truly as this earthly, mortal life here is an experienceable promise of the life that is eternal, immortal. If the divine Redeemer is himself present in this earth in hidden form, then the earth becomes the bearer or vehicle of his and our future.... For an eschatology that is christologically grounded and ecologically responsibly maintained, there is no better concept.

One of the contemporary writers who have argued eco-eschatology in the theology of Moltmann of new heaven and new earth is N. T. Wright,[197] the bishop of Durham. For him the coming of Jesus was not only an extraordinary miracle but it has ushered the beginning of new creation. The whole earth is God's holy land and one day in His appointed time and space, God will renew the whole created order where God's glory will be reflected and God's justice will prevail. This will set thing right the whole earth which is groaning form the slavery of oppression and exploitation to a new set of order. However, Wright affirms that God new creation will not happen from *ex nihilo* like the Genesis creation account but from the *ex vetere,* the existing one.

---

[193] Jurgen Moltman, *The Coming of God: Christian Eschatology* (London: SCM Press Ltd,1996), 273.

[194] He will wipe every tear from their eyes. Death will be no more; mourning and crying and pain will be no more, for the first things have passed away. (The Holy Bible, NRSV).

[195] Moltman, *The Future of Creation...*, 125.

[196] Moltman, *The Coming of God...*, 279.

[197] See N. T. Wright, "Jesus is Coming – Plant a Tree," The Green Bible (NRSV) (San Francisco: Harper Collins Publishers, 1998), 72-85.

James Lovelock's book on *The Revenge of Gaia: Why the Earth is Fighting Back - and How We Can Still Save Humanity*[198] has explained about how human kind has inflicted so much pain upon the living Earth, Gaia and as such the contemporary ecological crisis is the result of Gaia's reaction. Lovelock identified the apocalyptic disasters not as futuristic event which are yet to come but the present ecocrisis especially that of the global warming. The current climate change which otherwise is heading towards greater destruction if adequate measures of prevention are not initiated will reduced human survival to a minimum. In his own words of describing the condition of Gaia, he said;[199]

> As the sun grows ever hotter it will, in Gaia's terms, soon become too hot for animals and plants and many of the microbial forms of life. I think it unlikely that heat-tolerant bacteria, thermophiles living in the oases of a desert world, would be abundant enough to form the critical mass of living things needed for Gaia. It is also unlikely that the kind of Earth we know now would last even a fraction of those billion years. The harm done by a planetesimal impact, or even by a future, or even by a future industrial civilization, may drive Gaia first to one of the hotter and temporarily stable states, and finally to total failure.

Dean-Drummond was of the view that Moltmann's vision on building new life on the earth that include every creature that ever existed may not happen. However, the alternative suggestion and more realistic way can be[200]

> ...to envisage some form of inscription in the memory of God for creaturely beings, but a rather more robust interpretation of resurrection for conscious beings... for there are some things that we cannot know, since they are

[198] James Lovelock, *The Revenge of Gaia: Why the Earth is Fighting Back - and How We Can Still Save Humanity* (Oxford: Penguin Books, 2006).

[199] Lovelock, *The Revenge of Gaia...*, 59-60.

[200] Deane – Drummond, *Eco – Theology...*, 178.

> hidden in the heart of God. What we do know, however, is that since God is a God of love, the new experience will be one that is inclusive of creatures in some way, and that this life will be rich in its experiences, taking up the historical memory of different phases of our own history and biography, as well as wider in terms of the cosmos as a whole.

I would like to close this section with the concept and suggestion of Denis Edwards which is cited by Dean-Drummond. Perhaps this would also reflect my conviction and position on eco-eschatology. Firstly, the imminent location of the creation remains ambiguous and also surrounded in mystery. Secondly, the entire creation - humans and non-humans through the activity of the Holy Spirit are imprinted in the life of divine eternity. Thirdly, every creation - non humans and human finds their soothing and satisfaction in Christ. Fourthly, the redemption of Christ will vary depending upon the nature of the creation. God in His incomprehensible wisdom will relate to every creation in accordance to their positions. Ultimately, the action initiated by God for each creation will be the most appropriate to the particular creature.[201] All the creations are created in Christ and are also redeemed in Christ. Christian faith affirms that the earth is the Lord's as such overlooking the destruction of the earth and limiting God within the periphery of saving only human souls flatly denies the Biblical truths.[202] The redemptive purpose of God must be viewed in terms of saving the planet earth which ultimately begins with the cry of the poor and the cry of the earth as Leonardo Boff noted.

The study on the environmental issues explicitly shows that it is complex at the same time crucial. The discussion on biblical eco-theology has also given ample of substances that the Bible which was once castrated and regarded as the cause to the environment problems by the pioneers of environmental movement has major resources embedded within it to address the environmental problems. The *oikos*

---

[201] Deane – Drummond, *Eco – Theology...*, 176.

[202] Shantilal P. Bhagat, *Creation in Crisis: Responding to God's Covenant* (Illinois: Bretheren Press, 1990), 121.

is inflicted with many crises as a result of anthropogenic evil. With the advent of new scientific technologies, the ecumenical community is rather challenged to venture and contemplate on new approaches to combat the mounting global problem on ecology. I feel that one of such approaches that can be adopted is the model of eco-justice. Eco-justice model can be a pro-alternative response to the global ecological problems. It is vital for human community to consider the *oikos* as a habitat for all the species in which human beings are a part of that habitat. Learning to live in humility and harmony with other creations would further enhance, if not communicate humanity to adapt a just and equitable ways of living.

Through the discussions on ecology, I do not necessarily mean to neglect human's needs yet the arguments can be pointed more towards reviewing one's actions of greed, selfishness and power oriented programs considering the larger picture of the community of creation. I would undoubtedly consider that there are differences between human beings and the other creaturely beings. But, this difference should neither be taken for exploitation nor should it create barriers. On the other hand, I certainly would not elevate human beings as greater and unique beings than the other creaturely beings. However, I would suggest that this difference must be acknowledged, respected and as affirmed by Deane – Drummond the natural world must be regarded as mutual 'others.'

Chapter 2

Historical, Theological and Homiletic Development

1. Origin and Early Development of Preaching

The origin and beginning of Christian preaching can be trace back to the ancient oratory, Hebrew prophecy, the Synagogue worship and the Christian gospel. Even before the introduction of the Hebrew prophecy, Noah was mentioned as preacher of righteousness in his corrupt generation (2 Pet.2:5). As the history of Israel advances the prophets and the priest were responsible in repeating the law of God to the people.[203] The messages of the prophets begin with "thus said the Lord." When the conduct and messages of the prophets are examined thoroughly, one observes that each of the prophets appeared with distinct commission. However, one also noticed that there is uniformity in their preaching; reminding the people of their

[203] G. Isaiah, *Preach the Word: The basics of Homiletics* (Tiruvalla: Christava Sahitya Samithi, 2005), 34.

sins and exhorting them to repent. Their message also contains instructions on religious, moral, social and personal duties.[204]

The use and origin of oratory cannot be traced, yet what we know is that oratory grew out of conversation. Spencer assumes that oratory especially the religious oratory grew out of the laudatory address made to the war heroes upon their victorious return such as the acclamations of David on his victory over Goliath and the crossing of the Red Sea by the Israelites.[205] The Oratory of the ancient people before the Grecian and Roman times was neither very popular nor of the highest quality. However the Greek oratory was of great value and highest quality at the same time the gift of eloquence was also highly acknowledged. The growth and development of dialectic philosophy, art and literature, are flexible and powerful language of the Greeks and they contributed to the field of highest quality oratory. The Greco-Roman Oratory had no religious content but a moral one. While the Greco-Roman Oratory was in want for ethical and religious content, Christian Preaching steadily arose to offer oratory a new service. In the ancient Hebrew prophecy, the prophets were the preachers. They are orators with divine messages which were committed to the moral and spiritual culture of the people. Dargan points out that, " in the widely separated lines of development which the sacred and the secular oratory of the ancient world pursued before the coming of our Lord, God was laying the foundation for the use of public speech as a means in the spread and the establishment of Christianity."[206] In as way we can agree with Dargan and argue that the Hebrew prophecy was the preparatory period while the proclamation of Jesus and the apostles about the kingdom of God took the shape for the historic progress of Christian Preaching.

G. Isaiah opines that Synagogue worship might have had its origin either during or after the exile. In the Synagogue worship, two characteristics were very distinct – the reading of the portion

---

[204] DeWitte T. Holland, *The Preaching Tradition*: A Brief History, ed., William D. Thompson (Nashville: Abingdon, 1980), 14.

[205] Dargan, *A History of Preaching*...., 16-18.

[206] Dargan, *A History of Preaching*...., 21.

of the Old Testament and exposition of it by the elders (Luke 4:16-21& Acts 13:15f). These two distinct characteristics have been the core salient features of Christian preaching.[207] During the time of the introduction of Christianity, the service in the synagogues was mainly of oral instruction. Indeed, Jesus also took that opportunity to proclaim the Gospel. For the sermon in the synagogue until 200 B.C. (approximately) the Scripture lesson were chosen from the Pentateuch. Then slowly the work and messages of the prophets were also referred in the sermon. The Synagogue sermon was delivered every Sabbath, Friday night and Saturday morning and on special occasions as well. The Synagogue worship was arranged in such a way that the young rabbis will lead the other worship activities of the assembly and an elder rabbi will appear only during the delivery of the sermon.

In the New Testament, the earliest preacher noticed was John the Baptist from the wilderness. His preaching was on the preparation for the coming of the Messiah and repentance. Jesus Christ can be rightly considered the foundation, the graft and the substance of Christian Preaching. His preaching was on the Gospel of the Kingdom of God. Jesus tactically employed simple and natural language followed by plentiful illustrations, metaphors, parables, questions and answers in his proclamation about the Kingdom of God. He also spoke with authority. The Acts of the Apostles recorded that the preaching of Peter was direct and it witness the messianic personality of Jesus to the crowd (Acts 2). For the Apostle Paul, nearly half of the New Testament writings were attributed to him. This speaks volumes how he carried the rich heritage of preaching forward. Because of his intellectual knowledge and his unique background, he was able to use his oratory skills for preaching the Gospel. The great heritage of preaching was further passed on to the early Church fathers.

It is difficult to concretely bring out a systematic and well-proportioned discussion especially on preaching because of the limited resources. Yet I look forward that this limited presentation will surely enrich the readers especially in the field of homiletic development. I wish to discuss here the historical, theological and

[207] Isaiah, *Preach the Word...*, 35.

homiletical development briefly in accordance to the historical epoch.

2. The Patristic Age (A.D. 70-430)

2.1. Background

The birth of Christianity happened when the world during that time had its own religious, cultural, social and political structures. It was in this context that the new faith had to determine its relationship with its surroundings. One of the greatest challenges of Christianity was hostile attitude from the state, which later resulted in martyrdoms. The main reason for this persecution was because of the emperor worship. Thus, Christian teachings inclined more towards defence of the faith (from attackers) and formulation of the Christian Doctrine.[208] The Christian persecution in the second and third became very severe and it reached its worst persecution under Diocletian (284-305).

The Roman Empire was at the peak of their power at the beginning of Christianity. The Romans were highly skilful in their military endeavour which in turn helped them in establishing their strong political power very firmly.[209] The fall of Jerusalem in A.D. 70 resulted in the down fall of the Jewish commonwealth. Titus, the conqueror of Jerusalem extended his reign from Rome to the West including Spain and Portugal, Northwest it took France, Netherland and England, North it held the Germans, on the East it include Dalmatia, Greece, Asia Minor and Armenia, Southeast the lands of Egypt, Syria, Palestine, Persia; South it include the territories of Carthage and the Northern Africa in the West. He exhibited himself as an able ruler. In this period there were many corrupt rulers yet there were also few good rulers. By the end of the third century Christian was strong enough to endure the last furious persecution

---

[208] Justo L. Gonzalez, *Church History: An Essential Guide* (Nashville: Abingdon Press, 1996), 11-12.

[209] Martin Goodman, "The emergence of Christianity," *A World History of Christianity*, ed., Adrian Hastings (Grand Rapids: William B.Eerdmans Publishing Company, 2000), 8.

under Diocletian.[210] Christianity became a legalized religion during the reign of Emperor Constantine. Until now Christianity was a religion embraced mostly by the lower strata of the society, with the legalization Christianity begins to progress among the high officials. The rapid growth of Christianity brought in people of various religious backgrounds and this gave rise to the diverse interpretation of Christianity within the Church. The prominent groups of heretics were the Gnostics and the Marcion. Towards the end of the third century the polity and worship of the apostolic Church became more organized. The central act of Christian worship was communion and Baptism. Communion took place usually on Sunday and baptism on Easter Sunday after a long period of preparation for those who were to be baptised. The titles such as deacons, elders and bishops begin to appear in the church governance by this time.

2.2. Theological Development

The area in which the Roman did not excel and dominate during this era was in the field of writing and formulating theology. On the other hand, for Christianity this era is the age of the church fathers. The writings of the early apostolic fathers were precise which was aroused by the need of their contemporary situation. They do not exhibit concrete work of systematic theology even though it contains historical and literary interest.[211] The most prominent and intellectual centre of Christian theology was Alexandria. In the second and the third century, theologians like Clement and Origen both from Alexandrian developed a systematic and refined interpretation of the Scriptures and the relation of Christian beliefs to the culture and need of the current age. It was Origen who boldly made used of the contemporary philosophy in his writings rather than being too fundamentalist and confining himself to the repeating the past formulas.

The area of development and controversy was the Trinitarian theology. The problem faced by the early church fathers on Trinity

---

[210] Dargan, *A History of Preaching…*, 32-33.

[211] G. P. Fisher, *A History of Christian Doctrine*, ed., Hubert Cunliffe-Jones and Benjamin Drewery (Edinburgh: T&T Clark Ltd., 1978), 23.

was i) how can the Church escape from considering Christ as 'second God' and ii) how to explain the Triune God without sacrificing Christian monotheism. During this development, Irenaeus taught that the Son and Spirit participate in the divine substance. Tertullian using the word '*trinitas*' explain God as Father, Son and Holy Spirit. Origen considers 'logos' as person from all eternity and explained the doctrine of Trinity in a more philosophical approach.[212] Augustine was fully aware of the inadequacy of the medium of human language to explain about the absolute truth about Trinity, yet in his best possible expression he did explained the Trinitarian concept. Augustine explains Trinity through his great work *On the Trinity.* He affirms that the Triune God is one in substance, nature energy and will. He further explains that, "The Son and the Spirit are not sent because they are in any sense inferior or subordinate to the Father, but because they proceed from him. Each of the three persons is equal to the entire Trinity and the entire Trinity is not more than one of the persons."[213]

The most open theological controversies in this period were on the understanding of Christ in the New Testament writings. The Alexandrians stressed on the 'divinity of Christ' while the Antiochenes maintained on the 'humanity of Christ.'[214] The most severe controversy was the doctrine of Arius, a presbyter in the Church at Alexandria who denied that the Son, the second person in Trinity was fully divine. In his description the Son was the greatest of God's creation and mighty archangel but not God. Finally, Arianism was condemned at the Council of Nicea in 320 A.D. which was called by Emperor Constantine. The Nicean Council upheld the full divinity and the total humanity of Jesus Christ.[215] This Christological controversy did continued for another two centuries which the writer will discuss more in the next historical period of study.

---

[212] Otto W. Heick, *A History of Christian Thought*, vol. I (Philadelphia: Fortress Press, 1965), 144-145.

[213] Heick, *A History of Christian Thought*, vol. I…, 164.

[214] Adrian Hastings, "150-550," *A World History of Christianity*, ed., Adrian Hastings (Grand Rapids: William B. Eerdmans Publishing Company, 2000), 48.

[215] Jonathan Hill, *The History of Christian Thought* (England: A Lion Book, 2003), 58-59.

2.3. Preaching and its Significance

Many of the early Church fathers were notable and useful preachers yet because of the lack of written record of their homiletic work, their writings will be considered for determining the development of their homily. The homily was more inclined towards living a decent and righteous Christian live as that is the best they can do for Christ salvific sacrifice. They dwell mostly on Confession of Christ as the Lord and repentance. The style of preaching is natural, simple and appropriate even though they did not exhibit excellent oratory. They derived their sermons from the Scriptural text, however there was no exposition of the Scriptural text. The quotations from the Old Testament and the New Testament were frequently used. Writers have portrayed that preachers in theses period tried to practice what they urge upon others to do. Indeed their life itself was a preaching. Preaching occupied a part in the public worship. There was reading from the Gospels and also from the writings of the Prophets in the Old Testament. This was followed by a short discourse.[216] In the words of Dargan, "The interpretation and application are fairly good. There is no wild allegorizing or forcing of Scripture. The tone and spirit are admirable – faith, hope and love, with humility and sincerity, are apparent throughout."[217]

As Christianity began to grow into a more organised religion, Christian preaching also began to take it proper shape. By the end of the second century theologian and preacher like Origen and Clement from the Alexendrian School of thought, initiated an explanation and application of the Scriptural text in their homily. Origen expounded the sacred text and showed the importance of expository preaching. He followed grammatical, moral and allegorical method of interpreting the Scripture. He was simple and clear in the delivery of homily. He insisted on the ideology of preachers being doer of what they preach. Origen main interest was in Biblical interpretation. Using the Greek grammatical interpretation he analysis the text word by word and prepared his

---

[216] Alfred Ernest Garvie, *The Christian Preacher* (New York: Charles Scribner's Sons, 1921), 66.

[217] Dargan, *A History of Preaching…*, 45.

exegesis for the delivery of homilies. His application was moral at the same time mystical. In the moral application, he looked at the text for the meaning of the soul and the mystical sense the meaning of the passage in relation to Christ and the Church.[218] Origen made used of his sharp memory, excellent amount of Scriptural knowledge and abundant scholarship to teach spiritual and practical lessons through his sermons. He often concludes his homily with doxology. On the other hand Lucian and Dorotheus of the Antiochian School of thought began to teach on the literal, historical and grammatical interpretation of the Scripture. Prominent Antiochian school of thought preacher, John Chrysostom in his interpretation of the text followed the literal, grammatical, historical exegesis. Most of his homilies were expository in nature though at time he also preached topical sermons. In the beginning of the Ancient or Patristic Age since Christianity was an oppressed religion, the worship places were in secret places. But, by the beginning of the 4th century Church building for worship begin to be erected. Besides, the worship places, there was also a pulpit or platform for the preachers in the worship places. Gradually preaching took placed regularly on Sundays and festival days. The place of preaching became an important place in the Christmas, Easter and Pentecost days. As the Church in the East wrestles with the Trinitarian and Christological controversies, their preaching was also more inclined towards dogmatic. The West on the other hand with Church fathers like Tertullian, Ambrose and Augustine gave more emphasis on Soteriology; their preaching was evangelical and at the same time practical. Augustine was attributed a great practitioner and one of the first theoreticians of homiletics for his writings on the *De doctrina christiana*.[219]

---

[218] O. C. Edwards, Jr, "History of Preaching," *Concise Encyclopedia of Preaching*, ed.,William H.Willimon and Richard Lischer (Louisville: Westminster John Knox Press, 1995), 189.

[219] Augustine work on *De doctrina christiana* was the first significant work on homiletics that delineated differences and similarities in rhetoric and preaching. In his work he exhibited that sermon first of all was an exposition of Scripture. He suggested that the Bible is largely a kind of sacred rhetoric with its own ornaments, metaphors, and figures, which the preacher must learn to use.

In this period as mentioned above there were many outstanding preachers like Justin Martyr, Clement of Alexandria, Tertullian, Origen, Cyprian, Ambrose and others. However, the most outstanding personalities in the field of homiletics were Augustine from the West and John Chrysostom from the East. John Chrysostom earned the title 'golden–mouth' because of his oratorical skills. The Patristic period was a time of great achievements in preaching. It was a time where the writing on the homiletical theory and skills was developed rapidly.

In summary, the preaching in this period is firmly based on the authority of the Scripture with exposition and application of the Word. The doctrinal subjects on trinity, ordinance and baptismal regeneration also became an important part of homily. In the beginning part of the period, there was preaching yet it was informal type of conversation where even the lay Christians were also licensed to preach. Because of the informal conversation, the content and type of sermons were not recorded. However, in the middle part (A.D. 230-330) era as John A. Broadus opine, there was evidence that sermons were recorded and written yet because of the severe Diocletian persecution they were perished. Christian preaching entered into a new chapter with Constantine embracing Christianity as the state religion. Christians were able to participate freely in the field of education and social activities. Christian discourses could be freely published and widely circulated.[220]An overall evaluation of the period concerning preaching shows that the preaching was more inclined towards apologetic in nature.

2.3.1. Factors That Led to the Development of Christian Preaching

It was in this period of history Christian preaching in its ancient development reached its peak. One of the factors that enriched the enormous development of Christian preaching is the educational system at Greco-Roman World.[221] Dargan pointed out that, "if

[220] John A.Broadus, *Lectures on the History of Preaching* (New York: A.C. Armstrong & Son, 1893), 50-58.

[221] Dargan, *A History of Preaching….*, 65.

educated at all, a man was educated in rhetoric."[222] So be it lawyer, teacher or writer one must have had training in oratory. When Christianity became a legal religion, the schools were open for them and there was an opportunity for them to obtain training in their customary oratory from the best teachers of their era. Eventually Great Church fathers and preachers like John Chrysostom, Ambrose, Augustine and others who are trained under the famous teachers of their time entered the ministry. Prior to this external influence, there was a movement within the sphere of preaching to elevate Christian preaching to a higher quality of oratory which came to be established under the favourable conditions. The two great schools of thought - the Alexandrian and the Antiochian, practically accepted both the Old Testament and the New Testament as the inspired and the authoritative Word of God. Thus, the interpretation of the Scripture and the application of the text becomes the main focus of preaching. Another important area in the development of Christian preaching is the settlement and formulation of the Christian Doctrine especially the Nicene Creed in the Council of Constantinople in 381. This formulation of the uniform Christian Doctrine help in the presentation of great fundamental truths of Christianity in a more elaborative and formal manner during the discourse.

3. The Early Medieval Age (A.D. 430–1095)

3.1. Background

The early part of this era saw the exposure of the disintegrating ancient civilization flowing with the rough beginning of new and different stage of progress in history. The writings in the fifth and sixth centuries especially in the writings of Ambrose and Augustine lamented the painful decay and fall of Rome. After the death of Theodosius in 395, the empire was divided between his two sons who were weak ruler at the same time did not unite with each other. The political division was further followed by the division among the Churches which later began the down fall of Roman Empire. It was in A.D. 476 the classical civilization and the political power of the Roman Empire ended. As a result, drastic changes in the social and

[222] Dargan, *A History of Preaching….*, 65.

political life of the people begin to take place; travel became difficult because of robbery, wars and arson became common, there were also frequent famine, also education and the arts were totally neglected.[223] With the down fall of the Roman Empire and the confused beginning of the Medieval Monarchy, the religious and secular power of the papal authority was strongly established. The seventh and the eight century saw the rise and spread of Mohammedanism especially in the cities like Jerusalem, Antioch, Alexandria, Carthage, etc. At the same time Islam continued to gain and experience its greatest territorial expansion in the Western Europe. The society during this period was in total disorder and moral condition was in deplorable state. In the words of Dargan, "the ordeal and torture were common, the man who could not defend himself had not much chance for life, liberty and pursuit of happiness."[224] The Papacy by now independent from the Eastern Church, began to establish its political power in Italy and wisely made alliance with the king of France in order to strengthen its growth and power in the West. In the ninth, tenth and eleventh centuries there was a complete and powerful establishment of the Western Empire by the Pope. On the other hand, towards the end of the eleventh century the world history also witnessed the beginning of the first Crusade in 1095. One of the significant events in this epoch is the conversion of Russia to the Greek faith. Count Vladimir, the emperor who accepted Greek faith and married a Byzantine princess.[225]

This epoch witnessed Christological controversies among the Christians and pope like Leo the Great (440-461) and Pope Gregory the Great (590-604) intervened in the Christological controversies with outstanding administrative ability. The Third Ecumenical Council took Place in Ephesus in 431 and condemned the Nestorius position of two natures and two persons of Christ. The Fourth Ecumenical Council was held in Chalcedon in 451. This council condemned Monophysism, the doctrine which states that in Christ there is only a divine nature since the human nature is absorbed unto

223 Holland, *The Preaching Tradition…*, 31.

224 Dargan, *A History of Preaching…*, 131.

225 Dargan, *A History of Preaching….*, 154-156.

the divinity. This Council affirms that in Christ there are two natures joined in a single person.[226] The Fifth Ecumenical Council was held at II Constantinople in 553. The Council continued to condemned Nestorian and their writings. The Sixth Ecumenical Council was at III Constantinople (680-681). The Council condemned the teaching on Christology that in Christ there is only one will, although there are two natures united in a single person. The final doctrinal controversy in this era was in connection with the worship of the Holy images of Saints and Church fathers. This was finally settled in the Seventh Ecumenical Council (II Nicaea, 787). The Council declared that worship in the strict sense is due only to God. Sadly towards the end of this epoch, in 1054 the Church was divided into the Western or the Roman Catholic Church which acknowledge Pope as the supreme authority and the Eastern Orthodox Churches, which recognised the Patriarch of Constantinople as the leading ecclesiastical figure.

3.2. Theological Development

3.2.1. Christian Theology in the East

The Christian theology in the East in this epoch did not change much from the early Church fathers or the patristic period. Their approach to the Christian doctrine can be termed as '*paradosis*' means 'tradition' or literally it can be understood as 'that which is handed down.' They consider themselves as the heir of the rich Christian tradition from the past and obliged to transmit the 'tradition' without any distortion to the future generation.[227] This affirmation is clearly stated in the Seventh and the last Ecumenical Council (Nicaea 787) as "We take away nothing and we add nothing, the assembled bishops stated, but we preserve without diminution all that pertains to the Catholic Church… we keep without change or innovation all the ecclesiastical traditions that have been handed

---

[226] To this day most of the Churches held this Christological doctrine.

[227] Kallistos Ware, "Christian Theology in the East 600-1453," *A History of Christian Doctrine*, ed., Hubert Cunliffe-Jones and Benjamin Drewery (Edinburgh: T&T Clark Ltd.,1978), 231-232.

down to us, whether written or unwritten."[228] This reverence to the 'tradition' has made the Christian theology in the Byzantine mere compilers of other's work and follow the school of repetition. The prominent areas of theological activities can be noted moving from the 'Trinitarian theology' to the doctrine of Christ (431-681) and the iconoclast controversy (726-843), the controversy involve in the making and the worship of images. The veneration of the images of the saviour, Mother Mary and the Saints was the central issue. The other area is in the development of mystical theology. The Christian east vastly acknowledges that there is relation between mysticism and theology and spirituality and dogma. All theology must be mystical otherwise it becomes only a dry intellectual exercise and also all mysticism must be theological less it becomes subjective, illogical and heretical.[229]

The Christological controversy which we have seen in the above earlier epoch was finally settled at the Ecumenical Council at Chalcedon in 451 A.D. The Council advocate the two natures of Jesus Christ-divine and human. The Council of Chalcedon was challenged by the Monophysitism and the Monotheletism, yet it was not successful. In the seventh century, the area of discussion was not the nature of Christ but with the 'energy' and 'will;' Does Christ have two energies or one, two will or one? However, the third Council of Constantinople in 680-681 A.D. solved the matter by proclaiming that Jesus Christ has not only two natures but Christ has two wills and two natural energies without separation, change, division and confusion. Thus, the Council marked the end of an era of Christological controversies.[230]

3.2.2. Christian Theology in the West

For some years the development of western theology was a neglected historical topic because of inadequacy of great theologian. It is only after the seventh century some theologian like Leo the great and Tertullian appeared in the arena with the prominent theologian of

---

[228] Ware, "Christian Theology in the East..., 232.

[229] Ware, "Christian Theology in the East..., 184-186.

[230] Ware, "Christian Theology in the East..., 187-189.

their time. For the West the Iconoclast controversy began around 726 A.D. Emperor Leo III prohibited the worship of images and commanded for the total destruction. However, this prohibition was greatly opposed by Popes Gregory II and Gregory III. This issue was settled in the Council of Nicaea in 787 A.D. The Council pronounced that it is lawful to value the images, yet distinction need to be maintained between honour and cult and the adoration is due only to God. Meanwhile, Charlemagne, whose rule extended till the Northern Italy, came to exercise certain control over the papacy and regarded himself as the sole authority over the beliefs and the moral life of the people. Charlemagne at this time received a letter containing faulty Latin Translation from the Pope regarding the acts of the Council of Nicaea, which appears to have approved the adoration of the images. The King thus gathered on his theologians for deliberation and drafted *Caroline Books* which condemned worship of the images and also burning candles before the incense were prohibited. The Pope wrote back explaining the faulty translation and reaffirming the traditional doctrine, however, this could not be permanently settled until the Fourth Council of Constantinople in 869 A.D.[231] Another controversy was the Spanish Adoptionists propagated by theologian like Alcuin. They taught that Jesus was adopted as His Son by God the Father at the time of His baptism. But this teaching disappeared without resolving the controversy in the Spanish history. The development of the discipline of Penance was seen as one of the darkest chapters in the development of doctrine in the Christian history. Meanwhile there was also the development of Indulgences, debate over the Eucharist and Predestination. Most of the theological controversies in this epoch remained unsettled and continued in the next period of Christian history.

3.3. Development of Preaching and its Significance

The Dark or the Early Medieval Age was an epoch where the world history went through a phase of decline and unproductive centuries. For Christian preaching even though there were preachers of talent, character and influence, generally it was a period of

[231] Ware, "Christian Theology in the East…, 235-236.

decline in Christian preaching. The victory over paganism did not take Christian preaching to new heights. Outwardly the Church appeared to be more powerful yet inwardly less pure. Preachers yielded in seeking popularity than proclaiming the Kingdom of God. The rich heritage of preaching diminished and it was replaced by formal liturgies emphasising more on the mass. Christianity lost her passionate movement and inclined towards a more ecclesiastical institution – observance of rituals and duties. The epoch was evil indeed and corruption germinated within the church and state. Generally, the faulty living of the clergy men was more noticed and the hierarchical spirit of considering preachers as priest rather than prophets was explicitly evident. The fierce doctrinal controversy which was settled in the fourth century (Council of Constantinople 381) germinated ferociously in the fifth and sixth centuries. In the Council of Ephesus in 431, Chalcedon in 451 and Constantinople in 553, there was a prolonged debate over acceptable points in doctrine which resulted in violence. This ultimately projected the negative characteristics of the Christians and particularly the clergies. The Church indulges in highest form of violence and bribery to fulfil their selfish motives and interest. There were influential and talented preachers yet it is miserable to see the evil personalities of a person ruins and hinders their power of influence even though they possess the gift of highest qualities. It is said that the only new homiletics material produced were not preaching of new sermons it was rather the collection of the patristic sermons which writers and scholars have named as 'homiliaries.' Lamenting on the decline of preaching Dragan said, "In the West and in the East we find in this period a number of men whose characters and deeds are of considerable interest and importance in Church History, but when we look for any who are exceptionally influential or distinguished as preachers we shall look in vain."[232] In the Greek Church there was increased in the worship of the saints and angels, images and relics and the worship of the Virgin Mother of Jesus was excessive. There was no theological intellect and exposition of the Scripture was inadequate. The clergy are ignorant and corrupt at the same time. This resulted in poor

---

[232] Dargan, *A History of Preaching…*, 121.

quality of preaching with very little thought and less learning. In the West the preaching was no better than the East-preaching was much neglected affairs. The clergy were ignorant and wholly irreligious too. The worship services in the Church witnessed only ceremonies and chanting. There was no preaching from the Word of God. In the year 762 Chrodegang, the Arch-bishop of Metz, instructed that there must be preaching in all the churches of his diocese with numerous strict instruction on the duties of clergy and prescribed content and materials of the sermon to assume and preach to the people out of their own understanding and not according to the Scared Scriptures. This effort greatly affected in the fall of the frequency and quality of preaching in the end of the eighth century.[233] The only bright side of homiletics was noticed in the work of Charlemagne, king of Franks. When he conquered the conquered the German tribes the Holy Roman Empire began to establish. King Charlemegne opted for preaching as the primary tool for reform and building of a healthy society. He further assigned Alcuin, one of his ministers to set up training places for preachers.[234]

3.3.1. Methods of their Preaching

The content and form of homily remains the same which was developed in the fourth century. In the fifth and sixth centuries the nature of the sermon was expository yet the time for addressing in the homily became briefer. The allegorical interpretation mostly dominated the hermeneutics. Even though there were some like Theodore and some few others of the Antiochene school of thought followed historical and grammatical interpretation of the scriptures.[235] Most of the sermons were without text yet the contents are with introduction and a doxology at the conclusion. The seventh and eighth century epoch witnessed a very low profile of preaching that in fact there was no style to speak about. In the ninth, tenth and eleventh centuries, the style and content of sermon between the Eastern Church and Western church became so different. In the

[233] Dargan, *A History of Preaching...*, 134.

[234] Holland, *The Preaching Tradition...*, 33.

[235] Dargan, *A History of Preaching....*, 113-114.

Eastern Church, Praises of Mary and the saints became the content of homily. There was very little or no doctrinal preaching while there was little exhortation on moral life. The use of Scripture is all the more very scanty. Preachers became so dependent to the homilies which are at hand and read during the worship. More attention was given to the celebration of mass in the worship than the sermon. Most of the clergy were ignorant and many became utterly incapable of preaching an original discourse. Few of the preachers whose homilies contain exhortation with moral values and interpreted and applied the text with some skills were Christopher patriarch of Alexendria, Photius, patriarch of Constantinople, and Theophanes Cerameus the archbishop of Taorminia.[236] In the Western Church preaching continued to be much neglected and of poor quality. The clergy were much influenced by Monasticism. Many monks were ordained as deacons and priest and they were named as 'regulars' (because they live under monastic rule) and the other local clergy were called as 'secular' (as they live outside the monastic rule). Instead of the worship and preaching responsibilities the 'regulars' become victims of greed and luxury while the 'secular' along with the moral degradation, there was ignorance and superstition. The little preaching visible was in the part borrowing the homilies of the older preachers. Their discourse was not original. Church services consisted mostly of liturgy especially the celebration of the mass. There was very little exhortation and appeal for Christian virtues. At the end of the eleventh century the West Church began to revive the place of preaching in the worship services. Some of the preachers who devoted for reviving the Christian preaching were Fulbert, bishop of Chartres, Damiani papal legate at Milan and Anselem, a theologian.[237] Over all evaluation of preaching method exhibits that there was no spontaneity and freshness present in their preaching.

[236] Dargan, *A History of Preaching….*, 156-162.

[237] Dargan, *A History of Preaching….*, 162 – 171.

4. The Scholastic Age (A.D. 1095 – 1361)

4.1. General Survey of the Epoch

In the late eleventh and twelfth century, the firm establishment of territorial power in the political arena by the pope in Italy devastated the plan of establishing a very strong Western Empire by Italy, France and Germany. The political condition of Italy and Germany as different nations was in Chaos.[238]

In the thirteen century, England attained significance in the growth of parliamentary power and strengthening of constitutional monarchy. In France the monarchy grew stronger and powerful over the papal authority. Thus, she enjoyed a strong political power in Europe. In Germany there was confusion until in Rudolf of Hapsburg gave up the quench to subjugate Italy and concentrate on building proper Germany and with him a new dawn in the German history begins. In Italy the empire was fragmented into small and divided rulers; North, North - West, Central and South. By the end of the twelfth century the Southern part of Italy came under the rule of the Spanish king.[239] The monastic circles dissatisfied with the state of the Church, chiefly with the moral life continued their reform work with pace. They mainly insisted on clerical celibacy, poverty, obedience and condemned the selling and buying of ecclesiastical position.

4.1.1. The Crusades

This was also the period where the world history witnessed the time of war called the Crusades. The causes of Crusades are religious, economic and political, yet the most apparent motivations were religious cause; to recover the Holy land from the Muslims and to go for pilgrimage to the holy places in Palestine. It was Peter the Hermit a monk who led a first movement of crusaders. In this Crusade thousands of Peasants took active part, however these untrained Crusaders were massacred by the Muslim armies in Asia Minor. The First well prepared military forces Crusade was led by Urban II in 1096.

---

[238] Dargan, *A History of Preaching....*, 175-176.

[239] Dargan, *A History of Preaching....*, 218-221.

After much difficulties and struggles, the emperor in Constantinople seized Jerusalem in 1098. One of the visible outcomes of the first crusade was the establishment of several military monasteries. The Second Crusade was declared in 1146, when the Turks took the city of Edessa. As the news of the fall of Edessa reached pope Eugenius III, he issued a new call to Crusade in 1146. The most important leader here was Bernard of Clairvaux. He was considered to be one of the greatest preachers in the Christian history. It is recorded that through the preaching of Bernard of Claivaux, king Louis VII of France and Conrad III, emperor of Germany were inspired to go in the second Crusade to the Holy Land. The Third Crusade was launched in 1187 by Emperor Frederick I Barbarossa, King Philip II Augustus of France, and king Richard of England.[240] The Fourth Crusade (1204-1261), Christians were defeated and the opponents took the Christian city of Constantinople. The Fifth Crusade was in 1219 where the Christians attacked Egypt. The sixth and seventh Crusade was led by King Louis IX of France which ultimately has no result.[241] The Crusade which attracted a great wave of religious enthusiasm not only among the clergy but also to the king, lord, vassal and even to the children began to decline in the fourteenth century.

The rise of Crusade exposed the European nations especially Italy, France, Germany and England to accumulation of wealth. The merchants became wealthier and gained more recognized status in the society. The kings and the nobles remain at the top of the social order. With the inpouring of wealth, the educational system also was elevated to new highs of learning. Academic learning, art and literature had much influence in the society. Many Universities were established with crowded students for learning. Germany became the centre of learning in Europe with the foundation of the University of Prague in 1348. On the other hand the beginning of the thirteen century saw the ascension of Pope Innocent III into the Papal throne. He reduced England and Germany under his humble submission

---

[240] Dale T. Irvin & Scott W. Sunquist, *History of the World Christian Movement: Volume I,* Earliest Christianity to 14539 New York: Orbis Books, 2001), 396-403.

[241] Gonzalez, *Church History...,* 52-53.

yet faced with furious resistance in the hands of the French, Philip Augustus. However by the middle of the thirteenth century with the death of Pope Innocent III, the papacy entered the period of decline.[242] The beginning of the fourteenth century (1337) saw the beginning of the long century of war between France and England. Germany was thrown into a state of division and civil war and Italy still had no hope of unity.[243]

4.2. Theological Development

This period is a time of revival in the field of philosophy and theology and hence called Scholasticism. Scholasticism was rational in understanding and more scientific and objective in approach. The rise of Scholasticism definitely restricted the growth of monastic orders and development was shifted to schools which latter was advanced into modern universities. Some of the outstanding scholars were Anselm, Abelard, Hugo and Peter Lombard.[244] The major doctrinal controversy in this period was Berengar-Lanfranc controversy on Lord's Supper. Berengar wrote against the doctrine of Transubstantiation and Lanfranc argued in support of the literal presence of Jesus Christ on the bread and wine. The other was on the Doctrine of atonement. Anselm explains that all men have sinned in Adam and with him and it was impossible to remit this sin out of mercy therefore the incarnation of the Son was essential. Abelard and Bernard of Clairvaux severely criticized the position of Anselm. For them they taught that God can forgive without Jesus Christ being slayed. The controversy could not be settled in this period.[245]

In the twelfth century two great distinctions were simultaneously at work: at the abbey of St. Victor at Paris, Hugh was developing a summary of the economy of creation, redemption and sanctification while Gilbert de la Porree, bishop of Poitiers-a Platonist and a patristic scholar was translating the revealed truth into his own vocabulary and language. Alongside, the above work

[242] Dargan, *A History of Preaching....*, 221-226.

[243] Dargan, *A History of Preaching....*, 262.

[244] Heick, *A History of Christian Thought*, vol. I..., 265-266.

[245] Heick, *A History of Christian Thought*, vol. I..., 272-275.

Peter the Lombard, a student of Abelard the great theologian of their time published '*The Four Books of the Sentences*' where he described the whole content of the Jewish and Christian revelation and the economy of the Christian life. Later this writing became the sole text book for the students of theology, in fact for almost the next four centuries, students of bachelor in theology were made to read Lombard's *Sentences* regularly. It was in this century the academic teaching of theology began to take its proper shape both in the Students-Universities as at Bologna and the Master-Universities at Paris. These academic standards were later fortified in the thirteenth century.[246] Now the title master was also recognized to distinct person who qualified themselves through examination in certain subjects after undergoing a fix course of study. The universities gradually began to organise the essential elements like syllabus, examination, degree and distinction of faculties making the function and existence of the universities more systematic and scholastic.[247] One of the most prominent scholastic theologians in the thirteenth century was Thomas Aquinas. On the philosophical level he took the rational thought as the instrument for constructing theology. He followed Aristotle philosophy yet discarded the teachings of Aristotle that are not compatible with the Christian truth.

4.3. Homiletic Development and Significance

In the twelfth century the Crusade put the old Eastern Empire and the Greek Church more in contact with the West than any of the other ages, yet this did not help to revive the decayed preaching of the Greek Church. For the West there was a great revival in preaching. The clergy began to give much regard and importance to preaching. The classes of all people began to show much interest and respect towards preaching. Preaching becomes more popular as larger crowd begin to attend the discourse. The distinguishing reasons for the development and popularity of preaching can be noticed below.

---

[246] David Knowles, "The Middle Ages 604-1350," *A History of Christian Doctrine*, ed., Hubert Cunliffe-Jones and Benjamin Drewery (Edinburgh: T&T Clark Ltd.,1978), 259-260.

[247] Knowles, "The Middle Ages…, 266.

Firstly Clergy became more devoted in their moral live and live up to the standards of their office. Secondly, with the spiritual awakening more intellectual and philosophical theology was developed in their preaching. Thirdly, the heretics employed preaching as their means to broadcast their teaching while the Church also used similar means to counter their dangerous errors. Fourthly as mentioned earlier, the crusades were a powerful factors in motivating preaching. Fifthly, as always language played an important factor; Preaching was done in the language of the native people which attracted large number of people at the same time it also gain popularity.[248]

4.3.1. The Monastic Preaching

In the thirteenth century preaching continued to influence the life and conduct of the people of all classes. There was more conversion reported in the period. The foundation of two preaching orders of monk, Franciscans and Dominicians contributed much to preaching in the early period of the century. The Dominicans arose in Southern France in 1215 while the Franciscans in Italy in 1209. The Franciscans followed Francis of Assisi and denounced wealth and luxury; they confined themselves preaching to the lowly poverty spreading the message of love and grace. Both the orders came into being when the time was really pressing for the need of much preaching to deal with the deplorable condition of the Church as well as the state.[249] As the preaching of the friars' progresses, they began to show a real homiletical form in the history of preaching. Their sermons were not just a shapeless verse by verse comment on the biblical text but well-constructed sermon body. The sermon has sub-division having sub-points where the sub points were developed using established techniques with illustrations. The preaching orders of monk produced a new awakening in the missionary work. They also brought about a radical reformation in the Church. The monastic orders were also later influence by the universities and ultimately produced scholars of the century called the 'scholastic.'[250]

---

[248] Dargan, *A History of Preaching....*, 180-187.

[249] Holland, *The Preaching Tradition...*, 37.

[250] Gonzalez, *Church History...*, 15.

Though preaching attracted many people towards the end of this period, the drawback of preaching was noticed in its deviation from a true Biblical standard. Three types of preaching reached its strongest influence in the thirteenth century: The scholastic preaching which is a combination of philosophy and theology, the popular preaching which is concern more on the practical life and the mystic preaching which is incline into the deeper spiritual aspect of the religious life.[251]

The early period of the fourteenth century noticed in the sad decline of scholastic and popular preaching while mystic type became powerful and influential. The scholastic preaching lost its freshness of intellect and the popular preaching misuse the scripture. The preachers became only imitators of the past preachers and lost their originality. The growing corruption among the laity and the clergy and the search for earthly possession subsequently damaged the spiritual and fruitful work of the two orders of preaching. Mysticism gains its popularity and soon monasteries begin giving training for mystical training. Mysticism has similarity with feminine nature as a result it is seen that most of the distinguished preachers and teachers are women.

4.3.2. Characteristics of the Preaching

In the twelfth century, the old form of expository and hortatory homily was recollected. The use of illustration especially legend and tale was frequent event thought it was not used cleverly. The scriptures were quoted often yet it was misinterpreted and misapplied. They still followed allegorical principle of interpretation. Dargan points out four points of the characteristic of preaching in the twelfth century;[252]

i) The use of extra-biblical material as biblical, that is the Fathers of the church and legends;
ii) Gross and wilful errors of interpretation and application;
iii) Extreme use of allegory, even to the point of teaching things contrary to scripture;
iv) Frequent lack of any text at all.

[251] Dargan, *A History of Preaching…*, 228- 230.

[252] Dargan, *A History of Preaching….*, 190.

The thirteenth century also experienced the same characteristics of the twelfth century preaching. There was very little use of the scripture and there was wild allegorizing in the interpretation of the scripture. With the rise of scholasticism, in the early part of the thirteenth century, the form and content of the homily became more systematic and logical. The important figured person who practiced and advocated scholastic preaching was Thomas Aquinas of the Dominican order, a theologian who was highly regarded and recommended by the Pope of his time. The preaching was more intellectual rather than a talk to the heart or conscience and as such the common intelligence and reason could not comprehend the scholastic preaching.[253] In the late thirteenth and fourteenth century the mystical preaching was at its highest. Ecstasies, prophesies, nervous faints, abundant weeping were the frequent nature of the religious life. This indeed laid the platform for the hearers to listen with appreciation the mystic preachers. One of the typical features of the mystic preaching was on the doctrine of the union of soul with God.

5. The Reformatory Age (1361 – 1572)

5.1. Context

This period starts from the death of Wiclif and ends from the death of John Knox, the last of the great reformers. It is called the transitional or the reformatory age because this period marks the transition from the traditional medieval method to the modern times. It was a period of renaissance. Europe, England and France were at war. In Germany emperor Sigismund took hold of the affair strongly and over threw the papacy. However the following emperors could not held the political affairs potentially. The political confusion was followed by religious chaos which later brings forth the reformation. The political situation in Italy continues to be in the state of the old confusion. The papacy was in a deplorable state. The residence of the pope which was transferred from Rome to France in the beginning of the fourteenth century was brought back to Rome towards the

[253] John Ker, *Lectures on the History of Preaching*, ed., A. R. Macewen (London: Hodder & Stoughton, 1987), 125.

end of the century. But, there was a split, the Italian the Cardinals elected an Italian pope and the France too elected pope for them.[254] This is where the 'Great Western Schism' germinated. The two popes began to search for power and superiority. To protect their position, each pope had to escalate their income, thereby promoted to indulge more in exploitation and corruption. In order to solve the Schism and also to reform the church, the conciliar movement came into being. The First Council of Pisa (1409) tried to settle the schism yet it could not and the second Council of Constance (1414-1418) also failed to settle the issue. The schism was solved only in the third Council of Basel (1431-1449), yet this council resulted in the split of the conciliar movement into two.[255]

5.1.1. The Renaissance

The renaissance which originated mostly in Italy influences the pope. They were carried away by the spirit which pays more attention to building of Rome into the artistic and intellectual capital of the world. Their interest was diverted to building artistic palaces and making wars with other Italian monarchs than to the spiritual needs of the flock. This further requires abundant financial resources which eventually led into greater economic exploitation and corruption.

The transitional or Reformatory was a development age of trade and industry. Commerce grew with the discovery of new lands and places by Vasco de Gama, Columbus and others. It was also the period of invention of new technologies and machines. The invention of printing change the world of literatures and new avenues were opened for the world of letters. There was also new developments in the architectures as churches, castles, palaces, bridges etc. shows new outlook in the art. After the fall of Constantinople in 1453, many Greek Scholars were sent to the West and eventually Italy became the centre for the Greek scholars. Italy by this time, under the rule of Lorenzo the Magnificent became a flourishing centre of

---

[254] Dargan, *A History of Preaching...*, 290-292.

[255] Gonzalez, *Church History...*, 60-62.

learning which later spread into Germany, England and France in the beginning of the sixteenth century.[256]

5.1.2. Martin Luther and the Reformation

This epoch was the age where Christianity went through the most tremendous crisis in the history. The state of religion was very low. There was corruption in the doctrine and practices of the church where some became discontent with the corrupt practices within the church. The church believes practice magic and witchcraft .The worship of the relics of the saints were practiced. Ecstasies, vision and prophecies were randomly accepted as the divine revelation. The sale of indulgences and negligence of discipline all the more tarnished the image of the Church. The time was truly ripened for reformation in the church. After a long spiritual pilgrimage, Martin Luther, the father of Reformation, begins his reform work in October 1517 when he posted his famous 95 theses against the practice of indulgences. In the above mentioned lines there had been reform movements within the churches yet it was with Luther the movement of reformation gained an irresistible momentum and created a new chapter in the history of Christianity. Luther mainly opposes the sale of indulgence and the authority of the Church over the Scripture. Luther was asked to defend his theses in the meeting of the Augustinian chapter at Heidelberg in March 1518. Later in the following year Luther was engaged with a debate with one of the most effective Roman Catholic critic of the age, the Ingolstadt theologian Johannes Eck. However, Luther's theses were formally condemned in the papal bull '*Exsurge Domine*' in May 1520.[257] Luther's theology of reformation was further followed in Switzerland by Ulrich Zwingli and John Calvin. By the end of the 16th century Protestantism was strongly established in Germany, England, Scotland, Scandinavia and the Netherlands. In France, Protestantism was tolerated yet countries like Spain, Italy and Poland, Protestantism faced fierce persecution.

---

[256] Dargan, *A History of Preaching...*, 293-296.

[257] Andrew Pettegree, "Reformation and Counter-Reformation," A World History of Christianity, ed., Adrian Hastings (Grand Rapids: William B. Eerdmans Publishing Company, 1999), 244-246.

5.2. Theological Position

The major theological movement of the time was the 'nominalism.' The scholastic theology during this period turned to an understanding of the vast distinction between faith and reason. They argued that God cannot be subject of human reason and that God in His own Supreme power and will, can do anything, no matter how irrational it may be. In the words of Gonzalez, "On the basis of ever more subtle distinctions, and of a vocabulary ever more specialized, this theology lost contact with the daily life of Christians, and devoted significant effort to questions which were of interest only to theologians."[258] In response and sharp opposition to the reigning nominalist tendencies there was several reform movements led by John Wycliff, John Huss and Girolamo Savonarola.

The reformation has in its nature much of the content from the earlier Church fathers; from the ancient church it has the influence of Irenaeus, Origen, Athanasius, the Cappadocians, Tertullian, and Augustine. Among the Medieval fathers Anselm and Bernard influenced the reformers more. The light of reformation ignited when Martin Luther rediscover the gospel and attempted to make the gospel significant to all the needs and conditions of his contemporaries. The core interest of Luther's reform work was on soteriology. His theology was built upon the principles of the union between the divine and the human; it is demonstrated in the union of God and Christ in the incarnation of the Logos.[259]

5.3. Homiletic Development and Its Significance

We have already noticed that Scholastic and popular preaching have already decayed and also there was evidence of weakness in the mystic preaching. However, the mystic type of preaching had its share of minor influence in Netherlands and Germany for reform preaching. It was an age in which the world witnesses the rise of the wave of great reformation preaching. It begins with Wiclif towards the end of the fourteen century and Savonarola increased the intensity near

---

[258] Gonzalez, *Church History…*, 63.

[259] Heick, *A history of Christian Thought*, vol. I…, 316-319.

the end of the fifteenth century and reaches its full culmination with Luther in the sixteenth century.

Dargan describe the state of preaching in the fourteenth and fifteenth as struggling against the force of decline. There was little visible of scholastic, popular and mystic type of preaching yet not powerful for the very fact that preachers became just a mere imitators of their past great masters. This indeed made the method more ridiculous.[260] The art of copying others homily and imitating them was very popular. In fact there was a book like *Parati sermons* and *sermons Dormi Secure* which contains prepared sermons. These sermons were presented in simple and clear arrangements where the readers can easily memorized and present the discourse. This plagiarism was one of the nastiest symptoms of the decline of preaching ministry.[261]

Thought there was no great works on homiletics during this time, a visibly dim work available was Nicholas of Clemanges work on '*de studio theologico.' He* gave some important principles about preaching. Later Ulrich Surgant in his work '*Manuale Curatorum*' described about what is preaching, who should preach, how to preach, types of preaching, delivery of homily.[262]

In the second half of the fourteenth century, with John Wiclif new ray of hope and new note of sermon was heard. He preached against the corruption in the church and moral decay with more energy, courage, genuine freshness and originality. He used the Bible, which he had translated from the Vulgate into the language of the people as his weapon to fight against the corruption within the Church.[263] John Wiclif work clearly laid the strong foundation for reformation in the sixteenth century. Even though reforming preaching could not utterly supress the moral forces of decay in the society, their homily had powerful influence and a perpetual motivation to hope. It awakened the conscience of the rulers, statesmen, scholars, literary men as well as the preachers for the

---

[260] Dargan, *A History of Preaching...*, 300-301.

[261] Dargan, *A History of Preaching...*, 309.

[262] Dargan, *A History of Preaching...*, 304-305.

[263] Garvie, *The Christian Preacher...*, 117.

need of reformation of the church among the clergies as well as the members. John Wiclif was rightly called the 'Morning Star of the Reformation.' The followers of John Wiclif were called as Lollards, who went about expounding the Scripture and teaching the truth of the scripture to the people. They continued to sow the seed of Wiclif evangelical doctrine.

5.3.1. Reformation and Preaching: Its Relationship and Influence

Reformation and preaching has a distinct relationship in the sense that the achievement of the great movement was largely the work of preachers and preaching. It was by the Word of God through the preaching ministry people were enlightened and aroused in spirit for the great movement. Dargan while citing Christleib said, "The age of the Reformation makes the deepest cleft, the sharpest turning-point in the historical development of Christian preaching, as to contents and form, spirit and character."[264] History records that in 1529 Luther preached three to four times a week and in 1541 often four times on Sunday and two or three times in the week. Martin Luther used preaching as his best platform to reform the corrupt practices within the Catholic Church. With the amount of preaching Luther delivered and the impact he made upon the lives of the people, his followers like John Calvin in Geneva and Zwingli in Zurich were inspired to be zealous preachers. Broadus summarized the characteristic of the protestant preaching as;[265]

i) a revival of preaching.
ii) a revival of Biblical preaching
iii) a revival of controversial preaching and
iv) a revival of preaching upon the doctrines of grace.

---

[264] Dargan, *A History of Preaching...*, 367.

[265] Broadus, *Lectures on the History ...*, 113-117. i) In the earlier epoch there was no or very little preaching however much preaching happened in this era. ii) Instead of long stories about saints and martyrs and passages from Aristotle, there was preaching from the Bible. It is no longer what the Pope says but what the Bible says was the decisive authority. iii) Religious controversy is inevitable where living faith in definite truth is dwelling side by side with ruinous error and practical evils. iv) There was preaching on justification by faith, salvation by grace.

5.3.2. Method of Preaching

The type of preaching we noticed in the thirteenth and fourteenth century was firstly, it provided sound evangelical teaching. The second group are those who used the device of humour and sensational oddities to catch and attract the crowd. The third group are those who consider the humour and sensational oddities as the ends rather than the means of communicating the word of God. They are more concern in making impression with their humour. The content and form of the sermon was like the ancient homily. There was the invocation or a shot prayer for divine guidance and the reading of the scripture, then the explanation of the text. Sometimes the explanation was much in length but most commonly a brief explanation was used. The next step was discussion and elaboration with quotations from the earlier teachers. This is followed by illustration in the form of story, and fables which is drawn from the nature, from daily affairs, habits etc. Finally there is the conclusion with a brief closing prayer. As to the delivery of sermon, some preacher memorized the sermon, some employed extemporized type and some preached from notes.[266] The Protestant Preachers attacked the Roman Catholic doctrines of the mass, transubstantiation, penances, purgatory, and papal supremacy.

6. The Early Modern Age (A.D. 1572 – 1738)

6.1. Background

This age is the beginning of the modern era in the history of the world. It was an age of enlightenment as a result of the scientific and philosophical advancements. This was an era of Sir Isaac newton and Carolus Linnaeus where natural sciences were becoming the main cultural and intellectual force. The world was looked at from the eyes of reason. For the context of the Church, the Protestants in the previous period enjoyed religious tolerance in France but by the coming of Louis XIV (Edict of Fontainebleau 1685) the religious tolerance was put to an end. However Protestantism continued to

[266] Dargan, *A History of Preaching*..., 302-307.

exist in France in the deserts and other secret places, which later emerged as a small yet matured and well organised community. In England the Puritan Revolution[267] became very strong which later gave rise to civil war. There was not only news of wars but also an endless series of debate among the Catholics, Lutherans and the Reformed. The Catholics debated with the authority of the pope. For the Lutherans after the death of Luther, two groups erupted between the followers of Melanchthon-the Strict Lutherans and the Philipists Lutherans. The Reformed orthodoxy debated on predestination and grace. There were two councils for solving the debate-the Synod of Dort and the Assembly of Westminster. Those who did not accept the decision of the two meetings were declared heretics and expelled from the true Reformed Church. One of the reactions to these controversies within the churches was the growth of rationalism. Another consequence was the emergence of pietism within the Lutherans. While still others took the spiritual option and choose to seek God not in the Church or among the believers but in the inner and private life.

6.2. Theological Development

In this period within Christianity there was also a period of deep conflict. Among the Protestant Christianity there was persecution of the Arminians and religious independence like Baptist, Quakers and the Unitarians came into prominence. Christianity was intensely challenged by the enlightenment which tends to elevate human reason above divine revelation. Christian theology was made to think and re-evaluate the traditional doctrine of the Church and also the concept of the very nature of Christianity. In England, the so call rational theology[268] was significantly professed by three men who were close friends: Lord Falkland, John Hales and William Chillingworth. Falkland was open to rationalism in the sense of creating broader and more tolerant view of religion yet he did not undermine the grace of God which is necessary for

---

[267] The Puritans insisted on a Church that must be purified from all that was not biblical and they gained increasing support in Parliament.

[268] Rational theology stressed the importance of reason in matters of religion.

salvation. Hales and Chillingworth argued vigorously the need of reason for the interpretation of the Scriptures. The other group of theologians were the Latitudinarians. They taught on the freedom of will and universal redemption of Christ. They were rationalists in their principle of considering theology having no elements of truth where philosophy cannot prove its validity. For them theology must co-operate with philosophy, science must be recognized and masses must be conducted in accommodative manner. Burnet, Whiston, Spencer, Norris, Gale, Cumberland and Archbishop John Tillotson were prominent representatives of Latitudinarians.[269] In Germany among the Lutheran Churches they drafted the 'formula of Concord'[270] which was accepted by most German states. This became a definite Lutheran doctrinal and theological position in the seventeenth century. There was no major theologian who opposes the concord rather theologians were more on defending the concord in their writings and expositions.[271] The Churches of the Reformed Tradition wrestle with the question of the Church's position on Predestination. It was James Arminius, professor of Leyden whose deep studies led him to question the doctrine of Predestination. The teaching of Arminius and his followers, on salvation to all who believe through the Holy Ghost in the Son Jesus Christ was rejected by the Synod of Dordrecht in 1618.[272]

---

[269] Heick, *A History of Christian Thought*, vol. II..., 89-91.

[270] Formula of Concord is an authoritative Lutheran statement of faith. It is in two parts, *'Epitome* and *Solid Declaration'*. The *Epitome* is a brief and concise presentation of the Formula's twelve articles namely, Original Sin, Free Will, The Righteousness of Faith before God, Good Works, Law and Gospel, The Third Use of the Law, The Holy Supper of Christ, The Person of Christ, Christ's Descent into Hell, Church Ceremonies, The Eternal Foreknowledge and Election of God, Other heresies and sects. The Solid Declaration was the detail exposition of the articles. http://www.en.wikipedia.org/wiki/Formula_of_Concord.

[271] R. Buick Knox, "The History of doctrine in the Seventeenth Century," *A History of Christia Doctrine*, ed., Hubert Cunliffe-Jones and Benjamin Drewery (Ediburgh: T&T Clark Ltd., 1978), 431.

[272] Knox, The History of doctrine in the Seventeenth..., 433-435.

For the Roman Catholics the Council of Trent[273] had fortified its position yet it also left the gap between the Augustinian Thomism and the Pelagianizing doctrines of Franciscan. Michael Bajus, Cornelius Jansen and Bishop of Ypres reasserted the Augustinian theses. For instance, the natural will of human is sinful without God's help and no human is without sin. An outstanding leader of Pelagianizing movement was the Jesuit scholar Luis de Molina. He offered a rational explanation on grace, free will, providence and predestination. The Church of Rome overruled the Augustinianism and showed more tolerant attitude toward Pelagian teachings.[274] The other disputes between Curialism and Conciliarism also remain unsettled. The controversy was on "a) the question of the divine rights of the bishops as independent from the Pope and the conciliar rights as superior to the Pope; b)the question of Catholic tradition, whether the extent and content of tradition are to be determined by the principle of Vincent of Lerins or by papal decrees."[275] Overall the Roman Catholic theology was at the low position and the effect of enlightenment pushed the Roman Catholic Churches under severe spiritual decline.

6.3. Preaching after the Reformation: Its Significance

After the death of Luther in 1546, notably and visibly there was decline again in the Lutheran Preaching. Preaching lost in its freshness and it became dull. Furthermore the loss in spiritual power worsens the state of preaching. The unsettled state of Empire in Europe for many years certainly hindered the preaching ministry. Wittenberg after the death of Luther within a year came under the rule of the emperor, as a result many Lutheran compromised while others were very fervent in their old cause. There was also now division among the Lutherans. The situation was further aggravated by the constant theological dispute between the Catholics and the

---

[273] The Council met in three prolonged but non-continous period between 1545 and 1563. The council met to deliberate on reforming the Roman Catholic Churches and also fear for Protestant dominance.

[274] Heick, *A History of Christian Thought*, vol. II..., 146-147.

[275] Heick, *A History of Christian Thought*, vol. II..., 149.

Protestants. There was also internal conflict with the Protestantism between the Lutherans and the other reformed group especially on the understanding of the Lord Supper. In Germany, both the Catholics and the Lutherans opposed the Calvinists. In France, the persecution of the Protestants which begin in 1572 continued till 1598.[276] In England, this period was an era of glory in politics, philosophy and literature. The great name of Shakespeare appeared in the world of literature. Yet it is sad to notice the decline of Protestant preaching. Preaching was dejected by the effect of persecution by Queen Mary. Several protestant preachers mostly the best orators were slain or driven into exile as a result of the persecution.[277]

The situation of the Reformation saw the impact of preaching and henceforth, there was considerable impulse in the study and teaching on the theory of preaching. For the Roman Catholics there were an articles and writings on the art of preaching notably by Reuchlin and Erasmus. For the Reformers, Luther's work on his '*Table Talk*' contains some sermons, lectures and much consideration to homilitical principles. Melanchthon published his *Three Books on Rhetoric* which served as useful book for the theological students at Wittenberg. Nicholas Hermming also wrote a book on '*the art of preaching.*'[278] It is said that none of the above work on homiletics had much degree of value yet they cannot be neglected from the literature world of homiletics. After the Reformation particularly starting from the seventeenth century, the history of Christian preaching changed its complexion into the Roman Catholic preaching and the protestant preaching.

6.3.1. The Roman Catholic Preaching after the Reformation

In the later part of the sixteenth century, history witnessed some improvement in the quality and power of the Catholic preaching. The most important reason behind the improvement firstly can be attributed to the Council of Trent (1545-1563). Cardinal Charles Borromeo of Milan a sound theologian proposes enhancing the

---

[276] Dargan, *A History of Preaching*, vol. II…, 15.

[277] Dargan, *A History of Preaching*, vol. II…, 18.

[278] Dargan, *A History of Preaching*, vol. II…, 11-12.

quality of preaching in all the Catholic Churches in the Council. Eventually the Council in passing the Canons framed the first duty of a bishop was to 'to preach.' It also rectified certain abuses in the church and also passed rule for better education in the art of preaching. The other reason can be credited to the founding of the famous 'Society of Jesus' whose purpose was to promote preaching.[279]

In the seventeenth century 'the Society of Jesus' continued to lead the Catholics in preaching. There was also visible literature work on preaching and also produced high reputation preachers of excellent eloquence like Michael Staudacher, Victor Scheffer, Gerhard Pauli etc.[280]

6.3.2. The Protestant Preaching

The general Characteristic of the Lutheran preaching in the seventeenth century was noticed in the use of sufficient and variety of illustration. The prominent preaching during the seventeenth century was 'polemic dogmatism, scholastic pedantry, fanciful or sensational impressionism, or genuine and earnest spirituality.' Lutheran preaching also falls into either one or two of these above features. There was also treatises on the art of preaching from the Lutherans appeared. The treatises mostly deal with the different methods of preaching. One of the examples of the modes of preaching of John Gerhard as outlined by Dargan are as follows; 'i) the grammatical, ii) the logical, iii) the rhetorical, iv) the histrionic, v) the historic, vi) the ecclesiastical, vii) the catechetical viii) the scholastic ix) the elenctic x) the mystical xi) the heroic.'[281]

Towards the end of the seventeenth and beginning of the eighteenth century the Lutheran experienced the rise of Pietistic preaching. It is said that Luther was the reformer of its doctrine while Spener the reformer of the life of the Church in Germany.[282] Spener

---

[279] Dargan, *A History of Preaching*, vol. II..., 24-25.

[280] Dargan, *A History of Preaching*, vol. II..., 51-53.

[281] Dargan, *A History of Preaching*, vol. II..., 64.

[282] Garvie, *The Christian Preacher...*, 187.

passion and devotion for preaching was explicitly portrayed in his *Pia Desideria* as;[283]

> i) The larger circulation of the Word of God and private meeting of Christians for the study if it. ii) The diligent exercise of the Christian priesthood. iii) The earnest conviction that knowledge is not enough in Christianity, and that we must have life and action. iv) A right bearing towards unbelievers, so as to carry on discussion with heart-felt love, and to seek not merely to answer then but to gain them and do them good. v) Such as course of theological training as will make students feel that they should progress in heart and life as much in learning. vi) A new way of preaching, in which the great aim will be to show that Christianity consists in the inner or new man, whose soul is found in faith, with the fruits of a good life as the results.

This spiritual movement manifest nearly a revolution in both theory and practice. They exhibit great devotion and deeper spirituality. The biblical and evangelical preaching was much admired. Even though most of their sermons lack rhetorical form, it was their spirit, content and aim of their preaching that made it powerful and effective.

7. The Evangelical Age (A.D. 1738 – 1900)

7.1. Background

During the eighteenth century the rise of Russia to power, the spread and expansion of British Colonial enterprises to India and America, the independence and federation of United States and the French Revolution constitutes an era of significance in the history.

The nineteenth century has been called as the era of greatest progress in the history. There was major development and advancement in all the spheres of life. Religion and preaching also reached its culmination along with the other areas of development. Preaching in this era was significant not only in few areas but

[283] Garvie, *The Christian Preacher…*,188.

exhibited the heightening of power in all directions. It is also the period where United States came to its power in the pulpit along with other development and advancements. In Europe, after so many process of evolution especially after the reformation, preaching eventually reached the zenith. The preaching was less dogmatic and less formal with more flexibility and adaptation.[284] The rise of the British School of scientific speculation became one of the strong opponents of preaching in the nineteenth century. Nevertheless pulpit with courage and ability prevailed against the strong opponent. The century was also the great century of European colonialism as well as the great century of Protestant missions. The colonial success led to an awakening interest in mission by the churches. In Asia, it was India that drew the interest of the first missionaries which became visible by the arrival of William Carey, the father of modern mission movement to the Indian soil.

7.2. Theological Development

The Hesychast Renaissance in the Greece and the rise of the Russian theology were the significant theological development in the East. The Hesychast Renaissance was initiated by two friends, St. Macarius Notaras, Metropolitan of Corinth (1731-1805) and St. Nicodemus of the Holy Mountain. At the time when the Greek Church was decaying they started to retrieve the mystical theology of St. Symeon and St. Gregory Palamas. The main work and contribution of St. Macarius and St. Nicodemus was the publication of ascetic and mystical text, which modern orthodox history considers as one of the most influential books. The movement was more of spiritual rather than the doctrinal matters. The other development was the development of Russian theology. For the past many centuries Russia had been closely dependent on the Greek religious thought, yet by the middle of the 19th century (1850 A.D.), Russian Orthodox Church produced theology of its own. Two personalities that particularly changed the complexion of the spirit of the Russian religious thought was Alexis Khomiakov, the lay theologian and Philaret Drozdov,

[284] Dargan, *A History of Preaching*, vol. II..., 350-352.

Metropolitan of Moscow. They opposed the Western Roman Catholic thought as well as the Protestant thought and propagated on the return to the genuine tradition of the Christian east. For Khomiakov, he devoted much of his thought on the doctrine of the Church, its unity and authority. Metropolitan Philaret revived the patristic spirit in the Russian theological schools. It is attributed that Philaret laid the first foundation of the scientific theology among the orthodox Russian Church.[285]

In the Western Christianity, this is an era where the classical Roman Catholic and the Protestant theologies had to wrestle against pages of criticism from both insiders and outsiders. Theology was also seemed to be disturbed by the sociological changes of the time. However, with the development of technologies and scientific advancements there was also a wave that rejected the belief in the supernatural. The sociological and intellectual change has pushed Christianity from the centre making the study of Christian theology in the modern world as minority subject or an element of the study of religion.[286]

7.3. The Place of Preaching and its Significance

I will deal with each century (eighteenth and nineteenth) separately because of the complex and comprehensive account of history after the reformation.

7.3.1. The Roman Catholic Preaching in the 18th Century

In Spain along with the decline and loss of the state, preaching was at the low level. Preaching was considered as one of the rituals within the church with no influence. The Roman Catholic Inquisition was successful in supressing the Protestant completely and establishing the Catholic dominance. But the preaching ministry was at loss. There was no intellectual power or spiritual force noticed. Italy continues

---

[285] Kallistos Ware, "A Note on Theology in the Christian East: The Eighteenth to Twentieth Centuries," *A History of Christian Doctrine*, ed., Hubert Cunliffe-Jones and Benjamin Drewery (Edinburgh: T&T Clark Ltd., 1978), 455-457.

[286] John H. S. Kent, "Christian Theology in the Eighteenth to the twentieth centuries," *A History of Christian Doctrine*, ed., Hubert Cunliffe-Jones and Benjamin Drewery (Edinburgh: T&T Clark Ltd., 1978), 461.

to decline in the eighteenth century in the field of preaching as in other field too. The main causes for the decline can be evaluated from these reasons. Firstly the suppression of the Jesuits in 1773 removed many able and influential preachers from the Italian Pulpit. The other reason was the dominant of the foreigners in the moral and literature areas profoundly injured the Italian originality.[287] The preaching in Germany was neither so strong nor so diverse and unique. The Catholic preaching continued to be the accepted Romanist doctrine against Protestantism. However, it changes its complexion towards the end of the century by the rise of a more spiritual movement under Sailer and his school.[288] History indicates that the French catholic preaching during the eighteenth century lies between 1718 to1789. Dargan while citing Bernard gave five shorter period of French preaching "i)1718-1729, transition from the classic age to the new one; ii)1729-1750, rise of the so called 'academic' pulpit eloquence; iii)1750-1763, flourishing of the academic and rise of apologetic preaching; iv) 1763-1778, a critical period in which semi-philosophic essays were common in the pulpit; v) 1778-1789, period of reaction and effort to revive the better spirit and method of former times."[289] The content of their preaching include scriptural quotation where it is sometime misquoted and misapplied, rarely explained or expounded. While reviewing the French Catholic preaching in this century, we notice some transition in the methods of their preaching yet there was no clear evidence of a powerful force to re-structure the falling quality of the pulpit.

7.3.2. The Protestant Preaching in the 18th Century

The German Protestant preaching distinctly falls into three schools of preaching-the Pietistic, the Rationalistic and the Super naturalistic or Mediating. The influence of the Pietism decline and the rationalist movement gain its momentum with its implementation on the new critical method of the Bible study and exposition. The super naturalist or the Mediating method too arose

---

287 Dargan, *A History of Preaching*, vol. II..., 191-200.

288 Dargan, *A History of Preaching*, vol. II..., 204-205.

289 Dargan, *A History of Preaching*, vol. II..., 240.

as the result of their presupposition in recognizing the failure of both the preaching school of thought. And it gained its popularity in the middle of the century yet the rationalist school which was strong and aggressive reached its pinnacle toward the end of the century. The rationalist new critical method of interpreting the Bible had both positive outcome as well as the negative outcome. For some of the preacher this method help in better understanding and application of the Scripture while for others it came as a virtual denial of any divine intervention in the Bible rejecting the authority of the Scripture.[290] In France, the preaching of the Protestants shows more of true Scriptural content and spiritual appeal than the Roman Catholics. The Protestant preachers were in constant hunt, watch and pursue by Louis XIV. In spite of the fierce persecution they faced in France many of them remain loyal to Protestantism. The strongest challenges for the protestant preachers were to re-organise their scattered congregations, to minister to them as a pastor and organise worship services in secret places like mountains and caves.

7.3.2.1. The Revival Awakening

During the eighteenth century, the Revival Awakening (1734) played an important role in re-shaping and rebuilding the deplorable moral and spiritual condition of Christianity. In Britain the movement was called the Evangelical or the Methodist Revival. The Revival awakening was led by George Whitefield, Charles and John Wesley, which made a significant impact.[291] John Wesley was not an excellent orator yet his preaching was very effective because of his inclusive nature. He preached to all section of the people – to the coal miners, mill workers, prisoners, to soldiers and to mobs. The main theme of his preaching was on justification by faith, sanctification, new birth and about salvation. He was compared to as the Protestant Francis of Assisi because of his very nature of proclaiming the

---

[290] Dargan, *A History of Preaching*, vol. II…, 206-210.

[291] A. Skevington Wood "Awakening," *A Lion Handbook: The History of Christianity*, et al., Tim Dowley (England: Lion Publishing, 1977), 434.

Gospel.[292] On the other hand George Whitefield was a man skilled with the art of oratory. He mostly preached to the whole Anglo-Saxon Protestantism. The place of his preaching was in the open air, marketplaces, Churchyards and street corners. He mostly spoke extempore sermons. Like any other revival preachers his major themes were on righteousness, Sanctification and Redemption. In the American colonies the movement was known as the Great Awakening. The Great Awakening was led by Jonathan Edwards.[293] Jonathan Edwards was a well learned man. In his preaching there was no introduction, the sermon begins with the observation about the text which was followed by the explanation of the meaning of the text.[294] In evaluation, their preaching was very popular and Biblical. Their mode of preaching was simple and more evangelical in the content. The prevalent method of homiletics was more on topical type of composing sermons with a scholastic analysis.

7.3.3. Protestant Preaching in the 19th Century

In General the remarkable salient feature of the nineteenth century preaching is its variety. It can be mentioned that never before in the history of preaching was there more variety than the nineteenth century. The fact of liberty and freedom in the Christian circle added variety in doctrine and traditions. Hence, this variety also appeared in the method and style of preaching. The content of the sermon remain almost similar to the earlier period yet the interpretation was much improved with more scholarly exegesis. The preacher exhibited to interpret the exact Word of God without any dilution and this led to the exhaustion of the allegorizing or fanciful use of the text. The use of personal experience and infusion of humanitarian, social and ethical elements were visible. The literary quality of the sermon maintains a high standard. The thinkers or preachers in this epoch falls under three well known groups - the advanced, the mediating

---

292 Hughes Oliphant Old, *The Reading and Preaching of the Scriptures in the Worship of the Christian Church,* vol. 5 (Grand Rapids: William B. Eerdmans Publishing Company, 2004), 111.

293 Wood "Awakening," *A Lion Handbook...*, 434.

294 Old, *The Reading and Preaching of the Scriptures...*, 253.

and the conservative. The advanced group tried to harmonized and adjust the Christian doctrine with the theories of scientific hostility. They called themselves as liberals. The conservative on the other hand hold on the conviction that scientists and critics were destroying the very foundation of Christian faith and the true essence of religious life. The mediating thinkers are in between the two groups and tried to adjust and bring harmony of the truth and right held by the two opposed groups.[295]

In Italy with the establishment of the kingdom of united Italy there was also freedom of worship guaranteed by the government. This freedom gave much opportunity to the Protestant preaching to grow in Italy. The prominent style of preaching that developed was the evangelical preaching. The Germans, English and American established mission agencies and planted churches and learnt the native language where they use their linguistic ability for preaching. The native preachers also gained much significance as they presented the evangelical opposition to the papacy of Church of Rome. The three Great men who probably influenced the German pulpit were Luther, Spener and Schleiermacher. Their style and personality varies yet the great one common view was on the relation of a soul of a person through faith to Jesus Christ as the Saviour. Schleiermacher's writing on '*Discourses on Religion*' appeared in 1799 produced a profound impression throughout Germany. Preachers and hearers discovered that too much emphasis has been given on the intellectual and logical aspect and less scope on the faith and feelings. Henceforth a new beginning is felt in the German pulpit and later part of the century the evangelical preaching dominated the German pulpit.[296] The Protestant preaching in France also was not favourable in the beginning of the century yet gains its momentum from the middle-half of the nineteenth century onward. The beginning of the century till 1820, there was more of philosophic and moralistic preaching and less of spiritual and evangelical. From 1820-1850, there was a significant Awakening by the Evangelical preaching of Caesar Malan. The followers of Malan took his preaching to new heights. They

---

[295] Dargan, *A History of Preaching*, vol. II..., 351-358.

[296] Dargan, *A History of Preaching*, vol. II..., 378-381.

concentrated more on the authority of the Scripture, regeneration by the Holy Spirit and the divinity and atonement of Christ. The third phase from 1850-1866 was the development of Liberalism. Historical and exegetical study of the Bible along with the study of the progress of scientific thought took liberalism to higher standards.[297] In Britain the first third of the century was dominated by the evangelical preaching. Writers like Pattison, Overton and Dargan shows strongest evangelical preaching in this period. Preaching began to grow from strength to strength in the middle of the nineteenth century producing great preacher, writer and leader like Charles Haddon Spurgeon. Many have attributed him as one of the most impressive and permanently successful evangelistic preacher of the age. The closing years of the nineteenth century (1868-1900) was a period of much development in all the areas. Education was advanced, commerce and industries flourish, literature increased both in quality and in quantities and scientific and philosophic became more influential. It was also the period where Darwin work on *Origin of Species* (1859) and *Descent of Man* (1871) appeared. Three groups of preachers became distinctly visible towards the end of the century – the conservative Evangelical, the high churchmen who are associated with extreme ritualism and mystical piety and the liberals.

7.3.4. Roman Catholic Preaching in the 19th Century

Italy in the nineteenth century became a more stabilized nation. There was development politically, in the field of literature and in religion too. The Catholic preaching in Italy anticipated a more scholarly and academic style. With the preaching gaining its popularity, the Catholic pulpit also made attempt to defend the traditional faith or often undiscerning attacks against all modern ideas. This defensive attitude towards modern ideas forced them to neglect the moral and spiritual teaching. In order to advance religious teaching missions or evangelistic meetings continued to take often. There also arose a preaching style called the 'conferences' where free talks were held on popular theme rather than the careful studied and systematic

[297] Dargan, *A History of Preaching*, vol. II…, 437-439.

homily based on Scripture.[298] The study on certain biographies shows that most of the Roman Catholic preachers were person of high eloquence, intelligent, and educated.

In Germany after the reformation, there also has been a worthy and strong pulpit work. There was a progress in the evangelical direction as well as the independent line of thought. The Overthrown of the power of Napoleon help not only the Protestant but also the Roman Catholics to embrace the old faith. The more spiritual preaching of the Roman Catholics was mainly influence by the re-establishment of the Jesuits, among whom were number of good preachers. The general evaluation of the Roman Catholic preaching in Germany portrays that there were spiritual and orthodox preachers as well as more worldly and partisan kind. The beginning years of the nineteenth century France was unfavourable for the Roman Catholic preaching. However a new movement began about 1830, where there was a remarkable improvement in the pulpit of the Roman Catholic preaching. The general progress of the state of France helps in the development of the pulpit. France became one of the most advanced nations in Science, literature, political, social and industrial affairs. As in Italy, French Roman Catholic also introduced a popular addressed known as 'conferences' in order to enhance the pulpit. It is a topical address with no formal content and usually without a text.[299]

7.3.5. Type of Preaching in the 18th and 19th Century

I have attempted to evaluated the type of homiletics found in both the Roman Catholic and the Protestant together.

There was less amount of formal theology in Preaching. There was an ample use of Scriptural material which increases in the use of exposition of the Bible. The content of the sermons are much simpler and healthier in flavour. There is evidence of high standards both in homiletics and cultural ideas. The sermons demonstrate careful training, large knowledge, and strength of purpose. In Germany there was an excellent progress in the department of homiletics, especially through the writings and teachings of Schleiermacher,

[298] Dargan, *A History of Preaching*, vol. II..., 360-364.

[299] Dargan, *A History of Preaching*, vol. II..., 434-437.

Rudolf Stier and others. In their writings they emphasise on the proper pastoral training on homiletics and cure of souls. They insist on Biblical preaching with systematic presentation and earnest effort to benefit the hearers. The advancement of modern thoughts and ideas gave rise to a critical and scientific opposition to traditional Christianity. Thus, there was also certain measure of apologetic preaching in the middle of the nineteenth century. The homiletical principles are properly understood and employed. The style become more admirable coloured with clarity, flexibility, and elegant. Since the dominant preaching was the Evangelical type, sermons were mostly extempore without manuscript. The method of preaching specially in Britain was topical. The interpretation of scripture was neither technical nor meticulous; rather it was traditional and superficial. However at the closing years of the nineteenth century, the preaching mode sharply change (especially in Britain) to more exegetical and expository, and very little topical. The apologetic and polemic element of preaching continues to be visible towards the end of the nineteenth century.

8. The Post-Modern Age (A.D. 1900 Till Today)

8.1. Background

In the 20th century the Industrial Revolution of the 19th century was further developed with more sophisticated technologies. Thus, oil became an integral part in the economy of the century. Eventually the Islamic world became more powerful as a result of the available oil-fields in the region. One of the most horrors in the world history happened in the 20th century was the Holocaust which shocked the Western World. The dropping of atomic bombs on Hiroshima and Nagasaki and the destruction in Vietnam were also a major part of the bloodshed and destruction. Thus, the world at this stage became more inclined towards the question of the existence of God rather than the question of guilt, repentance and divine forgiveness.

The twentieth century witnessed the most destructive wars in the history of the world; The First World War (1914-1919) and the World War II (1939-1944). It was thought that the science, technology and progress will take the world of the twentieth century into new heights of peace and prosperity. The industrialized nations of Europe and United States were expected to lead the world towards a glorious time, yet it did not happen. In fact most of the wars in this century have used maximum modern technology producing great causalities than any wars in the past.

8.2. The Position of the Church

In the 20th century, Christianity went through a time of frustration as it was seen involving in every major conflict of the century; the Two World Wars, the use of nuclear bombs in Japan, wars in Korea and Vietnam, anti-colonial conflicts in Latin America, North Africa, South Asia and Middle East. Furthermore, the use of modern technologies drastically affected the balanced state of the world's ecology. The forest that stood for ages disappeared, the rivers and air became chemically polluted which made it even more difficult for sustaining life.

The Western Christianity started to move out of the European homeland to other continents. The Russian Church and the other Eastern Churches in various lands of Soviet Union live under hostile from the government first from the Muslim and then the Communist. Yet, they endured the period of trials and gave signs of strength and validity of sustaining the faith. This can be credited to the great degree of the liturgical and catechetical traditions of orthodoxy. For the Roman Catholics, with the election of Pope John XXIII and after the Vatican II, the Church became more open to the contemporary world and responded to the need of the people. The Second Vatican Council declared its solidarity with the suffering and turmoil of the modern world and formulated the liturgies according to each culture and situation and also licensed the celebration of mass in the vernacular language of the people. On the other hand the modern missionary movement realising the need of Christian unity since division among the Christians was a big hindrance to their conversion, formed the Modern Ecumenical Movement. As a result the most important conference, the World Missionary Conference took place in Edinburgh (Scotland) 1910. The Conference seeks for Christian unity and harmony among various Christian movements. The bishop of the American Episcopal Church in Philippines,

Charles Brent who was one of the delegates in the Edinburgh 1910 was convinced of a similar conference in relation to the faith and order professed by the Christians. With much effort the conference on Faith and Order was held at Lausanne in 1927. Parallel to this conference, another similar conference under the initiative of Lutheran Archbishop Nathan Soderblom, the primate of Sweden was also initiated. It was aimed to encourage the churches to put behind the differences and move forwards to relate the Christian faith to the society. Eventually, the first 'Life and Work' conference was held at Stockholm in 1925.

In the beginning of the 21st century, Christianity was challenged to wrestle with the problem of war and conflict, poverty, political oppression, scientific discoveries and a major challenge from the threat of climate change.

8.3. Development of Pentecostalism and Charismatic Movement

The Charismatic movement occupied a central place in the twentieth century Church. The growth of Pentecostalism was one of the significant developments in the Western Christianity in the 20th century. The Pentecostal Movement emphasises more on the Holy Spirit and the doctrine of personal holiness. They are more concern on 'baptism in the spirit' and give much importance to the speaking in tongues, singing and dancing.[300] The spirit and nature of Pentecostalism was strongest among the Scandinavian in Europe and the Apostolic Church in Britain. Pentecostals claims that it has its greater influence in Russia and China too. The most prominent province of the Pentecostal influence is in Latin America and South Africa. The Pentecostals preaching and teaching was based on Christ as Saviour, as the one who baptised in the Spirit, as the healer and as the one who is coming soon. One of the distinctive doctrinal teachings of the Pentecostals is the speaking in tongue as physical symbol of spirit-baptism. They are less concern with the social issues and have strict ethical standards.[301] The Charismatics preaching

---

[300] MacCulloch, *Groundwork of Christian History...*, 290-291.

[301] James Dunn, "The Pentecostals," *A Lion Handbook: The History of Christianity*, Tim Dowley, et. al., (England: Lion Publishing, 1977), 618-619.

lacks disciplined Bible study, systematic exposition or theological structures. The oratory is usually dynamic and style similar to that of the revival preaching. A Charismatic worship service usually takes place for around two hours with much of prayer and praise.[302]

8.4. The Field of Theology

In the twentieth century as liberalism began to take its proper shape some theologians also continued to defend the traditional orthodox position of the Church. Theologians like Darwell Stone and P. T. Forsyth were much involved in maintaining the traditional doctrines in the early twentieth century. The most prominent theologian who combined biology and Christian tradition was noticed in '*The Origin and Propagation of Sin*' by F. R. Tennant. He rejected the Genesis account of creation of Adam and the nature of human being. For him the story of Adam and Eve and the serpent was a theologically irrelevant fragment of folklore.[303] Tennant was more concern with the test of validity of the doctrine of human nature. He did not accept the view of Karl Barth and Emil Brunner on sin as a mysterious intrusion into the divine plan.[304]

Among the Protestants, Europe continued to be the centre of the Church's theological activity. The liberal Protestantism was challenged severely and the most outstanding theologian was Karl Barth who rebel against liberalism and propagated new-orthodoxy. It was based on this new theology the German Protestantism were able to meet the challenges of the Nazis. The most striking contribution of Karl Barth to the twentieth century theology was his '*commentary on the Epistle to the Romans.*' For him the Bible was the absolute source for defending Christianity. The Centre of Barth's theology is on the super-historical Christ and not just historical Jesus. He is more concern on the relevancy of the Gospel to the contemporary world. The fall of man is not only a historical event but a super

[302] Huges Oliphant Old, *The Reading and Preaching of the Scriptures in the Worship of the Christian Church,* vol. 7 Our Own Time (Grand Rapids: William B. Eerdmans Publishing Company, 2010), 394-395.

[303] Kent, "Christian Theology in the Eighteenth…, 568.

[304] Kent, "Christian Theology in the Eighteenth…, 568.

historical truth. In the 1960s liberal theologians like Bultmann, Tillich and Dietrich Bonhoeffer began to counter the neo-orthodox, ecumenical movement of Karl Barth. The core of Bultman's theology can be cited as,[305]

> Bultmann maintains that the New Testament reveals two line of thought. On the one hand, the New Testament demythologizes its message because, in contradistinction to other religions its central figure is a historical person both and dying in time. On the other hand, it clothes Jesus in a mythological grab the texture of which was suggested to the disciples by Jewish apocalypticism and the mystery religions of late antiquity. It presents him as pre-existent, born of virgin, and dying a vicarious death on the cross. What about resurrection? Bultman's answer is that it has no factual reality.

For Bonhoeffer, one can speak appropriately of Jesus only after knowing well the God of the Old Testament. He is more concern about bringing into unity and harmony the personal faith and the church- the confession of the church must be portrayed by witnessing Jesus Christ to the contemporary situation. For Bonheoffer supernatural and natural, religion and secular have already their harmony and unity in the Jesus Christ as the God-Man. Thus, one can speak of God without religion in a secular approach.

In the 1970s theologians like Karl Rahner and Jurgen Moltmann became an important figure. Karl Rahner might not have written any work on systematic theology yet he had hundreds of topics published in 22 volumes beginning from 1954. Rahner was convinced at his heart that the existence of human life is totally impossible without God.[306] On the other hand Moltmann with his profound intellect went much deeper than Karl Barth and Bultman into the nature of God and salvation. Simultaneously with much

---

[305] Heick, *A History of Christian Thought...*, 285-286.

[306] Hill, The *History of Christian Thought...*, 299.

insight he describes Christian theology tackling the contemporary problems.

For the United States, the country witnesses the crisis, conflict and struggle for civil rights of the African American, under the leadership of Martin Luther King, Jr. The rife between the traditional and new learning Christians created unrest situation within the Church. The theology is captured by either extreme liberalism or extreme conservatism.[307] In Asia, Africa and Latin America the ethnic and cultural minorities within the church claim their traditional theologies which eventually resulted in the development of Black Theology, Latin American Liberation theology and Feminist theology.

8.5. Preaching in the Post-Modern Christianity: It's Significance

After the World War II, there was a revival of interest in the religious activities in America. There was rapid growth in the membership of the Church and a new generation of evangelical preachers appeared. The most outstanding evangelical preacher was Billy Graham, a Baptist minister from North Carolina. The Women movement demanding their equal treatment in the political and economic field extended their demands for supporting women in the pulpit. There was also the development of evangelical preaching and liberation preaching.

This epoch is the period on the development of the model of biblical scholarship preaching in Germany, Great Britain and the United States of America. Major work on homiletical theology was the publication of '*The Servant of the Word*' and '*God and Me*' by H. H. Farmer, a Cambridge theologian. The modern liturgical movement was also taking its shape within the Roman Catholic Church; the use of vernacular instead of Latin and celebration in which the priest faced the people. On the other hand, the Roman Catholic biblical scholars in their homilies were using historical-critical method for the exegesis of the Biblical text and started making use of their findings. This led to the rediscovery of the pulpit by the Roman Catholic priests in Europe and then in America. The

---

[307] Heick, *A History of Christian Thought...*, 409.

movement soon influenced the other tradition like the Anglicans, Lutherans and others as well. Eventually, it resulted in the use of lectionary in both the Protestant Churches and the Roman Catholic Churches.

Shortly after the World War II, Billy Graham became a very prominent evangelistic preacher ever since his first big Crusade in Los Angeles in 1949.The central theme of Billy Graham's preaching was on salvation, faithful Christian living and warning of the final judgment. He used very effectively the style of oratory. In fact, the style of Bible belt oratory enabled him to reach out to thousands of people. Billy insists his listeners to hold the Bible as they come to receive the Word of God. He neither used Biblical commentaries nor have much concern with the developments and movements of the modern biblical scholarship. Billy's Bible Belt oratory style was profoundly populist in nature. He established a strong rapport with his listeners. He was sensitive to common feeling and spoke the mind of the multitude of people who were deeply grieved over the situation of their country.[308] Billy Graham soon adopted in using the modern mass media for preaching by using the electronic amplification of his voice where over 100,000 congregations can hear his preaching. Later he expanded his ministry by using a network radio broadcast named '*hour of decision*' and a columnist on a nationally syndicated newspaper *'My Answer.'* He made use of the facility of scientific technology by telecasting his Crusades through television.[309]

The other area of preaching in the post-modern Christianity was on social issues. With Walter Rauschenbusch's effort to preach on social Gospel new era was inaugurated in the 1960s as civil right movement, the peace movement, the student movement, the women's right movement and the war of poverty became much prominent. The seriousness of Christian commitment was evaluated in their commitment to social activism. As a result of this movement two homiletical responses followed. The hermeneutics of suspicion

---

[308] Huges Oliphant Old, *The Reading and Preaching of the Scriptures in the Worship of the Christian Church*, vol. 7 (Grand Rapids: William B. Eerdmans Publishing Comnpany, 2010), 75–79.

[309] Edwards, Jr, *Concise Encyclopedia of Preaching...*, 224.

– there was a decline of respect for all forms of public speaking particularly the preaching ministry. The other response was the development of new homiletical genre in the form of 'prophetic preaching' as it exhibits a powerful medium for social change. In the middle of the twentieth century the African-American preaching known as the black preaching took the stage. The nature of their homilies was chanted sermon which is still prevalent in Kentucky and Tennessee. They practice poetical language and powerfully preached the Gospel. The African-American preaching reached its most eloquence in the civil right movement of Martin Luther King Jr., when he preached on 'I Have a Dream' in Washington in 1963. Since then Gardner C. Tylor, James Forbes, James Earl Massey, Henry Mitchell and others have made an impression of the progress of preaching outside the African-American community. All throughout the centuries Christian preaching was mostly a patriarchal oriented activity yet women preaching which was slightly visible in American starting from the seventeenth century became fully recognized in the twentieth century. In America, the ordination of women began among the Methodists and the Northern Presbyterians in 1950s, Southern Presbyterians in the 1960s, Major Lutheran groups and Episcopalians in the 1970s. Eventually women gradually is now developing homiletical models of their own and feminist homiletical literature is now appearing. The significant elements of feminist preaching are the use of gender-inclusive language, the use of liberation hermeneutics in the interpretation of the Bible and imagine God as not only masculine yet feminine too.

In Asia through the efforts of the Western missionaries, Churches began to grow. There was also the establishment of mega churches in many countries. This growth can be attributed to the high quality work of preaching ministry. Toyohiko Kagawa from Japan, Watchman Nee from China, Kyung – Chik Han and David Yong-Gi Cho from Korea and D. T. Niles from Sri Lanka were some of the prominent preachers in Asia.[310]

---

[310] Old, *The reading and Preaching of the Scriptures…,,* xiii-xiv.

9. An Overall Evaluation of the Homiletic Development in the Various Continents

In this section, attempt has been made to evaluate homiletics in relation to the theologies of various continents and reflect how homileticians have developed homiletic theories basing on the theological position. I will focus the evaluation, North America, Africa, Asia and Latin America as the visible literatures on homiletics are noticed mostly from these continents. I will deal with the European homiletics and also some particular homiletic theories in the next chapter.

9.1. The North American Continent

The history of homiletics in North American Continent falls under four historical eras; 1639-1800 A.D., 1800-1928 A.D., 1928-1960 A.D. and 1960 A.D. to the present. In each of these periods homiletical theory was developed basing on the theological climate and in harmonization with the cultural changes.

The period from 1639-1800 A.D. witnessed the introduction of printing which helps the American Churches in making copies of American Ordination sermons which basically deals with the instructions on effective preaching. The parish ministers were attracted to these ordination sermons in order to enhance their preaching ministry in the Churches. This was later fortified by the work of some notable English men on homiletics and volume of sermons collections joined the American ordination sermons which later form into a small early American homiletical literature. The nature of sermon in North America in this period contains elements of Enlightenment scholasticism. As suggested by Cotton Mather in his homiletical work in 1926, preachers were scholars who deliver a well-studied sermon. The homiletics was structured on reason rather than sermon built around a single theme or purpose. The manner of delivery was no an important matter of discussion, however a well reason material was ever more important and valued.[311]

In between 1800-1928 for the first time among the North American preachers the passion for reaching out to the ordinary

[311] Wardlaw, "Homiletics and Preaching…, 244.

people with the Gospel was ignited. John Witherspoon in his '*Lectures on Eloquence*' made the connection between scholasticism and common humanity. Another significant area of homiletical development was the founding of theological seminaries in USA and Canada which enhanced the systematic study and teaching of homiletics especially for the Protestant Churches. The teaching depended more on rhetoricians both ancient and the modern. Meanwhile, for effectively reaching out to the people in the pew, Ebenezer Porter and Henry Ripley published texts which have exegetical and theological concerns. Towards the end of the 19th century, the establishment of annual Lyman Beecher lectures on preaching at Yale stimulated North America to ascertain its own voice. Eventually, the separation between speech and rhetoric were established in the department of homiletics. Another threat to the Christian preaching in this continent was the rise of secularism. Homileticians like Henry Van Dyke called this as 'an age of doubt.'[312] Don M. Wardlaw while citing P. T. Forsyth wrote, "The age and much of the Church, believes in civilization and is interested in the Gospel, instead of believing in the Gospel and being interested in civilization."[313] Preachers failed to hold firm to the biblical foundation and began to draw their inspiration for the spiritual message in the others literary arts.

The period from 1928-1960 A.D. the world of homiletics realises the need of rediscovering the biblical root. The North American homileticains were more inspired by Karl Barth's theology of the Word of God. Barth writings and theological thought was a sharp reaction to modern liberalism. His work diverted homiletics to a new agreement with the Scripture.[314] For Barth as cited by Wardlaw, "Proclamation is human language in and through which God himself speaks…."[315] C. H. Dodd a New Testament scholar also published homiletics work on '*the Apostolic Preaching and Its Development*'. In this book Dodd describes preaching not just a moral instruction

312 Wardlaw, "Homiletics and Preaching…, 244-246.

313 Wardlaw, "Homiletics and Preaching…, 246.

314 Wardlaw, "Homiletics and Preaching…, 247.

315 Wardlaw, "Homiletics and Preaching…, 247.

or *didache* but it is a *kerygma,* the proclamation of the Gospel. His work was much influential as it adds theological character to the development and collection of the preaching materials in North America.

Beginning form 1960 to the present age, the Continent had experience a number of social turmoil. There was the civil right movement, the wars in Vietnam, urban riots, appearance of feminism etc. Homileticians exhibited shift in their approach by developing dynamic homiletical theologies by being sensible to the experiences of the people. By the year 1970, the hermeneutical in homiletics began a drastic shift from historical-critical method to metaphors and myth. As a result, there was the rediscovery of imagination in the interpretation of the text and hermeneutics from liberation and feminist theology. North America has been reading the Bible from the perspectives of the privilege and the power, yet this hermeneutical revolution has made the homileticians to discover the scripture from the perspectives of the poor and the oppressed. Here, the major discussion on homiletics concentrated on rhetoric, imagination and social analysis. Publication on homiletical work rapidly increased, graduated program in homiletics were initiated and Academy of Homiletics was formed which later began planning for annual meeting in order to produce their own scholarly resources. The most extensive discussion on rhetoric was on narrative and imagery. Homiletician like Fred Craddock opined narrativity as the basis for constructing new theory for preaching. However several thinkers and homileticians preferred imagery as the ultimate answer to the rhetorical nature of the postmodern homiletics. Frederick Buechner in his lectures '*Telling the Truth: The Gospel as Tragedy, Comedy, and Fairy Tale*' has described the superior role of imagery over story. David Buttrick further enhanced the superiority of imagery in the new homiletics through his book on '*Homiletics: Moves and Structure.*' The second major theory in new homiletics was on imagination in preaching. Paul Wilson and Thomas Troeger have explored the potentialities of imagination in the pulpit.[316] They placed "imagination at the juncture of human spirit and Holy

[316] Wardlaw, "Homiletics and Preaching…, 248-250.

Spirit, channeling divine creativity through human creativity to fashion new visions of the kingdom."[317] The third area of discussion in the new homiletics is the kind of sermon based on social hermeneutics. The development of liberation theology and feminist theology and the introduction of social analysis in the discipline of theological studies have made the social hermeneutic theory distinct and significant in the homiletical arena.[318]

9.2. The African Continent

The exact origin and expression of African Theology is vague yet the development can be trace back to the ideas disseminated by the North American blacks such as E. W. Blyden and W. E. B. Dubois in the 19th century. Initially their main concern was political issues concentrating on slavery and colonialism while on the other hand they were also interested in the importance of the religious and cultural practices of Africa. These ideas took shape and resulted in the development of different ideologies. Colonialism as in any context, for African context was to reject African personality and accept Western Civilization. The same ethos and practices was adopted by the European Christians for evangelization outside the Western World. Thus for the African thinkers and theologians, they were convinced that Christianity that is not based on the tradition and culture of Africa has no real connection with the lives of the people. The message of the Gospel is not rooted in the ethos and practices of the people. This thinking and struggle led to the emergence of a branch of theology called the Black theology.[319] The African theologians insist on rehabilitating their religio-cultural heritage and experiences into the Christian life of the people.[320] The African Theologian maintains that, "they had a genuine knowledge of God

---

[317] Wardlaw, "Homiletics and Preaching..., 250.

[318] Wardlaw, "Homiletics and Preaching..., 250.

[319] The crust of black theology consists in the systematic and conscious theological reflection f the Africans based on their unique experience which is characterized by oppression and suffering under the white racist societies in North America and South Africa (Matthew Illathuparampil et al., 293).

[320] Illathuparampil and Vincent Kundukulam eds., *The Contemporary Theologians*..., 292-293.

and that they had their own ways of communicating with deity, ways by which they were able to speak authentically as themselves and not as imitators of others. They were aware of the great store from which they could fashion new ways of speaking to and about God, and new styles of worship consistent with Christian faith."[321] The African theology emerged as a result of their struggle in social and political liberation from inequality and oppressions. One of the examples of such theologian was John Samuel Mbiti, who is also called as the 'father of contemporary African theology.'[322] Beliefs, ceremonies, sacred items and places, values and holy people are very important elements of Africa's religious life. Mbiti projects a close connection between the biblical language and the African culture in relation to images, pictures, rhythm, vividness and beauty. He advocates that the Bible can be interpreted in the light of the African religio-cultural context as they exhibit a very close connection. For instance, the teaching of Christian rites and values one can use the cultural practices like visions, exorcisms, healing and traditional dances and folk songs. Therefore, for the African theologians the liberative potentials within Christianity is the most significant and foundation for Christianity in the African context. The Word of God as it is revealed through the incarnation does not divides people on class, caste, creed, nation etc., rather it is for the unity for the whole humanity.[323]

The African homileticians basing on the above theological understanding have developed their homiletics upon their traditional and cultural understanding of religion mainly from liberation perspectives. It is said that the most important theological work for Africa is found in the sermons and in the preaching.[324] Aylward

---

[321] Illathuparampil and Vincent Kundukulam eds., *The Contemporary Theologians...*, 293.

[322] Illathuparampil and Vincent Kundukulam eds., *The Contemporary Theologians...*, 291.

[323] Illathuparampil and Vincent Kundukulam eds., *The Contemporary Theologians...*, 295-297..

[324] Aylward Shorter, "Homiletics and Preaching in Africa," *Concise Encyclopedia of Preaching*, ed., William H. Willimon and Richard Lischer (Louisville: Westminster John Knox Press, 1995), 229.

Shorter while writing on the homiletics about Africa commented that "the African preacher tends to adopt the hermeneutical methods favoured by the New Testament, imparting a typological function to biblical events and traditions and reinterpreting these in relation to contemporary existence. Historicity is played down, while emphasis is placed on symbolical and allegorical explanation."[325] The African preacher while explaining the biblical message uses folk tales, proverbs, traditional myths and symbols as illustrations in their sermons. In the African traditional religion, ancestors are essentially the mediator between God and humanity, taking this understanding the African preachers clarifies the doctrine of Christ and establishes better Christian understanding.[326]

In the contemporary, African continent churches the preaching in the mainline churches are doctrinal, liturgical and has sociological elements. The Reformed Churches follows evangelical preaching while the Roman Catholic or the Orthodox tradition preaching appears to be liturgical. Among the African Independent Churches there is significantly doctrinal in content and form in their sermon.[327]

9.3. The Asian Continent

Ever since the World War II, the Asian theologians have been considering an Asian theology away from Western theology.[328] So, the Asian theology germinated because the European theology was unable to provide the concept of religious understanding from Asian perspectives.[329] The Asian Theology was developed to make the Gospel more relevant to the life and situation of the people. The development of Asian theology is closely linked to the development of 'indigenization' and 'contextualization' in the early 20th century.[330] The Asian theology was strengthened by the emergence of creative

---

[325] Shorter, "Homiletics and Preaching ..., 229.

[326] Shorter, "Homiletics and Preaching ..., 230-231.

[327] Shorter, "Homiletics and Preaching ..., 229.

[328] B. R. Ro, "Asian Theology," http://www.mb-soft.com/believe/txo/asian.htm.

[329] James M. Cone, "Asian Theology Today: Searching for Definitions," http://www.religion-online.org/showarticle.asp?title=1236.

[330] Ro, "Asian Theology," http://www.mb-soft.com/believe/txo/asian.htm.

conference such as the conference in Wennapura, Sri Lanka on the theme, 'Asian's Struggle for a Full Humanity: Toward a Relevant Theology.'[331] Asian Theology therefore as described by J. A. Veitch states that, "An Asian Theology is a way of talking about what is created out of the Christian interpretation and appreciation of the living faiths as genuine ways of experiencing the divine and as they can be theologically interpreted in the light of the resurrection of Jesus Christ from the dead."[332] M. M. Thomas further explains Asian theology as a response to make the faith relevant in the situation of social revolution in Asia.[333]

The continent of Asia is very huge designed with diverse cultural backgrounds and different historical, religious and political context. Asia is also a continent where the number of Christians is very low in terms of the ratio of the total population in the Continent. It is said that only Philippines in the whole of Asian Continent is regarded as Christian nation. The Christian percentage is above tenth per cent of their total population only in Korea.[334] As such it is difficult to evaluate the early development of homiletics generally about the whole Asian Continent. Firstly, there are very little or no literatures on homiletics available and so it is difficult to do a scientific survey. Secondly, in countries like India and Philippines after a long colonial period English language became a major educational and cultural language. Thus, mission work in English was easily carried out. However, countries like China, Japan and Korea uses their own languages and the Gospel message followed transculturation into the thought pattern of the masses. Thus indigenization of the gospel happened through different ways and means in every Asian Country. After the Post World War II, the Asian Churches became more independent and there was a

---

[331] Cone, "Asian Theology Today: Searching for Definitions," http://www.religion-online.org/showarticle.asp?title=1236.

[332] S. Batumalai, *An Introduction to Asian Theology* (Kashmere Gate: ISPCK, 1991), 2.

[333] Batumalai, *An Introduction to Asian Theology*..., 2.

[334] Robert Mikio Fukada and Tsuneaki Kato, "Homiletics and Preaching in Asia," *Concise Encyclopedia of Preaching*, ed., William H. Willimon and Richard Lischer (Louisville: Westminster John Knox Press, 1995), 231.

gradual development of theologies and education basing on the Gospel which is rooted in Asia. Today, survey shows that country like Japan follows biblical exposition with systematic exegetical work of the Scripture giving much attention to ethical implication. On the other hand the Korean preaching is significantly carried out in topical methods.[335]

The Asian Churches have developed their own theologies basing on their context and have attempted to establish their homiletics theory upon the various contextual theologies. For instance, the Korean Churches developed the Minjung theology affirming the Korean culture and history. The Indian Churches have developed theologies like the Dalit theology and the tribal theology affirming the dignity and identity of the oppressed and neglected section of the country. The Asian homileticians have developed their homiletics in accordance to their contextual needs upon the various theologies developed within a particular country. Therefore, the interpretation of the Scriptural text is more oriented towards the poor and struggles of the people.

9.4. The Latin American Continent

The historical development of Latin American theology which is also called the liberation theology goes back to the earliest colonial period in Latin America where the evangelists and missionaries were very prophetic with the unjust treatment of the indigenous people, blacks, mestizos and the other poor section of the people in the rural and the urban masses. During 1950s and 1960s nation like Argentina, Brazil and Mexico were more engaged in significant industrial development. This process benefited only the middle class and the urban public but left the huge section of the peasantry into deeper rural marginalization. Therefore, the liberation theology or the Latin American theology had its origin in the context of the dialogue between the church and the society, between Christian faith and the urgency of transformation and liberation need for the people. One of the most outstanding Latin American theologians is Gustavo Guterrez, who is also considered as the father of liberation

[335] Fukada and Tsuneaki Kato, "Homiletics and Preaching ..., 233.

theology. His work and attempt was for the massive injustice and oppression and enable the cry of the poor heard in theology.[336] For Gutierrez, "Theology must be contextual....Theology must be intrinsically linked with a specific social and cultural situation.... A critical reflection on praxis.... To know God is to work for justice...."[337]

For the development of homiletics, initially Latin American Continent was under the Spanish colonial power. Thus, the major portion of the missionaries preaching was against the mistreatment of the native converts by the ruling colonial class. So, far the Franciscan and the Dominican was dominant preacher. However after the political independence from the colonial supremacy Protestant Churches began to establish. The Latin American early Protestant Christians were soon sent to North America where they inherited the fundamentalist evangelical theology of preaching for the Protestant Churches in Latin America.[338] The writer observes that as homiletics took its proper shape, the Gospel and the context was the central focus of preaching in Latin America. The context during the initial formation of their theology was liberation from all powers of oppression. As one observes the context in which the Latin American liberation theology was developed, it is noticed that the theology was developed out of the struggles of the marginalized people socially, economically and politically. Therefore, the Latin Americans homileticians upon their yearning for social liberation have developed their homiletics from the liberation dimension presented in the Bible.

Preaching has sustained the growth and ministry of Christianity throughout the centuries. Christianity went through thick and thin, rough and smooth, low and high period throughout the centuries. There were number of theological controversies throughout the

---

[336] Illathuparampil and Vincent Kundukulam eds., *The Contemporary Theologians...*, 195.

[337] Illathuparampil and Vincent Kundukulam eds., *The Contemporary Theologians...*, 198.

[338] John L. Kater, Jr., "Homiletics and Preaching in Latin America," *Concise Encyclopedia of Preaching*, ed., William H. Willimon and Richard Lischer (Louisville: Westminster John Knox Press, 1995), 242.

centuries and divisions had prevailed within Christianity. Christian faith was also challenged by secularism, natural sciences and scientific advancements. Yet Christian preaching has adapted to each of the needs and conditions of the unique and different situations effectively and exhibited in making preaching utmost relevant to all the epoch in the world of Christianity. Careful evaluations of the history of Christian preaching show that the wide spread and growth of Christianity both geographically and numerically can be attributed largely to the work of preaching. Christian preaching has been significant in each of the era in its own creative way hitherto in a nut shell one can pen down its major significance in the growth of Churches and Christian population. It is estimated that the Christian population grew from 1.236 billion in 1970 to approximately 2 billion in the year 2000. Which means the year 2000 census records that Christianity covers 34.4 per cent of the total world's population.[339] Therefore, with the changes of time, lifestyles and understandings of the world, Christian preaching is challenged to constantly develop and discover new hermeneutics so as to make homiletics relevant to the demands of the times.

---

[339] Winston Crawley, *World Christianity, 1970-2000: Toward a New Millennium* (California: William Carey Library, 2001), 36.

Chapter 3

An Overview of Homiletic Theories

1. The 'Word:'[340] It's Functionality in Preaching

The 'Word' in the Old Testament was considered as powerful and active (Isa. 55:10-11), powerful agent in the creation which thus forth give lives (Gen.1: 3ff.), its carries divine authority (Ex. 4: 10ff.) and it is through the 'Word', the ministry of the prophets were ordained and authorised. In the New Testament the 'Word' continued to have its significance having either the Old Testament connotation or development from it. The 'Word' is identified with the reveal will, plans and purpose of Jesus Christ for humanity (cf. Lk. 11:28, Rom. 2:6, Col. 1:25-27) and to the word spoken by Jesus Christ which of course was powerful indeed (cf. Lk 5:1).[341] Jesus Christ is the Word of God, the Truth and the Revelation of the redemptive work of God to the world. John presents in his prologue the 'Word'

---

[340] By the term 'Word' I refers to the Word of God and hence forth would use the term to mean the latter.

[341] J. N. Sanders, "Work, The,' *The Interpreter's Dictionary of the Bible*, vol. 4, George Arthur Buttrick et. al. (Nashville: Abingdon Press, 1962), 868.

or *logos* as eternal, divine and originator of everything (John 1:1ff). As Jesus declares "Whoever listen to you, listen to me, and whoever rejects you rejects me and whoever rejects me rejects the one who sent me" (Lk 10:16). The book of Hebrews also explains that "God spoke to our ancestors in many and various ways by the prophets; but in these last days… has spoken to us by a Son" (Heb.1:1-2). There was definitely a close connection between the proclamation of the Church and the proclamation of Jesus. Consequently, like the prophetic ministry in the Old Testament, the apostolic office in the New Testament is also a divinely ordained ministry (Lk. 1:2, Acts 6: 2-4, Col. 1:24-26).

The 'Word' found its significance in the Jewish Synagogue worship in the reading and preaching. Christianity being accorded as preaching religion, the 'Word' played a vital role in sustaining the life of the Church among the early Christians. The reading of the Law and the prophets continued even as the early Christian met for worship yet deeper ministry of the 'Word' begin to take place. The 'Word' is more proclaimed as the fulfilment of the Law through Christ. In other words the kerygmatic dimension of its worship was most evident in the early church. The historical document of the early Church, the *Didache* (80-110 ca.), *The Teaching of the Twelve Apostles* tells of the life of the second and third century Church as devoted to the preaching and teaching of the 'Word.' This preaching of the 'Word' was not mere elementary instructions but more directed towards maturing Christian members in the Lord.[342] The ministry of the Word was highly regarded and hence bishops and deacons were honoured for their sacred services. Christian preaching was understood and identified with the 'Word' during the patristic period till the early middle age period of John Chrysostom and St. Augustine. As preaching decline the understanding and identification of preaching with the 'Word' receded, until it was revised and established during the reformation period by Martin Luther and John Calvin. Preaching as witnessing the divine 'Word' was further

[342] Hughes Oliphant Old, *The Reading and Preaching of the Scriptures in the Worship of the Christian Church*, vol. 1, The Biblical Period (Grand Rapids: William B. Eerdmans Publishing Company,1998), 255-256.

affirmed by theologians like Emil Brunner, Karl Barth and others. Thus, preaching can be considered as the extension of the 'Word' revealed through Jesus Christ. The identification of preaching as the extension of the 'Word' finds its affirmation in two fundamental truth; God's desire to communicate and not only spoke in the history but continues to do now.[343] Thus, preaching becomes the Word only if it preaches the Word – preaching God's revelation through the Son and preaching the will and way of God.

2. The New Hermeneutics

The word 'New Hermeneutics' in preaching was developed on the ontology of language proposed by Martin Heidegger, a German philosopher which was later expanded and propagated by a German theologian Gerhard Ebeling. Ebeling explains that the power of language is measured by the fact of experiencing the world as time. One cannot speak without the power of the language which was hand down through time and also experience the world without this language. Thus for Ebeling word/language is understood "not simply as a vocable or even as a grammatical sentence, but rather as the totality of statement that is word as an event…embracing the situations in which it arises, into which it is spoken, and from which it is answered….Language does not merely point to or signify actions; language performs and elicits actions."[344] Ebeling further employed the term 'word-event', the other term used for the 'language' which travels along with time for the proclamation of the Word of God.

New Hermeneutics is also accorded as post-Bultmannian since it was taken forward, as mentioned earlier by Gerhard Ebeling one of the students of Bultmann. New Hermeneutics reflection on the language or the word-event in the kerygma of the Word was more of a refined process of the demythologization theory of Bultmann. Bultmann claims supernatural act by Christ in making the ordinary language into extraordinary effective. For him, in Christian preaching,

---

[343] John S. McClure, *Preaching Words: 144 Key Terms in Homiletics* (Louisville: Westminister John Knox Press, 2007), 151.

[344] Gerhard Ebeling, *God and Word,* translated by James W. Leitch (Philadelphia: Fortress Press, 1967), 20-21.

Christ the crucified encounter us, in other words in the kerygma of the Word, the continued revelation of God through Jesus Christ in the human word takes place. So, what is new in the New Hermeneutics informed by Heideggerian theory of language is this. It has taken Bultmann's demythologizing one step further by denouncing the supernatural intervention and giving utmost position to the language in the kerygma of the Word. For Heideggerian's New Hermeneutics, language has performativity power inherent in itself. The New Hermeneutics draws it distinctive parallel to the parables of Jesus. For them just as language or poetry performs pure speech so does the parables in the Gospels functions the purest form of speech of Jesus. The interpretation process of the text is no longer taken as its simple task but New Hermeneutics critically understands this process as the 'interpretation of existence by means of the texts.'[345] The phenomena is not the understanding of language but understanding through language. Word does not function as an object of understanding as such it needs proper solution through exposition. Word mediates and takes to the state of understanding.[346] The homiletic movement of the New Hermeneutics is concern with the transition of the scripture to the spoken word. Thus, the homiletical task is making the text become God's Word by interpreting the scriptures as word. I observed that the New Hermeneutics follow the form criticism and redaction criticism as an interpretive tool of interpreting the Bible.

3. The New Homiletics

The New Homiletics is a movement started after 1950s by homileticians who deviated from a rational argument and persuasion model of homiletics to a homiletics where preaching will enable people to encounter God in their own situations and experience God. New Homiletics advocates that sermons are not a presentation of rational-cognitive opinions to the world of faith but it is the revelation of the hidden meanings of the Bible to the faith community. New homiletics is also a move away from the traditional homiletics of topical, expository and problem-oriented sermons. In

---

345 James F. Kay, *Preaching and Theology* (St. Louis: Chalice Press, 2007), 86.

346 Kay, *Preaching and Theology*..., 87.

1969 initially the movement was categorized as the New Homelitics by an educator and scholar, David James Randolph and later got the attention of many homileticians who had similar concerns. Homilitician like Dick Eslinger attribute the New Homiletics as the 'Copernican revolution in preaching' in North American Homiletics. Paul Scott Wilson considers the New Homiletics movement as the most 'dramatic homiletical shift' ever since the reformation movement in the Christian era.[347] New homiletics is least bothered on what the sermon say but rather concern on what the sermon do. The New Homiletics follows the New Hermeneutic philosophy of the word-event in the kerygma of Word. The German origin New Hermeneutics theory influenced homileticians in North America like Fred Craddock and others. Thus, the New Hermeneutics was modified and termed among the North American Homileticians as the New Homiletics. Most of the contemporary homileticians also suggest that the New Homiletics and postmodern homiletics are identical and synonymous. Paul Scott Wilson has shown few identical characteristics of the New Homiletics and the postmodern homiletics.[348]

1. Engage the experience of the hearers.
2. Seek to confirm rather than to prove.
3. Value concrete experience over abstraction.
4. Conceive of form as an extension and expression of content.
5. Are inductive and employ narrative.
6. Allow for participation and disagreement.

As I deal with the New Homiletic theory, indirectly the study of postmodern homiletics[349] will also be inculcated. The New Homiletics emphasis firstly on the theory of preaching not as

---

[347] Eugene L. Lowry, 'Arrangement,' *The New Interpreter's Handbook of Preaching*, Paul Scott Wilson et al. (Nashville: Abingdon Press, 2008), 347.

[348] Paul Scott Wilson, *Preaching and Homiletical Theory* (Missouri: Chalice Press, 2004), 137.

[349] For introductory study of Postmodern Preaching, see Ronald J. Allen, Barbara Shires Blaisdell and Scott Black Johnson, *Theology for Preaching: Authority, Truth and Knowledge of God in a postmodern ethos* (Nashville: Abingdon Press, 1997).

a simple exposition and information about God through certain ideas or themes but it performs the Word of God. Secondly, New Homiletics takes seriously the work of biblical exegesis which allows the preacher to take forwards the intention of the text to the contemporary hearers. Unless this is accomplished, preacher surely misses the point in preaching. Thirdly, the New Homiletics takes into serious account the theology of preaching. Preaching is not a plain talk using persuasive rhetoric or mere duty of a pastor to do self-promotion, propagation or even it is not an opportunity to make public relations. God is to be spoken of in a manner that He really is expressed as God. Fourthly, the New Homiletics encourages deeper devotion into the homiletical task, to ponder on the biblical text with renewed attention and deeper theological reflection.[350] The North American Homileticians have mostly limited the New Homiletics movement to the homiletical theory such as, phenomenology, narrative, conversational and imaginative.

3.1. Phenomenological Theory

Phenomenological theory in homiletics is often attributed to David Buttrick mostly on his work on *Homiletic: Moves and Structure.*[351] Buttrick remarkable position in the world of homelitics was the description of how sermons happen in consciousness- the investigation of listener's consciousness as the basis of designing the sermon. Basing on this research, he put forth rules for the design of the sermon. Buttrick design is primarily aim at communal consciousness rather than individual consciousness. He explain that 'language' functions in human consciousness and as such preachers must design their sermons intentionally so as to allow language penetrate and form in the consciousness. Preachers thus can create sermons, that can lead to develop 'faith consciousness.' For developing the phenomenological theory in homiletics, Buttrick offers two major parts of sermon – the moves and the structures.

---

[350] Kay, *Preaching and Theology*..., 101-102.

[351] David Buttrick, *Homiletics: Moves and Structures* (London: SCM Press Ltd, 1987), 78.

Buttrick names the occurrence of sequence of language in modules in sermons as 'moves.' Sermons are made up of a series of moves, for instance, in a twenty minutes sermon, preacher can have five moves with each having three to four minutes. These moves must be developed in a sermon with conversational logic connection between each step. Buttrick was more inclined towards sermon moving from one step to the other rather than maintaining points by points where there is void of rational connection. Preacher can developed the ideas of the sermon using images, symbols and metaphors. In his development of the whole sermon structure, Buttrick outlined that preacher's intention of the sermon can be carried out by means of a plot. For him, plot is a series of moves constructed to establish the intention of the sermon. Buttrick explains three process in a sermon structure through which consciousness moves. First is the mode of immediacy. This is the stage where the plot of the biblical text immediate a narrative movement in human consciousness; consciousness hears the story. Second is the mode of reflection. Here reflection of the meaning of the biblical passage in the contemporary understanding in the listeners' consciousness takes place. Thirdly, the mode of praxis comes into play when human consciousness realises 'what am I on the earth is doing? What should I do then? Buttrick explains that in this mode of sermon hermeneutic of lived experience happens, in other words preaching begins with the human experience and relate it to the gospel rather than gospel relating to the lived experience.

3.2. Narrative Theory

Narrative theory is one of the most basic ways in which human beings expresses their knowledge and their worldviews. It is basic yet the contemporary homiletics has turn towards narrative methodology for effective sermonic development in the recent homiletical scholarship. Narrative methodology has restructured the field of homiletics particularly after 1970s with the publication of Fred Craddock's book *As One Without Authority.* Barbara K. Lundblad, an American professor of homiletics, explains that narrative theory proposes different way of interpreting the text and different way of preaching.[352] Narrative theory would view the whole Bible both the narrative literatures as well as the non-narrative literatures as one encompassing narratives. Narrative scholarship identifies that the total meaning is found in the text as whole rather than in isolated sections. While the historical development of the passages/stories is crucial for interpretation, narrative method focuses on the narrative representation of the text for interpretation. The primary objective of narrative method is not on the existence of any historical person/s[353] mention in the story/ies in the Bible or the author but concentrates on the Biblical text about the person/s. The text is given the focal point for the study to discern and know those values and theological perspective put across by the original author in a particular text.[354] The most basic element in narrative theory is to follow close reading of the text or to read the text thoroughly so as to grasp the drama and power of the story/ies. There are two different approaches of narrative theory especially in the field of homiletics – contextual narrative and biblical narrative. Scholars and homileticians who advocates contextual narratives emphasises more on deriving the narrative sermon from life experience of the people and move towards the biblical text. In other words, it is taking a particular context to the interpretation of the Biblical text. On the other hand, theologian who advocates biblical narratives emphasise on the biblical text/passage for narrative performance. Fred Craddock, the father of modern narrative theory discusses the contextual narrative approach in his inductive method. The inductive method proposes that the starting point of the sermon begins from the life experience of the people and lead the listeners to discover the truth of the Bible in their own situation. Eugene L. Lowry in his homiletical plot, talks of sermon as a process. Sermons begin by upsetting the equilibrium where the root of existential issues is unearthed or discovered and then lead to resolution from the Bible. For Biblical narratives, David

[352] Barbara K. Lundblad, "Narrative theory," *The New Interpreter's handbook of Preaching*, Paul Scott Wilson et al. (Nashville: Abingdon Press, 2008), 203.

[353] The sentence does not demythologised or rejects the historic human personality of Jesus in the Bible.

[354] Grant R. Osborne, *The Hermeneutical Spiral: A Comprehensive Introduction to the Biblical Interpretation* (Illinois: InterVarsity Press, 1991), 154-155.

L. Larsen talks of such narrative approach in his book *Telling the Old Story: The Art of Narrative Preaching.* This methodology approaches every biblical text from narrative perspective - reading the text as narrative and preaching it as narrative sermon. The theory emphasise on narrative performance in the Biblical interpretation and also in the proclamation from Genesis to the Revelation. Narrative approach to the biblical interpretation underscores that the narrative passage/ text itself hold the meaning. This approach follows the text-centred hermeneutics, which is propagated by Paul Ricoeur. In other words, narrative theory focuses on the current shape and meaning of the text rather than dwelling extensively on the historical critical method.

Narrative theory would thus help the preachers to retell the biblical stories/passages in a way that will enable the listeners to experience the biblical stories as their stories and connect them with the narratives of their lives. It is allowing the listeners to enter into the biblical stories imaginatively as they retell. On the other hand, in the narrative theory, non-biblical narratives such as drama, folklores, movies etc., can also be re-narrated as a way that leads to the biblical stories/narratives. The character of narrative also retells and re-narrates the story of the people. It begins with the re-narration of the contextual realities and experiences of the people towards mediation from the Bible. The story and experience of the people were re-narrated bring new hope and the possibility of new living. Thus, re-narration ultimately would have new perspective and new ending for the hearers. This contextual narrative process does not lose the authority of the Bible because the Bible take control of the entire movements of homiletic plot.

3.3. Conversational Theory

Initially at the beginning of the New Homiletics movement, conversational homiletics was more concern with the interaction of the preachers and the congregation during the sermon or after the sermon. In some cases, preachers organises the congregation into small groups to converse during the sermon. However, in recent years conversational homiletics has made a move from the traditional practice to a more refine practice of the theory. Ronald J. Allen, explains that Conversational homiletics today is more concern with the theological method and content of the sermon rather than the style.[355] One of the notable contemporary homileticians who have made visible contribution to conversational homiletics is O. Wesley Allen Jr. He proposes that preaching cannot be understood and define in hierarchical terms where preacher speaks from the above to the congregation below. For him the Church is a conversational community. Thus, instead of placing preaching above or at the Centre of the Church's proclamatory conversations, it can function as one conversational voice among many and one conversational partner among many that are involved in the proclamation of the Gospel. Preaching is not the beginning, the centre or the end of the conversation in the Church. In order to make preaching as one conversational partner or voice, preachers must stick to the conversational ethics and etiquette of the Church. He insist that, "preacher must be trusting and trustworthy, sincere and honest; value both common points of view and asymmetry; and be committed to the conversation beyond moments of either consensus or utter tension."[356]

Wesley Allen further clarifies that the foundation of the pulpit is the give and take relationship that exist among the congregation. In other words, the 'covenant of egalitarian reciprocity'[357] takes place in the Church's conversational community. Conversational theory also finds its similarities with the principles of dialogical theory and collaborative theory. In the principle of egalitarian reciprocity, preachers must not just be on the giving side but must be on both sides of the give and take nature of proclamation. The preachers' listening must be genuine, open-minded and willing to listen not only on the ground of the professional vocational task and call but

---

[355] Ronald J. Allen, "Conversational Preaching," The *New Interpreter's Handbook of Preaching*, Paul Scott Wilson et al (Nashville: Abingdon Press, 2008), 372.

[356] O. Wesley Allen Jr., *The Homiletics of All Believers: A Conversational Approach to Proclamation* (Louisville: Westminster John Knox Press, 2005), 41.

[357] Egalitarian reciprocity means if the preachers' wishes to be heard, then they must listen to others as they proclaim their experience and interpretation of God, self and the world in the Church.

also as fellow Christian struggling in the interpretation of God, self and the world.

3.4. Imaginative Theory

Imaginative theory advocates the use of cognitive faculty to design a particular image in the sermons. The theory is interested in poetic and artistic characteristic of homiletics; as such this approach is less interested in the older rhetorical theories of homiletics and more inclined towards an imaginative theology. Implementation of creative theories and critical imagination in the interpretation of the Scripture play a major role in this theory. Images and symbols are the means used in the imaginative homiletics to probe the mysterious meaning behind the biblical passages. Imagination provokes the preacher to experience cognitive conflict and tension which later steers the preacher to work towards creating resolving images or the sermonic resolution. John S. McClure has prescribed Richard Eslinger four steps of homiletic imagination in biblical preaching as,[358]

> First, the preacher's imagination conforms deeply to a tradition and worldview. Second, preachers exercise patience as they attend carefully to the biblical witness, identifying the range of issues or problems raised by the text. Third, preachers begin to think sermonically as they wrestle with the tensional convergence of tradition, scripture and their own preaching context. Finally, preachers begin to think paradigmatically as they undergo paradigm shifts and discover new insights that will shape the thought and imagery of preaching.

4. Post Liberal Homiletics

The post liberal homiletics emerged in the 1970s and 1980s. Post liberal homiletics is basically a reaction to the liberal theology and homiletics. The Post liberal homileticains affirms the uniqueness of the biblical faith and counter the liberal view of correlating the Bible with the philosophical and existential experiences of the world. Post

---

[358] McClure, *Preaching Words…*, 60.

liberal homileticians emphasises absolutely on using the Bible to deal with the human experience rather than attempting to 'experientialize biblical texts.'[359] Postliberal homileticians express reservation and they are critical with the popular New Homiletics inductive theory and narrative theory as their homiletical focus is grounded on the human experiences rather than the biblical faith. Post liberal homileticians seek to improvise the biblical character to the social settings and take the biblical text in solidarity with the sufferings of the world and preach the message of hope from the biblical character. Post liberal homiletics searches the Christian claims as is expressed in the scripture and tradition and work towards engaging the listeners in shaping their faith through the scriptural claims.

Some of the prominent work of postl iberal homeliticians are Hans W. Frei, *The Eclipse of Biblical Narrative: A study in Eighteenth and Nineteenth Century Hermeneutics*[360] and *The Identity of Jesus Christ: The Hermeneutical Bases of Dogmatic Theology,*[361] George Lindbeck, *The Nature of Doctrine: Religion and Theology in a Postliberal Age*[362] and Charles Campbell, *Preaching Jesus: New Directions for Homiletics in Hans Frei's Postliberal Theology.*[363] The postliberal homiletics operates with the hermeneutics of cultural-linguistic theory of religion and doctrine. If one has to understand what Christian means when they say God, one has to really immersed into attending the rituals, liturgies, hymns, prayers and other Christian religious practices. It is only in this process God can be understood. The postliberal critics the historical Jesus constructed by the academic historiography which tells more about the authors than about Jesus. Jesus the saviour has to be the principle character and not the academic historiographical construct. So, for postliberalism the

---

[359] McClure, *Preaching Words...*, 111.

[360] Hans W. Frei, *The Eclipse of Biblical Narrative : A Study in Eighteenth and Nineteenth Century Hermeneutics* (New Haven: Yale University Press, 1974).

[361] Hans W. Frei, *The Identity of Jesus Christ: The Hermeneutical Bases of Dogmatic Theology* (Philadelphia: Fortress Press, 1975).

[362] George A. Lindbeck, *The Nature of Doctrine: Religion and Theology in a Postliberal Age* (Philadelphia: The Westminster Press, 1984).

[363] Charles L. Campbell, *Preaching Jesus: New Directions for Homiletics in Hans Frei's Postliberal Theology* (Grand Rapids: Eerdmans, 1997).

task of theology is to unfold this principle character of the crucified and the risen Lord to interpret and 'help the church enact it, ritualize it and preach it with assurance.'[364] Hans Frei derived the identity of Jesus Christ from the canonical form of the text rather than applying the method of historical criticism. He stands against Bultman's view of sharing the Gospel story as Christ myth and argued the Gospel story can be approached through the genre of 'realistic narrative.' For Frei the Gospel narrative fictionally describes and gives identity the factual existence of Jesus of Nazareth as a historical person who now exists factually as the Risen One.[365] Charles Campbell[366] in his work on preaching Jesus accorded that preaching must include expositional work of Jesus' story enabling the preachers to assist the listeners understands the Biblical story as their stories.[367] Preaching is not about locating individual needs and assuring solution but it is more about building up the community of faith, the Church. Campbell's core work is noticed in his argument on his homiletical conviction 'preaching as an act of non-violent resistance' against dominion and power.

5. Homiletics in German Speaking Europe

I would like to discuss the homiletics in German speaking Europe because of their in-depth theological work in the field of homiletics. In fact much of the new developments in homiletics were basically the work of the German speaking European homileticians. Homileticians in other parts of the continent developed their homiletics theory basing on the homiletics theories which were already in the world of homiletical literature by the German Speaking Europeans. I shall discuss the homiletical theory of some of the most prominent theologians and homileticians from

---

[364] Kay, *Preaching and Theology*..., 108.

[365] Kay, *Preaching and Theology*..., 116.

[366] My analysis of Campbell's homiletics here mostly depends on the work of James F. Kay *Preaching and Theology* (St. Louis: Chalice Press, 2007).

[367] For instance, the reflection of the Bible story about the Pharisees should let the listeners realized that I am modern day Pharisee.

the modern era onwards as it will not be possible to discuss the homiletics theory of all the theologians and homileticians.

One of the outstanding personalities who ushered German modern homiletics a fresh impulse was F. D. E. Schleiermacher. He understood the homiletical task in the context of three religious languages – the poetics, the rhetorical and the descriptively didactic. Nevertheless his reflection on preaching went beyond the phenomena of religious language of logical and philosophical advices. Preaching is a testimony of one's experience with Jesus Christ and the scripture. He advocated the homiletical theory of worship. For him, sermons are meant to serve the community of faith and so he argued from the homiletics viewpoint that sermon should be parish-related to meet its purpose for the congregation, rather than reasoning and lecture oriented presentation. Sermon act as a mediator or mediates between the preacher, scripture and the congregation and as such preaching on theological themes must grapples along with the non-theological language of the congregation. After Schleiermacher, a liberal theologian Friedrich Niebergal developed the homiletics of the role of the listeners in preaching. He proposes developing the homiletical theory inductively from the empirical observation of the life condition of the contemporary hearers rather than simple homiletical theory from dogmatic principles. This psychological dynamics in homiletical communication became one of the most extensively researched areas in the post- modern homiletics especially in the new homiletics movement.

Another important homiletician to consider is Karl Barth. Barth homiletics argues against the homiletical theory of Niebergal which gives the central role of the listeners in a sermon undermining the scriptures. For Barth nothing can substitute the primacy of the Word of God in preaching. His homiletical theory is based on this following homiletics conviction;[368]

---

[368] Jan Hermelink and Friedrich Wintzer, "Homiletics in Germany and German-Speaking Europe," *Concise Encyclopedia of Preaching*, ed., William H. Willimon and Richard Lischer (Louisville: Westminster John Knox Press, 1995), 236.

> 1. The sermon is the Word of God spoken by Himself by means of an explanation of a biblical text to contemporaries . . . delivered by a person called by the church. 2. The sermon is the ordered attempt of a called person . . . to serve the Word of God itself by explaining a biblical text to contemporaries as an announcement of what they have to hear from God himself.

Karl Barth emphasised on the conviction that the Bible is neither a myth nor a history. For him the resurrection of Jesus is an event which took place in space and time. Thus, this Resurrection account cannot be considered neither as a prescientific myth nor scientific history, nor is it the amalgamation of both. Barth branded it as a genre called the 'biblical saga or legend.'[369]

Dietrich Bonhoeffer along with Karl Barth Neo-orthodoxy considers the authority of the Scriptures, the Bible as the Word of God. For him Christ is present in the sermon which is the spoken word of God. In other words, in and through the Bible one can locate God's revelation and thus it is the sole source for preaching. Basing on this understanding, Bonhoeffer relentlessly urges his congregation and students towards the Bible. Bonhoeffer homiletical theory was built upon his understanding on the word, church and the world. Sermon is the spoken Word of God where Christ himself reveals and communicates to the listeners as the Word. The Church is the visible body of Christ on earth and as such she becomes the particular place where Word of God happens, the risen Christ meets. It is only through the kerygma of the Word, the world can attain it true worldliness, i.e., a world as God intended it.[370] Bonhoffer was more concern on worldly than religious preaching as he was convinced that religion is a way human being have developed to fit God into human wants and meet one's ends. The logical meaning behind Bonhoffer's worldly preaching unveils that God meets human kind in their world of space and time. He followed Christocentric

---

[369] Kay, *Preaching and Theology*...,112.

[370] Clyde E. Fant, "Bonhoeffer, Dietrich," *Concise Encyclopedia of Preaching*, ed., William H. Willimon and Rochard Lischer (Louisville: Westminister John Knox Pres, 1995), 39.

hermeneutics as such for Bonhoffer, preachers are witnesses, bearers of testimony to the biblical faith. Jesus is not only found in the Word but He is the Word. His life, death and resurrection are the interpretive keys. He affirms that only where "Christ is preached God is present."[371] Bonhoffer although regarded the authority of the scripture, he ultimately gives essential importance to the sermon. The scripture is meant to be interpreted as it is, so that through the kerygma, the Word of God might go forth into the lives of the listeners. Thus interpreting the scripture from the viewpoint of what does the text tells about God? about ourselves? And allowing God to speak to the hearers is the homiletical task of the preacher.

Rudolf Bultmann another liberal theologian made a great impact in the field of hermeneutics. In some ways his theology of preaching is related to Karl Barth and Dietrich Bonhoeffer, but I found that Bultmann's homiletics is more motivated towards liberalism. He followed the form criticism and redaction criticism in his hermeneutics especially in the New Testament interpretation. His homiletic theory was more incline towards the significance of the biblical text to the contemporary existence. Bultmann argues that the narrative of the historical Jesus is only a historical event, in a sense that it does not have any significance in the contemporary situation. Bultmann's homiletical theory can be best understood upon his following theological conviction. Firstly, he does not believe in the literal pre-existence of Jesus with the God-head prior to his earthly mission and the virgin birth of Jesus. Secondly, the resurrection of Jesus literally happening in flesh is a myth and not reality. Thirdly, the eschatological happening in the Bible is a mythological one and it cannot happen. Fourthly, he does not believe in demons, the demons in the contemporary situations are the political, social and technological evils which possess us. Fifthly, He does not believe in miracle, because miracles cannot be proof scientifically and thus become illogical and impossible. Basing on this theological conviction, Bultmann introduced his homiletical theory of 'demythologization' which attracted much attention. Bultmann argues that the first

---

[371] Dietrich Bonhoeffer, *Christology*, introduced by Edwin H. Robertson and translated by John Bowden (London: Collins, 1966), 105.

century Christians have presented the New Testament within their mythodological world views which need to be review from modern scientific perspectives. In the contemporary scientific age the first century myth of the New Testament becomes scientifically illogical and irrelevant. Thus, Bultmann, through his homiletical theory of demythologization attempted to serve the contemporary scientific world. He did not try to eliminate or remove the myths in the New Testament but interpret the New Testament myths in the modern terms. Another reason for his demythologization is that through mythology God is objectified and limit in terms of space (Heaven) and time (Eschatology). Nevertheless, Bultmann sees the Gospel as God's liberating work on humanity and thus objectifying God distorts the reality of God. Bultman's homiletical theory was grounded on the philosophy of human existence.

6. Recent Homiletical Theories

6.1. Deconstruction Theory: John S. McClure

John S. McClure homiletics theory went beyond the movement of new homiletics and he proposes a homiletics theory of deconstruction build upon the philosophy of 'otherness,' a v theory propounded by Emmanuel Levinas, a French philosopher. McClure's homiletics theory is thus oriented more towards the 'others' in other words preaching must recognize the responsibility and obligation towards others – our neighbours and strangers. McClure in one of his prominent books which of course depicts his homiletics theory in detail, *Other – Wise Preaching: A Postmodern Ethics for Homiletics* shows that homileticians must exit the house of scripture/canon, tradition, experience and reason as these houses of preaching enterprise were constructed by modernity and enlightenment without taking into consideration about the 'others'. Thus, McClure proposes a homiletics theory that deconstructs these frameworks in homiletics which is influenced by modernity and enlightenment. McClure's other – wise homiletics is related to some of the recent homiletics of Justo L. González and Catherine G. González's *Liberation Preaching: The Pulpit and the Oppressed,* William Sloane

Coffin[372] and Christine Smith[373] homiletics on ethical and social issues, Leonora Tubbs Tisdale[374] homiletics on the 'local theology' and other feminist preaching. However, McClure homiletics theory went deeper than these theories into homiletical consideration of the human others, preaching oriented towards a new vision of all humility – compassionate, resistance, justice and hope.

McClure homiletics theory is directed more towards a practical model of preaching. For instance in the ethical preaching he stresses the importance of exiting the biblical, theological, social, experiential and cultural hegemonies that is prevalent within the faith community and beyond. Then adopt language of critical-justice from the biblical text. Then he called upon the need of re-examining the language and theology of the preachers, new theological reading and also new biblical commentaries. In order to establish his theory, McClure proposes exegetical model of listening to the textual margins asking certain questions such as: Who doesn't speak in the text? Who is missing in the text? Who goes nameless in the text? Where is the voice of the voiceless in the text? Then in the next step of the exegesis he proposes to apply the deconstructive biblical criticism that moves beyond the textual margins to listen to what he calls the 'erasure-testimony' within the biblical text.

6.2. Biblical Literary Theory: Thomas G. Long

Thomas G. Long introduces the homiletics theory which is oriented towards the literary forms and the rhetoric of the biblical text. Long like John S. McClure moved beyond the principles and approaches of inductive, narrative and other approaches of the New Homiletics into the genre of the text for biblical preaching. He follows text centred approached confining to the literary forms and interrogating the text in the exegetical and homiletical process. Thomas Long's homiletics theory is visible described in his impressive book *Preaching*

---

[372] See William Sloane. Coffin, *A Passion for the Possible: A Message to U.S. Churches* (Louisville: Westminster/John Knox Press, 1993).

[373] See Christine M. Smith, *Preaching as Weeping, Confession and Resistance: Radical Responses to Radical Evil* (Louisville: Westminster/John Knox Press, 1992).

[374] See Leonora Tubbs Tisdale, *Preaching as Local Theology and Folk Art* (Minneapolis: Fortress Press, 1997).

and the Literary Forms of the Bible.[375] Long particularly focuses on the role of the different literary forms like proverb, narrative, psalm and parables in a sermon. He insists that neither the literary dimensions in the biblical text are for mere decoration nor the texts are packages that contain ideas. He considers that through the literary rhetorical theory it is vital to unveil the total impact of the text upon the readers. Long did not totally negate the traditional approach of historical criticism in exegesis, however, he introduces that in the movement from the text to the sermon along with the traditional historical critical approach to the text discovering the literary and rhetorical dynamic of the text must take place. Interrogating the text from the literary and rhetorical aspect, Long has put forth the following question,[376]

1. What is the genre of the text?
2. What is the rhetorical function of this text?
3. What literary devices does this genre employ to achieve its rhetorical effect?
4. How in particular does the text under consideration, in its own literary setting, embody the characteristics and dynamics described in question 1-3?
5. How many the sermon, in a new setting, say and do what the text says and does in its setting?

One of the most interesting aspects in Long's book is crafted in his presentation in taking the readers through the various genres of the biblical text such as the Proverbs, Psalms, Narratives, Parables of Jesus and the Epistles in the light of the above question supported with examples.

6.3. Aesthetic Theory:[377] Grozinger Albrecht

Aesthetic theory is a theory which explains about the beauty of reality. Creativity is the first mode of the functionality of the theory

[375] See Thomas G. Long, *Preaching and the Literary Forms of the Bible* (Philadelphia: Fortress Press, 1989).

[376] Long, *Preaching and the Literary Forms...*, 24.

[377] Aesthetic theory in homiletics is one of the recent trends of theory in postmodern homiletics, yet resources related to this theory are very limited.

while imagination forms the next. Fixing the creativity and the imagination within the reality of that which is explained is one of the primary ways this theory operates. Creativity and imagination do not disturb or dilute the truth of the reality but adds flavour to the truth of the reality for better and contextual understanding of it. Aesthetic theory is concern with the aesthetic of language, environment, worship, human behaviour, creation, culture of creation etc. For instance, in Psalm 104, aesthetic theorists would concentrate more on the beauty of creative and imaginative language used by the poet such as "…you make the clouds your chariot, you ride on the wings of the wind" (v. 3b). The theory also concentrates on the culture of the creation in the Psalm 104, where the poet had expressed the beauty of birds and animals living in peace and harmony in their own assigned places.

6.4. Contextual Theory: Alfred Stephen

Contextual theory generally assumes that there are different forms of human experiences which have to be addressed in the proclamation of the Gospel. This theory considers the different forms of human experiences in the process of homiletics and made relevant the proclamation of the gospel to all section of the people. I here would particularly concentrate on reviewing the contextual theory of Alfred Stephen firstly, because of its dynamic applicability to the diverse socio-religious and cultural context of India. Secondly, Alfred Stephen has approached the theory from new and wider perspectives and has taken it beyond the traditional understanding of contextual preaching. Alfred Stephen has extensively and logical reflected his contextual theory in his book '*Homiletics from the Underside: The Art of Contextual Preaching.*'[378] To comprehend the theory clearly, one needs to understand his definition of preaching. For him preaching

Grozinger Albrecht, a swiss theologian and homiletician has published number of articles on Aesthetic theory yet mostly in German. I have written about the aesthetic theory from the class lecture of Dr. Alfred Stephen on July 14, 2016 at Tamilnadu Theological Seminary Madurai.

[378] See Alfred Stephen, *Homiletics from the Underside: The Art of Contextual Preaching* (Madurai: Ecumenical Centre for Homiletic Orientation Forum for Ecological Spirituality and Sustainable Turnover, 2014).

becomes the 'Word of God' only when it participates and enters into the dialogical interaction with the existential reality of human beings so as to bring about meaning and hope to the listeners for harmonious community. In formulating his theory, he has grappled with the question of the role of human experience in preaching. He is concerned with analysing and recognizing the experiences of the listeners and telling them to understand the Gospel as their story. He proposes that the existential realities of the listeners must be part of the hermeneutic process in preaching. He claims that only when the biblical texts are interpreted along with the existential realities and ushers meanings to the listeners then only it becomes the Word of God. The Word of God is located in the dynamic interaction between the text, preacher and community. I observed that the core of his arguments is in taking the context of the listeners into the interpretation of the text yet without losing the authenticity of the biblical text. The scripture must control the movements of the homiletic plot. For the homiletics process of his proposed contextual theory, Alfred Stephen has named and explained the theory of resurgence, convergence and relevance for doing the cited theory. In the resurgence homiletic process, preachers are to have a pre understanding of the history, culture, lives and experiences of the people through revisiting and rereading with new insights and perspectives. In convergence, the preacher takes the existential reality of the listeners towards the meditation of the scripture searching for new possibility of living. Relevance will materialise the new possibilities in this homiletic process. In other words relevance is the application of the theological reflection developed in the homiletic process.

7. Rhetoric

Rhetoric is generally understood as the study, art or skill of speaking effectively and persuasively. In rhetoric, truth is not the primary objective but the crux is employing a skilful art of speaking to win and convince the heart of the audience persuasively even if it is in the absence of truth. According to Aristotle, "Rhetoric may be defined as the faculty of observing in any given case the available means of persuasion."[379]

Contemporary writer, Karlyn Kohrs Campbell defines rhetoric as "The study of all the processes by which people influence each other through symbols, regardless of the intent of the source."[380]

In the classical Greco-Roman world where the use of rhetoric was at its highest, rhetoric was considered as an art of speech oriented with persuasion and as such people were train in this art to defend themselves in the courts of law. Thus, rhetoric initially originated in the context of how to defend a case or how do present a case in the civic discourses. Nevertheless, it has been regarded as one of the most important area of oratory theory since the classical Greco-Roman world and has also influenced Christian preaching to a large extent especially with the theories of rhetoric. To take the discussion further, I would concentrate on three ancient rhetoricians and would refer at different stages of the discussion in relation to homiletics.

7.1. Aristotle (ca. 384-322 B.C.)

Aristotle defines rhetoric as "seeing the available means of persuasion."[381] He insists on making plausible persuasive arguments for winning over the audience rather than the issue of 'truth' of the matter. Aristotle rhetoric is different from logical argument, which is based on 'valid' or quest to prove. It is also different from dialectical arguments a way of reasoning towards the truth through using probable valid reasons. In Aristotle rhetoric, the valid argument is not the matter of truth present but how reasonable the argument would appear to the audience.[382] Aristotle rhetoric is audience centred rather than truth centred discourses. Aristotle did not limit

---

[379] Cited in Fred B. Craddock, "Is There Still Room for Rhetoric?" *Preaching on the Brink: The Future of Homiletics*, ed., Martha J. Simmons (Nashville: Abingdon Press, 1996), 69.

[380] Karlyn kohrs Campbell, *The Rhetorical Act* (Belmont: Wadsworth Publishing, 1996), 8-9.

[381] Aristotle, *On Rhetoric: A Theory of Civil Discourse*, translated by George A. Kennedy, 2nd edition (New York: Oxford University Press, 2007), 16.

[382] Lucy Lind Hogan & Robert Reid, *Connecting with the Congregation: Rhetoric and the Art of Preaching* (Nashville: Abingdon Press, 1999), 29.

the understanding of rhetoric to a particular subject matter, for him anything that has oral address resides within the subject of rhetoric. Rhetoric is an art and a skill where the discipline can be taught and at the same time acquire. Aristotle rhetoric is mostly considered a descriptive which is rather more of prescribed theories which were not practically experimented. In Aristotle rhetoric these three dynamics – *ethos, pathos* and *logos* forms the key factors in determining the means of persuasion in a speech. *Ethos* determines the authenticity of the person. *Ethos* is related to what character the speaker projects in other words how listeners thinks about our persona. *Pathos* is related to understanding the setting of the audience and the aptitude to move and shape the emotion of the listeners. The *logos* is related to using good and convincing reasons. In other words it is framing what is needed to say and how to say.

7.2. Cicero (ca. 106-43 B.C.)

Cicero a Latin rhetorician has been considered as another important figure after Aristotle. He built upon Aristotle's work and expanded rhetoric to persuading the audience with a valid truth which is already proved through reasoning. For Cicero, students of rhetoric have superior ability to effectively move and persuade the audience. He appears to have a more systematic description on rhetoric than Aristotle. He is more oriented towards practical oratory rather than the theory of rhetoric. Cicero based his rhetorical understanding on the five principle of rhetoric and has worked through these principles of winning and moving the hearers; invention, arrangement, style, memory and delivery. It is fascinating how Cicero has developed these principles and behind each principle there are volumes of logical reflection embedded within. Speaker should discover in other words invent the content of the oratorical discourse, and then the invented contents needs to be arranged with focused intention. The speaker then must furnish the thoughts with language in style and restores in memory for effectively persuasive delivery.

7.3. Quintilian (ca. 40-95 A.D.)

Quintilian simplified the rhetorical description of Aristotle to a good person speaking well. There is no doubt the element of *ethos* and *logos* in his description. However, Quintilian emphasises more than Cicero on the persuasive dynamic of style and arrangement in the plausible oratory discourses. With Cicero, Quintilian expresses that effective orators are the diligent student informed by the art and skill rhetoric. Like Cicero, he broadens the understanding of rhetoric beyond the periphery of persuasion and included instruction as well as speeches which gives pleasure.

7.4. Rhetoric and Homiletics: Its Influence and Relationship

Rhetoric beyond doubt has influenced Christian preaching since the first century A.D. onwards. The main targeted group in Christian preaching is the audience so also the rhetoric. Thus during the early Greco-Roman world it is likely that every public speaking is expected to have the principles of civil discourse of their own world. Any public speeches that lack such principles might have negative treatment from the hearers however good, valuable and insightful the speech might contain. Into such context, I assumes that even Christian preaching which had its origin in the Jewish synagogue were in some ways influenced by the rhetoric of their times.

As Christianity expanded, the early church leaders rejected rhetoric vehemently. One of the reasons being, rhetoric had its pagan origin. The early proponents of rhetoric were pagans and as such they held that it's for secular discourses outside Christian preaching. The other reason was on the issue of 'truth.' The persuasive act in the absence of truth is contrary to Christian teaching. For the early Church leaders the Bible is the divine truth and thus preaching is the communication of the authoritative truth where the Holy Spirit bore as the witness. Therefore, the early church leaders distance themselves against the art of plausible persuasive discourse as this art will undermine the work of the Holy Spirit to witness the divine truth to the listeners. However, since the beginning of the 4th century A.D. to the middle ages and throughout the history of the church, rhetoric and homiletics have travelled parallel to each other with Christian preaching drawing more influence from the art of rhetoric.

The most important persons in the early period of Christian history where rhetoric influence was noticed in their work on homiletics were John Chrysostom and St. Augustine of Hippo. John Chrysostom who underwent the training on rhetoric in persuasion of his law career before his priestly vocation saw the value of effective art of speech in rhetoric to the task of preaching in his clerical vocation. In his voluminous work *On the Priesthood,* Chrysostom outlines that Christian can not only use rhetoric in the defence of the faith from the attackers but also employ the art of rhetoric in the ministry of the Word. St. Augustine was profoundly influenced by the Latin rhetorician Cicero school of rhetoric. He was a teacher of rhetoric before his call to the church ministry. In his famous work on the Fourth *Doctrina Christiana,* which is rather attributed as the first handbook of Christian rhetoric, he employed rhetoric as the means of persuading the Christian to live a holy and righteous life. Augustine argued against the contemporary church leaders that knowing the truth alone do not make one an effective communicator of the truth. Thus he reclaimed Cicero's rhetoric theory of style in his work yet exclusively in the literary styles of the Bible.[383]

7.5. The State of Rhetoric and Homiletics from 18th Century Onwards

As homiletics became more inclined towards the theory of arguments, evidences, intellectual enthusiasm and the role of the audience towards the end of the 18th century, the platform was established for preaching to reclaim the art of rhetoric at the highest ever in the history. The most prominent proponents of this stage were mostly Britain clerics and rhetoricians George Campbell (1709-1796), Hugh Blair (1718-1800), and Richard Whately (1787-1863).

George Campbell in his work on the *Philosophy of Rhetoric* broadens the understanding of the function of rhetoric by pointed

---

[383] Craig A. Loscalzo, "Rhetoric," *Concise Encyclopedia of Preaching,* ed., William H. Willimon and Rochard Lischer (Louisville: Westminister John Knox Pres, 1995), 410-411.

out the relationship between the speaker, the listeners and the subject. Campbell demonstrated the role of psychological analysis in an effective rhetorical theory. He explains how imagination moves the emotion of the audience. Campbell constructed his homiletics through four steps of persuasive theory-instruction, imagination, passion and motivation.[384] Hugh Blair with Campbell defines rhetoric as "the Art of Speaking in such a manner as to attain the end for which we speak."[385] Blair most productive work in rhetoric is found in his three volume work on the *Lectures on rhetoric and Belles Lettres* which became very popular work in rhetoric. His work entails an elaborative discussion on rhetoric in civil discourse as well as pulpit oratory. Richard Whately relates his rhetorical understanding to logic and arguments. Whately rhetorical theory was based on reason, will, style and delivery which are very closely related to Cicero's rhetorical theory. But, Whately deviated from Cicero's theory of 'invention' and rather he explains that speaker needs to start with proposition where the proposition will be supported progressively by different evidences. Whatley book *On rhetoric* advanced the rhetoric of Campbell and ushered the Christian world in pulpit oratory and Christian apologists the theory of argument to stand for the rationality of the divinely revealed truth.

In the 19th century, one of the pupil of Whately Oxford school of rhetoric was John Henry Newman. Newman's work on rhetoric was carefully detailed in his work on, *An Essay in Aid of a Grammar of Assent* and his *Oxford University Sermons.* Like his mentor, Newman emphasised on logic and enlightenment reasoning yet his insistence on the use of 'invention' as key factor in public discourses is the method which deviates him from Whately. Meanwhile, in America, John Broadus advanced the rhetoric theory of Whately. He embraced the rationalistic rhetoric theory of Whately. Broadus along with Aristotle, Cicero and Quintilian affirms the ethic of labouring hard to acquire the skill for any effective public discourses.

---

[384] O. C. Edwards, Jr., "History of Preaching," *Concise Encyclopedia of Preaching*, ed., William H. Willimon and Rochard Lischer (Louisville : Westminister John Knox Pres, 1995), 219.

[385] Loscalzo, "Rhetoric," *Concise Encyclopedia of Preaching*..., 412.

Rhetoric teaches preachers the code phrase of effective public discourse in the classical rhetoric 'what to say and how to say.' For Broadus, homiletics is considered as a branch of rhetoric and kindred of art. This understanding was evident in his famous work *On the Preparation and Delivery of Sermons* which was used extensively with revisions in the later part of the century as well. Another well-known homileticain Philips Brooks also echoed the influence of rhetoric in homiletics. He was convinced that sermon should have presentation on argument to prove the divinely revealed truth. In the 20th century, neoclassical rhetoric study of Aristotle, Cicero and Quintilian was established in Cornell University. I. A. Richards work on *The Philosophy of Rhetoric* (1936) became prominent. He argued against the classical rhetoric theory of persuasion as having limitations as this confined understanding denies the full scope of rhetoric. He was more influenced by Whately's rationality argument and Campbell's psychology of the audience. His particular interest was in the use of 'language,' how it works in the psychology of the audience to produce understanding.

7.6. Contemporary Movements: Search for Balance Between Rhetoric and Homiletics

As discussed earlier language, reasons, audience, arguments and psychology plays an important role throughout the history of rhetoric which homileticians in some periods deviated yet many embraced the art of rhetoric in supplementing the homiletical theory. The recent development of homiletic theory like the new homiletics which gives renewed attention to the listeners, the role of language and imagination, certainly demonstrates the deep influence of rhetoric. On the other hand, theology has also question the creditability of rhetoric role in homiletics. For instance, Barthian homileticians such as Richard Lischer, James kay and others argues against the persuasive nature of rhetoric and the special attention and the role accorded to the audience. For them to much attention on human element will undermine God as the subject and cease the role of God in the witness of the Word of God. I am of the opinion that in order to make preaching more meaningful in the world of modern science, communication and technology, homiletics must be open to renewed skills and art that will enhance the theory of communication. Thus, rhetoric and homiletics needs to co-exist with each other without the former overshadowing the latter. Homiletics and rhetoric must function as partners and take the steps together to perform the Word of God. I would prefer to use the phrase 'dance' of two partners from Robert Stephen Reid for the relation between homiletics and rhetoric. He further cited that, "Homiletic's collaborative dance with rhetoric provides the preacher with a discursive means to express thoughtful reasoning in contingent theological matters while also expressing his or her witness to God's divine revelation in the person of Jesus Christ."[386] For the contemporary world, to establish a balance role between rhetoric and homiletics is to embrace rhetoric along with John Broadus that rhetoric and homiletics are kindred and they have relations. In an attempt to draw this relational element between rhetoric and homiletics. I will retrieve Aristotle's classical rhetorical theory of persuasion through *ethos, pathos* and *logos* and discuss in the light of contemporary homiletics theory. Lucy Lind Hogan & Robert Reid has produced an elaborate discussion on this classical rhetorical theory and I would refer to them as the discussion expands.

Ethos for Aristotle is related to the persona of the orator – how listeners level us. Establishing ethos can be considered as one of the most crucial demand for a preacher. Lucy and Reid have discussed elaborately on maintaining the external ethos as well as internal ethos. Along with our external virtues how do preachers developed character within the sermon is very important. But, then it is universally known that the concept on *ethos* is culturally shaped. As such understanding or the interpretation on *ethos* especially from homiletics viewpoint needs to consider the theology and the cultural practice of a particular context. For instance, for the Naga tribal Baptist churches where the designation of pastor is highly revered, mostly preachers are accorded the authority from their pastoral calling to the church ministry rather than their ethos within the sermon which

---

[386] Robert Stephen Reid, "Rhetoric," *The New Interpreter's Handbook of Preaching,* Paul Scott Wilson et al., (Nashville : Abingdon Press, 2008), 345.

otherwise may not be the same in the Western world. In other words external *ethos* overshadows their internal *ethos*. Nevertheless, the vital importance of internal *ethos* cannot be neglected or undermine even if the congregation perception is oriented more towards the external *ethos.* Sermon delivery unlike other public discourses demands character and personal virtue of a preacher to influence the community of faith. In fact developing a personality or quality of character and gaining the confidence of the congregation is all the more important in the homiletical task. Quintilian definition on rhetoric, 'good man speaking well' definitely speaks volumes for preacher's virtue in sermons. Lucy Hogan and Robert Reid in their discussion on the contemporary rhetorical theory and contemporary theology came to conclusion that "We cannot speak or preach unless we recognize the power of the community to grant us authority, and they will not grant us authority unless we are able to demonstrate that we are virtuous and worthy of their respect."[387]

Pathos – For Aristotle *pathos* is related to the understanding of the audience and arousing the emotions and the feelings for the audience. The classical rhetoricians were fully convinced that reason and emotion moves human to action. In a sermon motivating the congregation to do something by steering their emotion and feelings is crucial. At this point, I will coin the title of Lucy and Robert book, connecting with the congregation which is the essence of *pathos* in a sermon. Taking measures in the process of sermon preparation not to create the psychological picture of the listeners somewhere out there. Understanding the core realities of the congregation members - knowing the situation they are going through, moving the listeners that you care. This is how sermon's emotional appeal will move the feelings and emotions of the listeners to be receptive. Lucy and Robert have furthered the conversation on the role of pathos in the sense of creating sermon that moves and not manipulate. One of their suggestions is to create an imagination in the head of the listens and move their emotions in their hearts.

Aristotle *logos* is concern with the content of the good reasons in a speech, in other words what to say logically. *Logos* in the classical

---

[387] Hogan & Robert Reid, *Connecting with the Congregation…*, 65.

rhetoric is concern with the critical analysis of the situation and using appropriate words and arguments fitting for the listeners.[388] The essence of *logos* always direct us to understand that homiletics takes place in a particular context, the *sitz im Leben,* setting of life situation. Rhetoric art of *logos* offers homiletics theory a broader horizon of imagination. It is critical for preachers to ponder on the *logos* i.e., what to say in different life situations and context of the listeners. Words are powerful means they can build up, can destroy, can create tension, can heal, can comfort, can injure, can wound and so on. Contemporary preachers must ponder on whether their *logos* can be good reason for the listeners to logically reflect and convince them or in other words does the argument in the sermon bears meaning to the listeners? The crucial issue for homiletics unlike rhetoric is that the good reasons should not be manipulative but truthful and yet compelling. Homiletical task always needs to take seriously the movement of words. The very purpose of preaching is to interpret the Word in such a way that the Word is relevant to the lives and experiences of the people having salvific power. Contemporary Homiletics needs to blend together the classical rhetoric persuasive means of *pathos* and *logos* in the move and structure of the sermon.

[388] Hogan & Robert Reid, *Connecting with the Congregation…*, 91.

Chapter 4

Towards Eco – Homiletic
Crafting Narrative Preaching

The core essence of pulpit ministry is not listing downs 'dos' and 'don'ts' and giving of pieces of advices. It goes beyond these surface level arguments. Theological interpretation is required for theological reflection. Alfred Stephen has broadly discussed the importance of theological interpretation in his book *'Homiletics: Handbook for Teachers and Learners of Preaching'.* He states that, "Theology generally understands human efforts to understand the revelation of God within the context in which one lives. God revealed God's self in a particular context in a specific way....Human beings try to understand this revelation of God in the present context and make meaning of the record of the revelation and derive the message out of it."[389]

[389] Alfred Stephen, *Homiletics: Handbook for Teachers and Learners of Preaching* (Mokokchung: TDCC & ECHO – FOREST, 2017), 50.

1. Major Ecological Themes for Preaching

The Bible describes about God's activity towards the creation and has used the images of God as Majestic, Creator, Owner, Provider, Sustainer, Giver and Controller. Here, I am deducing some of the ecological themes from the Bible which can be used as the main theme in eco-homiletics. It is beyond doubt that the Bible is embedded with inexhaustible resources for deriving ecological themes, yet here I am pointing out only few themes to give clear perspective. Preacher can select any of the themes for constructing and developing sermon on ecology using the narrative homiletic methodology.

1.1. Dominion

The concept or the use of the word 'dominion' in the Genesis account of creation has been misunderstood by many and especially so by the environmentalist where it is viewed as Christianity sanctioning domination over the whole creation and exploit the earth especially citing the Genesis creation account Gen.1:26-28. This has been evident in the early movement of environmentalism - American historian Lynn White in 1967 blames the Judaeo-Christian tradition for the environmental crisis. However, a careful and systematic study of the Bible reveals that it does not license humankind to destroy the earth without any limits. Creation is a gift of divine love and as a gift; the natural world needs to be treated with respect. The Genesis account calls for human kind to exercise their dominion as the image of God who has willingly and humbly gave up his life for the reconciliation of the whole creation (cf. Colossians 1:15-20).[390] Loren Wilkinson is of the opinion that Genesis 1 and 2 describes human kind as two different kinds-a part of nature and apart from nature doing or functioning two different things namely 'ruling nature' and 'serving nature.' He argues that human kinds are both superior to the nature as well part of the nature. It is this superiority which enables them to subdue and dominate the nature also; it is their interrelatedness that enables them to understand, to share and to sympathize in serving and preserving nature. Thus, human

[390] Sarkar, *The Bible,Ecology...*, 139-140.

superiority should be exercised in the sense of serving and preserving the earth.[391] For Jürgen Moltmann, "having dominion is linked with the correspondence between human beings and God, the creator and preserver of the world – the correspondence which is meant when the human being is described as being the image of God."[392] The creation of God was designed in such a way that human kinds and animals are to depend on the fruits from the plants and trees. A dominant power over the nature is not the intent of the Genesis account. Dominance can be understood in the sense of human rule of peace without any power over life and death. In fact human beings are entrusted to play the role of maintaining justice and peace with the natural world without any force of dominance.[393] W. Bruggemann understands 'dominion' in Genesis account form the servant hood leadership of Jesus of Nazareth (cf. Mk 10:43-44). The one who rules is the one who serves and looks after the welfare of the sheep (Jh.10:11).[394] The commission in Genesis (1:26-28) does not intent to abuse and destroy the creation, rather it can be best understood in the sense of the responsibility for human kinds to extend maximum care and love for the nature and animals. If only human kind does not intrude in the peaceful existence of the natural eco-system, then only the earth will also produce its sustaining vegetation for the survival of human kinds and animals. Therefore, the core idea of 'dominion' in the Genesis account is the responsibility ushered to human kind to maintain harmony amongst the whole creation of God. Human's effort and vision should be enveloped with the concern on how to co-exist with the rest of the creation in this wonderful planet earth without causing any destruction and damage on either side.

---

[391] Loren Wilkinson, et at., *Earth Keeping: Christian Stewardship of Natural Resources*, ed., Loren Wilkinson (Grand Rapids: William B. Eerdmans Publishing Company, 1980), 208-210.

[392] Jurgen Moltmann, *God in Creation: An Ecological Doctrine of Creation* (London: SCM Press Ltd, 1985), 29.

[393] Moltmann, *God in Creation…*, 29-30.

[394] W. Bruggemann, *Genesis* (Atlanta: John Knox Press, 1980), 321-323.

1.2. Eco - Justice

The theme 'justice' is very prominent in the Biblical literatures because it is the very heart of God. The Biblical account explicitly displays how God executes justice and how God expects humanity to practice justice. God was always in favour of the oppressed, the poor, the exploited and the marginalised community of the creation. The Old Testament echoed the just initiatives of the Creator God for Creation. The Exodus account of liberating the oppressed community of Israelites from the Egyptian bondage of slavery depicts how God is concern with the poor and the unfortunate ones to share in His resources of milk and honey. I would refer to the earlier discussion on dominion where it is argued that dominion was in the sense of executing justice and peace to all creation. God has delegated humanity to carry forth His justice in the world. The natural world is not placed outside the realm of God's justice but very well within the reign of God's justice. God strictly instructed the Israelites that "You must not distort justice. . . . Justice and only justice, you shall pursue, so that you may live and occupy that land that the Lord your God is giving you." (Deut. 16: 19-20). They were also instructed to maintain justice towards the land and its produce through the law of Sabbath (cf. Ex. 23:10-11). The Biblical understanding of justice goes beyond conceptual framework of justice within human's community to the entire creation as God is the creator and the author of all life. One of such fascinating examples of God's justice is found in the book of Psalm 104. In this poetic description, the psalmist presented the attributes of God and his reign of justice to all His creation. God demonstrates His just governance in His providence to the entire creation with justice without granting special status to any part or section or group of the creation. Indeed, the psalmist has included human kinds with the community of creation as kindred to the other natural creation. Interestingly Jesus set the tone in the New Testament, in the Nazareth manifesto by declaring that He came to bring justice to the poor, the oppressed and the downtrodden (cf. Lk. 4:18-19). Jesus echoed the Old Testament tradition of Jubilee for justice and liberation. He proclaimed liberty and justice to the marginalized section of the society. His message of liberty was for those who have lost status in the society and those who have event lost their land through corrupt practices to all return into their original state through the proclamation of the year of the Lord's favour.

The world experiences the constant presence of God in all forms of life and walks of life. This depicts how exclusively God is much concerned in the relationship with the universe. Psalm 104:27-30 explains the direct, immovable and intimate relationship of God with all the creatures. So, God's presence or involvement is not facilitated by any king or institutionalised temple activity, yet the Creator God is close and intimate to every creation. A fascinating picture of liberating element is the mention of Leviathan in Psalm 104:26. In the ancient Near East, military leaders occasionally use the demonic picture of Leviathan as military power to threaten their enemies and rule over them. However the Psalm projected Leviathan not as a primordial enemy to the entire creation or to God but Leviathan was a playmate to God. The more liberative and clearer picture of just society is also described in Psalm 104:35. The Psalmist senses the cry and pain of the creation from oppression. As a result of human's greed and carelessness, the creation's harmony is disturbed and is subjugated to bondage. I agree with the interpretation of Walker-Jones[395] that in the last verse, the Psalm depicts the vision of a new 'paradise' where there will be intimate relationship of the Creator and creation in the absence of dominance, empires, kings and armies.

Since God's good and perfect creation is exploited, oppressed and subjugated, the continued activity of the Creator God is on liberation. For the cosmos to experience the integral liberation, human kinds has to involve in a new relationships of kindness, compassion, cosmic solidarity and deep reverence to the rights and life of the whole cosmos.[396] Human kinds are called to play the role

---

[395] See Arthur Walker-Jones, *The Green Psalter: Resources for an Ecological Spirituality* (Minneapolis: Fortress Press, 2009).

[396] Leonardo Boff, *Cry of the Earth, Cry of the Poor* (New York: Orbis Books, 1997), 115.

of co-creators and co-workers and contribute to the building of the earth's community of love, justice and togetherness.

The act of God, calls us to respond to the ecological chaos, crisis and disorderliness in the world and promote love and harmony for the earth's community. *A true ecological undertaking has deep concern for equality, justice and accountability for the future generations.* The Bible advocates justice extended to the entire creation, irrespective of their appearance, stature and nature. God the Creator distributes food and strength to all equally, those who are in need and provides the best suited habitat for all the creatures. God maintain justice in the divine governance and providential bounty. The Creator does not sanction any special status or special provision at the expense of the other fellow creature to any part of the creation. The perspective on ecological justice can be further clarified by the four norms of ecojustice - sustainability, sufficiency, participation and solidarity enshrine within the Psalm.

i. Sustainability

Sustainability can be understood in terms of having sufficient resources for survival and preservation and conservation of the natural communities. In modern world of civilization where the exploitation and manipulation of natural resources is at ramping pace, the norm of sustainability teaches diligent protection for the world of nature. The fertility of the earth is renewed by God for creating sustainable habitation by God. All creation exist and live by His divine sustaining life giving energy, therefore any forces or activities that disturbs the existence of the divine life sustaining order interrupts God's original systematic order. Exploitation and destruction on any segment of the creation destabilises the perfect order of God's creation and denies them their rightful living.

ii. Sufficiency

Sufficiency accentuates that all forms have the inherent right to share in the properties of the creation. In other words, it is having the basic needs and security for life. The norm advocates the life style of equality and turns away from luxury as well as poverty. In the original design of God, the entire creation shares the resource among themselves and there is no oppression and exploitation in the created order of the God. All the creations are eligible to participate in the abundance and sufficiency of God's blessing for food and habitation. The contemporary world today which is saturated by the ideology of consumerism and capitalism needs to review the biblical spirit and teaching on contentment (cf. I Tim. 6:6-8). The global community must learn to share and live in humility and equality to save the planet earth from further destruction and exploitation.

iii. Participation

Participation affirms the admiration, respect and value for all forms of life. In this model of eco justice, there is no marginalization and disregard. In fact it gives right and opportunity for all creation to participate in the life and existence of the earth's community. Every part of the creation has the legal sanction from the Owner and Creator to participate in the web of life. The right to participate in the web of life is also extended to the voiceless section of the human community as well as to those species whose voice cannot be heard. In fact human beings as neighbours to the fellow created beings must speak and stand for those who cannot defend themselves against the dominant forces.

iv. Solidarity

Solidarity recognises the kinship of all God's creation and affirms the relationship and interdependence of all creation. The entire creation of God is considered as a community. Human beings and the entire creation of God are neighbours and as such one has to identify with the cost and struggle of the oppressed community. We are to extend mutual support and maintain the harmonious integral relationship with the rest of the world.

1.3. Stewardship

Genesis 2:15 explains that Adam was expected to *serve* the garden and *keep it.* The Hebrew word for *keep,* is *shamar* and *shamar* is translated as 'guard', 'safeguard', 'take care of', or 'look after.' It indicates the idea of caring, loving and sustaining.[397] Humankind as one created in the image of God does not possess the energy, the power or the resources to recreate the good creation of God. Yet human kinds are projected to be '*Earth keepers*', by being sensitive to the will and purposes of the sovereign God the Creator who sustains the earth in accordance to His covenant. Human domination can be understood in the sense of responsibility and exercising the role of servant hood to all creation.[398] Human kind's responsibility for the earth must always start with an acknowledgment that it is not the humans' effort but only God gives fertility to the earth and the fertility and fruitfulness can be understood in terms of God's abundant blessings. Human kinds are purely entrusted to facilitate and relish the blessings and bounty. In short humans are stewards to manage the household of God. This stewardship is to be executed with accountability and responsibility to the Creator God. One of the best examples one can draw is the stewardship of Jesus Christ which is servant hood model of service. Christ Lordship was explicitly expressed in His servant stewardship. As discussed earlier, human dominion of love and justice over the creation should be well understood with the framework of servant hood model. Humans need to acknowledge that the dominion accorded to us in the Genesis account is to be understood in the sense of delegated dominion and thus as stewards' humans are servant and are accountable to God. God only delegated human towards His creation and as such the authority of the Creator God was neither transferred to humanity nor was part of the stewardship. Humans are just managers and I would reiterate the Biblical declaration which was mentioned earlier that "The earth is the Lords.... (Ps. 24:1), and "all the earth is mine" (Exod. 19:5). Stewardship calls for the management that include the welfare of the creation and the glory of God. Stewardship in the real biblical sense is executing the creative rule that is intended by God for the whole creations by the human kinds.

---

[397] DeWitt, "Reading the Bible through..., 28.

[398] Robert P. Meye, "Invitation to Wonder: Toward a Theology of Nature," *Tending The Garden: Essay on the Gospel and the Earth*, ed., Wesley Granberg-Michaelson (Grand Rapids: William B. Eerdmans Publishing Company, 1990), 45-46.

The Pentateuch in the Old Testament contains ample of instruction for the day of Sabbath for the whole creation. Deuteronomy 5, Exodus 20, 23:10-12 explicitly proclaims time of rest for the people, animals, nature, land and the whole atmosphere. The Sabbath principle is laid in the Bible to protect the earth from persistent exploitation, and allow to rejuvenate, to give rest and restoration to all creation. Indiscipline act towards the strict observance of Sabbath law has its consequences too. The book of Leviticus 26:14-15, 33-35 and Isaiah 58:13-14 describe both the dual consequences of obedience as well as disobedience for observing Sabbath. The instruction of Moses in Lev. 25:2-4 also clearly depicts the observance of Sabbath in the promise land. Any measure of disobedience to the instruction of the Law was treated as complete sin and offense against God. On the other hand keen observance of the Law was a blessing for the people of Israel. It is on the Sabbath rest the creation completes and is crowned as God's creation. The Leviticus further imparts us that just as humans need rest so do the land and the entire creation. In other words Sabbath is both for the human as well as the entire natural creation. The three dimension of Sabbath in the biblical literature – the Sabbath day, the Sabbath year and the Jubilee year speaks about God's justice to the entire creation. The principle of Sabbath protects the creation of God from exploitation. Biblical Sabbath teaches the ethics of respect, reverence, conservation, and contentment. Indeed as Moltmann cited, "It is the Sabbath which blesses, sanctifies and reveals the world as God's creation."[399] Thus, the observance of the Sabbath rest for the entire creation is a sacred hope for the redemption of the whole cosmos.[400] It is the proclamation of liberty to the whole creation – humans and non-humans alike. The principle of Sabbath invites us to join with God in declaring the glory of God through His creations and invites us to appreciate the intrinsic worth of all creation.

---

[399] Moltmann, *God in Creation* ..., 6.

[400] Moltmann, *God in Creation* ..., 6.

1.4. Creation Care

Human care of the earth has been one of the most deliberated biblical themes on ecology. The biblical narratives on ecological concern affirm the need for creation's care. The book of Psalm 104 supplements the Genesis account of creation story, making it explicit that the Bible talks on the relationship among the creation in the whole universe. It stands out as clear reaction to the accusation made on the Judeo-Christian Bible by the American historian Lynn White in 1967 in the early environmental movement, which has been dealt elaborately in the first chapter. The Bible describes more about goodness, blessings and wellbeing of the entire creation. God's care for the creation is also reflected in the divine providence and sustenance. It is also reflected in God's continued work of creation and renewal of life. Human beings are to enjoy God's good creation and not to destroy. As been kept under care by God, one has to extend the care of the Creator by being human earth keepers. Creation looks up to God for their existence because God renews life through the divine 'breath.' God directly extends the divine relationship not only to human beings but to the universe and the entire species of the earth. Every creatures from that of the lion to the small bird and creeping creatures, prays to God for divine care (cf Psalm 104). All these exemplify that the psalmist recognises the absolute dependence of life on God.

The book of Leviticus (Lev. 25) further reaffirms how the Israelites were entrusted with the responsibility of caring and protecting the Promised Land especially by the observance of Sabbath and Jubilee. In Deut. 11:12-15, God's care and protection for the entire creation are apparently visible. It was not by the human efforts that the crops grow out of the land but by the constant and direct care of God. The psalmist was very particular in Psalms 24 in reaffirming the belongingness of the earth to the Creator. Human beings are entrusted with greater responsibility to care and protect the cosmos against the threat from chaotic forces.

1.5. Status of the Creation

The book of Psalm 104 affirms that within the umbrella of God's creation, the Creator treated all the creation equally. There was no special status given to any part of the creation including the human being. In a way the Psalmist was proclaiming the egalitarian community among God's creation in the whole cosmos. God equally provides, give habitation and sustains. No part of the creation however big or small is considered superior or deemed inferior. Human beings are not given any special status over against the other creaturely beings. In fact, the Psalm explicitly co-relates almost all the six eco-justice principles developed by theologians and scholars through the Earth Bible Project. The first principle is intrinsic worth. The psalmist shows that every creation has special status. Their worth is not view simplistically from moral values but more importantly their worth is reflected from the perspectives of God's wisdom and God's artefacts. The second principle is interconnectedness. The Psalmist beautifully articulated how God's creation interconnects themselves. For instance, the Psalm 104:14-17 described the interconnected nature of the creation. Grasses are grown for cattle, plants and food from the earth for the human and trees for the birds to sing, habitat and build their nests. The third is the principle of voice. This principle is interpreted from the view point of listening to what the earth might have to say; to have kinship attitude rather than as alien from human community. Modern scholars and theologians today have move beyond the traditional concept of stewardship towards embracing the other creation as mutual kinsfolk. The psalm 104 for sure has depicted all creations as functioning one family under the outstretched arms of the creator God. Under God's providential care every creation looks up to the Creator longings for parental care. So, a close knitted family is explicit. The fourth is the principle of purpose. It claims that the universe, the earth and all its components are part of the dynamic cosmic design. Each part of the creation has its unique purpose. The Bible shows that God has designed all the components of the earth and the entire universe with the divine wisdom with a purpose. The fifth is the principle of *mutual custodianship*. This principle redirects the role of human beings not as master to the rest of the creation but as mutual creatures and partners. It includes respecting the mutual difference among the creatures and maintaining a close relationship. The sixth is the principle of *resistance*. It claims that the earth and its components resist human assault and injustice inflicted upon them. The Bible teaches that human beings are to identify with the rest of the creatures and resist the evil forces that assault and exploit the artefacts of God's wisdom.

In the New Testament, the apostle Paul affirms the co-creation or partnership of the entire creation. He further describe that because of human greed for power and dominance, subjugation and oppression, the status of the creation is in the state of 'groaning in labour pain until now' (Romans 8:22). He explains that the entire creation is looking towards with hope the coming of Christ to liberate them from this pain. Interestingly in the letter of Paul to the Colossians (Col. 1:15-20), he states that Christ coming has ushered freedom and liberation to the entire creation. Christ is the agent of the cosmic peace because He has reconciled everything in heaven and on the earth to God. The atoning sacrifice of Christ has brought forth peace not only to human beings but also to the whole creation. In other words, the whole creation was made through Jesus Christ and it is through Christ all things were reconciled to God. Thus the coming of Christ has restructured the status of the entire creation and has liberated all from the cosmic bondages as has been hope for.

1.6. Eco-theodicy

A theodicy seeks to explain how God's goodness and power can coexist with a world of suffering and evil. As discussed in the first chapter, theodicy justifies the work of God on the earth even in the situation of suffering. For explaining the eco-theodicy I want to focus particularly on Psalm 104. Psalms 104 presents a comprehensive over view on creation theologically, cosmologically, ecologically and biologically where all these areas are related by the doxology.[401] The Psalm is an expression of an act of religious obligation in praising and glorifying God for His majestic handiwork of creation. The psalmist presented a concrete logic of God's direct involvement in the natural

[401] Brown, *The Seven Pillars of Creation...*, 145.

world. The Psalm is a sketch presentation on creation rather than an analysis of the creation. For the Psalmist, the world is a community of diverse and complex creation, they exist in different forms, habitats and life style and yet they are interdependent and interrelated.

The psalmist presents a persistent theocentric argument. The Psalmist affirms the philosophy of equality and justice among the creaturely beings attributing the handiwork and wisdom of God in the existence of the entire creation. The author of life is attributed to God. Every part of creation is germinated and sprouted by God. God the creator is responsible for the growth, renewal and death of the entire creation. God is attributed as the Royal Majesty who is endowed with divine authority to rule over the entire cosmos. Furthermore, no part of creation is given the authority to rule over the other. The psalmist in fact recognises the intrinsic worth of every creation. Creations are interdependent and have definite purpose. The Psalmist did not mention the details of the origin or beginning of the existence of the creaturely beings. Rather the psalmist emphasis more of the harmonious and peaceful living of the entire creations under the divine authority of the Royal Majesty. The psalmist denounced the ideas of manipulation, oppression, subjugation, exploitation etc., which are in fact the root causes of ecological evils in the contemporary world. Creations are perceived as the artefacts of God; result of the divine wisdom and the Creator God rejoices in the existence of the earthly beings and continues the divine act of creation.

The psalmist presents God as Creator, sustainer, giver and renewer of life where justice and equality forms the integral attributes of the divine Creator. Under the divine rule there will always be peaceful co-existence and mutual respect among the creaturely beings. The psalmist enhances the final satisfaction of God in Genesis over the creation as 'good' (cf. Gen. 1:21). Thus God rejoices in replenishing and renewing this good creation and also forbids any form of forces that would inflict destruction which eventually will lead into the chaotic state. The Psalmist did not give a place to the wicked, rather the Psalmist entreated God for consummation of the wicked from the face of the earth. Therefore, the psalmist did not anticipate for moral evils and anthropogenic evils on ecology as the hymn is artistically crafted in portraying peace, harmony, relationship and inherent interdependency of the earthly creaturely beings. The Psalmist did not give space event for the occurrence of the natural evils because the creator God is portrayed as having control over the whole cosmos (cf. Psalm 104:6-9). There is no picture of the presence of suffering and evils in the Psalm as it is well functioned and inhabited under the divine rule of the divine royal majesty. Henceforth, the psalmist pleaded for God's continues involvement on the earth so as to keep the earth safe from the evil destructions.

1.7. Theocentric Ecology

The Bible presents an unquestionable account attributing God as the author and owner of the whole cosmos. Psalm 24:1-2 states that, "The earth is the Lord's and all that is in it, the world and those who live in it; for he has founded it on the seas and established it on the rivers." Everything belongs to the Lord and every creaturely being is sustained by the Creator God. The Lord has established the cosmos from chaotic state to a state of order by his wonderful handiwork. Therefore, human beings cannot exercise their rule over the other creaturely beings as the owner. God alone is attributed as the creator, owner and ruler of the entire cosmos. The Lord laid the foundation of the earth, determined the dimensions of the earth and the boundaries of the sea, and made the animals, stars, weather, and other aspects of nature (Job 38:4-11, 31-33; cf. 26:12-14). The Lord has authority and control over his created beings.

The Bible describes about the interconnected or kindred of all the creation in the household of God. In other words they are woven together by God to co-exist and establish God's purpose. The Greatest commandment of God is to love Him and second is to love the fellow creaturely beings. The entire creation in fact is the manifestation of God's image to the world. As such how can we love God completely when we do not love God's image which is manifested in the life of the other creaturely being. One tends to lose the aesthetic imagination when one fails to see the beauty and the greatness of God's creation.

1.8. Earth is Sacred

The Lord declares in Numbers 35:33-34 that, "You shall not pollute the land in which you live; for blood pollutes the land, and no expiation can be made for the land, for the blood that is shed in it, except by the blood of the one who shed it. You shall not defile the land in which you live, in which I also dwell; for I the Lord dwell among the Israelites." The earth is clearly the dwelling place of our Lord and if so the earth is made holy and sacred by the very indwelling of the Lord within it.

Review of the earlier chapter displays the explanation of James Lovelock's theory of the earth having life. The earth possesses 'life' which has been instrumental in constantly maintaining the temperature and gaseous composition of the earth and also adapts to the environmental conditions. The Bible teaches that the whole creation groans and toils under the weight of sin and longs for liberation and freedom (Romans 8:18–22). The entire creation longs for the redemptive work of God. The Bible also affirms that, the revelation of Jesus Christ in flesh has also redeemed and reconciled the whole creation to Himself (Romans 8:21, Colossians 1:20).

1.9. Love and Harmony

The redemptive act of God through Jesus Christ was purely established out of love for the world (cf. Colossians 1:15-21). God's decisive cosmic covenant with Noah in Genesis 9:8-17 that established a realistic account of relationship between humans and non-human creatures was purely out of God's love for the creation. Love was the basis of God's sacrificial work towards his creation. Thus to maintain love and harmony among the creaturely beings becomes the primary responsibility for humanity.

2. Homiletic Concern

The primary requirements for a preacher to preach on ecology must have deep and wide knowledge and understanding on the subject matter. This requirement must be enhanced by the preacher's sense of an inherent ecological spirituality and commitment.

The important area of discussion centres on how these ecological themes address the global ecological crisis. The ecological themes discussed earlier are instructive in providing a system for reshaping the theological commitments towards the creation in such a way that nurture ecological sensitivity among the people. The themes reminds human community to live in complete responsibility and regard other creaturely beings as mutual others created by God as partners. The themes can be a means of encouraging the people to reshape their perspective on God and the natural world, thereby relate themselves in a particular way to God and also to the natural world. The themes ultimately declare that humanity as assumed and perhaps understood in many ways is less the crown of creation. It directs us to go beyond considering the natural world not just as only 'good' but also 'sacred' and move beyond 'stewardship' to the principle of intrinsic worth perhaps listening to the voices of the other creations as mutual partners. It points to the very fact that the display of God's creative wisdom in and through the creation is for God's glory.

For instance, the theme on 'creation care' addresses the issue of difference, distinction and separation between humanity and the natural world. Out of the divine love and care, the Creative God brought the universe from chaos to a proper form (cf. Gen 1:2). God's act towards the creation was always accompanied by the divine care. The theme invites humanity to extend the love and care of God which they have experienced to the natural world of creation as well. The theme on 'status of the creation' addresses the issue on ecological exploitation and inequality. The theme on eco-justice perhaps explicitly speaks on the issue of assault and injustice towards the other creaturely beings. It speaks about the inherent right for all the creation to live on the universe. When justice fails to prevail between the creaturely beings, then the plan and purpose of God the creator becomes distorted. The theme on stewardship concerns about 'keeping the earth' based on Genesis 2:15. It talks about the idea of guarding, safeguarding, caring, loving and sustaining the survival of the earth as faithful managers. The theme on eco-theodicy shares the role of the Creator God in the face of ecological suffering. As created beings made in the image of God, human can become co-redeemers through the sharing in the sacrifice of Christ's self-emptying act on the cross. Therefore, the most appropriate way is to stand along with the sufferings and pains with the love of God. The purpose of God for the entire creation was to live as one interdependent community. They were created to live as kinsfolk. The theme the earth is sacred has deep theological root. The earth has life within it because it produces resources for the other creatures to survive in the cosmos. Thus earth ultimately becomes a sacred entity since the supernatural creator God dwells within the earth.

Thus, these themes adequately and theologically address the ecological problems of the global community. It reminds us to re-locate the place of humanity with the rest of the creation with sensitivity and utmost respect. We are to appreciate the very principle of mutual custodianship and understand the interconnectedness of all the creation. Also take active steps and measures to promote resistance to the exploitation and injustice towards the rest of the creation. As mentioned earlier the themes such as creation care, the status of the creation and eco-justice certainly are instructive in providing an approach for reshaping the theological commitment and it can be included in the liturgical handbook of the Church for building ethos on ecological spirituality. For instance one of the common ecological crises is deforestation. Looking at the book Psalm 104, the Psalmist describe that the trees and forest as planted by God the Creator and the divine Creator waters them abundantly for the other creatures such as birds to make their home and build their nest (cf. Psl. 104:16-17).

3. Towards Eco-Homiletics

Human injustice has already violated God's vision of maintaining healthy wholeness and peaceful life and as such to preach about eco-justice is to call upon the people/community to the original purpose and destiny of God. Eco-preaching is a new trend of preaching in the post-modern world and so it is challenging task for any writer to venture this path because eco-justice issues are deeper and broader than mere human projects and thus it demands a whole new spirit from the preachers. Environmental responsibility and challenges are at the centre stage for our new millennium world. The degrading environment is a major threat to the life and existence for the future generation and as such when the environment and the earth are sick, people cannot have an abundant life and healthy economy. Any contemporary Christian theological proclamation must be holistic in approach and cannot neglect the ecological issues. The task of Christian preaching must be oriented towards the contribution of Christian community to help turn and rectify the pattern of the world which indeed is moving towards ecological destruction. The liberating Word of God needs to address not only the issues concerning the forms of human's liberation but also inculcate how humanity must engage in liberating the whole creation from human exploitation and oppression. It is fundamental to view the earth and the entire nature as equal subject of God's love and as co-creature where we are bound in mutual dependence, mutual care, mutual nourishment and mutual well-being. In the covenant relationship of God, the fauna and flora are also included as Genesis 9:9-10 states "As for me, I am establishing my covenant with you and your descendants after you, and with every living creature that is with you, the birds, the domestic animals, and every animal of the earth with you...." Only when the earth is cared and protected, only when the earth's atmospheres is not polluted and only when the earth's environment is cautiously look at as co-partners by human beings, then the well-being of human being becomes visible and possible. Maintaining an eco-just society will elevate us to the formation of a new social paradigm, new supposition, new standards and values. Our planet earth groans under the excessive demands of the modern industrialism and consumerism.

The Bible expresses fundamental concerns about ecology as discussed in chapter one and how would the Church translate this understanding into our context is vital. It is important to see how the Bible has been shaping our perception about the ecological crisis of the world as we consider the resounding Biblical themes on ecology. I wish to reiterates the discussion in the earlier chapters that preaching ecology would demand understanding creation holistically as integral parts of human existence. Preaching on ecology in the contemporary world may not be fully sufficient with the traditional theological resources. Preachers need to work hard and keep updating with the new developments and trends. The Church needs to take up the challenge and motivate people to be open to the entire creation of God as interdependent beings. Homileticians and theologians are challenged to think deeper and ponder on finding relevant homiletical methodologies for eco-preaching. The Bible is concerned about the God - human - world relationship. Inter-discipline and inter-connectedness of God's creation needs to be acknowledged, sustained and enriched. The dynamism which disturb and distort this wholeness should be identified and denounced in Christian preaching. The Christian preaching is challenged to preach on building and construction new lifestyle that will nurture and respect the integrity of creation. Preaching on ecology is further challenged to inculcate the fresh affirmation which reflects God's pleasure on the totality of the creation. Creation is not simply an ordinary substance to be misused and oppressed; it has divine purpose which needs to be protected, conserved and cared. Preaching on ecology demands right attitude and right understanding because we cannot truly love and truly respect when we don't see other creation in the cosmos as partners and co-dependent beings. In the post – modern world, homiletics can no longer be limited primarily to the anthropocentric understanding of sin, forgiveness, redemption and personal salvation. It should point beyond and include the existential issues and realities of the world.

For the narrative method, I wish to explain the methodology by referring to the context of an indigenous group of people from North Eastern part of India called the Lotha Nagas. Taking the rich contextual resources especially on ecology, I will explain how preachers can construct narrative preaching from the Lotha Naga Tribal perspective. This methodology can be applied to other context as well. Depending on the social and cultural practices of the hearers, preachers can craft the narrative preaching on ecology using this methodology. The pre-literate Lotha Nagas has resourceful ecological insights embedded in their socio-religious and cultural life. Perhaps this meaningful ecological insights needs to be relooked and consider for deeper theological reflection. Before explaining the narrative method, let us briefly look at the eco-theology of the pre-literate Lotha Nagas.

3.1. The Lotha Naga Eco-Theology

The Lothas believe in the benevolent god of the heavens and the earth who created everything including the humans. They called the benevolent god as *Potsow* which literally means great father. The benevolent god is also called *Joyingpvui*, which literally means 'one who hammers out in the sense of a blacksmith's work. The Lothas believes that the benevolent god, *Potsow* or *Joyingpvui* inhabits beyond the sky yet as the Creator God, *Potsow* or *Joyingpvui* also inhabits among and within the creation - humans, land, mountains, valleys, trees, rivers and rocks. He is the one god who protects the people from the other gods. The Lotha Nagas knowledge on ecology may not be technical and scientific but their eco- theology was mostly rooted from their daily lives' experiences and their empirical observation through their intimate interaction with the natural world of creation. For the Lothas, there is no idea of dichotomy. They perceive everything holistically; there is no distinction between secular and sacred, earthly and heavenly and spiritual and physical. They advocate wholeness of life. The Lothas religious ethos, folklores and folksongs never teaches superiority of humans to that of the other creations. They co -exist together in an inter-related web of life. The existence of the entire universe is attributed to the handiwork of the Creator God, *Potsow* or *Joyingpvüi.*

3.1.1. The Lotha Nagas Cosmo-Centric Spirituality

Like the other the indigenous peoples around the world, the Lotha Nagas socio-religious and cultural life is founded on the Cosmo-centric spirituality. Human beings are considered as an integral member of the whole cosmos and not as superior or dominion force for exploiting the cosmos. The whole cosmos is integrated and interlinked with one another. If one part of the creation is inflicted with pain the rest will be affected. One of the interesting facts about the Lotha Nagas socio-religious and cultural life of Cosmo-centric spirituality is its originality. Unlike, the Hebrew peoples whose cosmology is much influenced (as history reveals) by their surrounding worldviews, the Lotha Nagas developed their religious-cultural practices in and through their relationship with the creation.

Thus for them if there is no God's creation they don't have their root. In other words, their entire life is solely dependent and built upon God's creation. They perceived themselves as an integral part of the cosmic life and existence. Humans and nature are created as mutual dependents on each other's. Like other indigenous people, the Lothas Cosmo – centric spirituality is built on some of the following conviction mentioned below.

3.1.2. Nature is Sacred

It is also believed that the spirit of the Creator God inhabits among the trees, rocks, rivers and mountains. Ultimately the whole nature is considered and treated as sacred, to be contemplated upon and revered. This belief directs to the understanding that the whole creation is the handiwork of *Joyingpvüi,* the Creator God and it is through the nature the creator God operates. It is through the nature, the Lothas relates and have communion with *Joyingpvüi,* the creator God. Nature is the divine expression of the Creator God and thus is considered as sacred. For instance, the Mount Tiyi Peak for the Lotha Nagas is a living example of such spirituality. It is told that the spirits/souls of dead persons go through this Mountain Peak to the valley of the dead, consequently the land, the flowers, plants and other creation were treated as sacred as they belong to the spirits. The other reason can be drawn from the experiences of the people. The landscape, the natural vegetation and the tense forest of the mountain Peak provides suitable growth for their agricultural crops. Thus, they uphold the sacredness of the mountain Peak because it preserve and sustain life through its natural cycles. This is how, the Lothas connect and relates themselves to the *Joyingpvüi,* the creator God whose spirits dwells in the mountain Peak and sustains their life. This is how they revere and respect the flora and fauna of the mountain Peak as sacred.

3.1.3. Nature is Life

Nature is life for the Lotha Nagas because it sustains life. Without nature humans cannot exist and life will be directionless. Humans are dependent on nature as such there is no sharp distinction and they are inseparably related. Nature occupies an integral part in the human community. The pre-literate Lotha Nagas dependent everything on nature such as food, shelter and cloth as such nature enhanced the existence of their life. They derive their medicine, knowledge, history from the nature. Nature is their home and there is no human life when this intrinsic nature centred life is disturbed.

3.1.4. Creation as Divine Manifestation

The Lothas perceive God as transcendent as well as immanent. Consequently, the immanent nature of God can be mostly perceived through the whole creation. For the Lothas, God cannot be understood without considering the whole creation. In fact God is seen in and through the wonderful and beautiful creation that is displayed on the earth. The mysteries of God is revealed and manifested through the whole creation. "Creation is the exegesis of God."[402] In other words, creations are the artefacts of God's handiwork where the God inhabits. Creation demonstrates God's act of revelation. Thus without the trees, vegetation, wind, water, rocks, sky, day, night, animals and humans God cannot be perceived. The Lothas view every creation as having life within which indeed is endowed by God. This life must be cared and protected. God reveals and communicates the fate of the village or family or individual through the signs and symbols from the natural creations. It is believed that the creator God reveals and warns about disasters such as natural calamities and death in the village thought the natural creation. At the same time, God's life sustaining self to the people is also revealed through the agriculture crops which sustain the people.

All creation is view as creatures having minds, feelings and emotions. The Lothas perceive the whole creation as fellow partner, family and akin. The pre-literate Lothas never consider themselves as superior being but the community social structured governs their lifestyle. Every being is considered equal, having its own distinct rights. All the creations are interrelated and interconnected as such

---

[402] A. Wati Longchar, *Returning To Mother Earth: Theology, Christian Witness and Theological Education An Indigenous Perspective* (Tainan: Programme for Theology and Cultures in Asia, 2012), 35.

no separation is maintained between humanity, creatures and other entities. The distinction is maintained only at the physical existential level yet this distinction is regarded with respect and reverence. They deeply perceive that any part of assault on any creation affects everyone, in other words if one part suffers the rest of the creation gets affected. Their kinship is further interwoven through their beliefs on totem, intermarriages and interchange-ability between humans and the natural world.[403]

3.1.5. The Lotha Naga Land Ethics

I wish to articulate that the Lothas Cosmo – centric spirituality is mostly founded on land. Land plays a very important role in the socio-religious and cultural life of the Lotha Nagas. Without land there is no life and history. For the Lotha Nagas land is their identity, their source of survival, their intimate friend, their mother and ultimately gift from the Creator God. They have the belief that the Spirit of the Creator God dwells in the soil and so they worshipped. For the Lotha Nagas land is regarded as sacred and central to their life existence. As rightly pointed out by Wati Longchar, in contrast to the colonial understanding of the land as wilderness and empty space, for the Lotha Nagas, land is their temple, university and hospital.[404] The land is their temple because they regard it sacred and they congregate on it and worshipped. Their folksongs, folkdances, ceremonies, rituals and festivals are centred on land. Their religion does not centre on a well-structured shrine or temple but the whole earth is considered sacred and animated by the spirit.[405] Land teaches them the dignity of life and it is a university for them because they

---

[403] Intermarriages and interchange-ability between human and the natural world are expressed through their folklores and folksongs. We can derive most of their eco-theology from their folklores and folksongs.

[404] Wati Longchar, "Green Theology: Resources From Primeval Traditions," *Green Theology* ed., Wati Longchar (Kolkata: SCEPTRE, 2014), 226.

[405] K. Thanzauva, "Community Ownership and Management of Land and Forest: The Mizo Perspective," *Tribal Ecology: A Search For Ecological Values From The Cultures And Practices Of The Tribes Of North East India,* ed., Razouselie Lasetso, Marlene Ch. Marak & Yangkahao Vashum, Tribal Study Series, No. 20 (Jorhat: ETC Programme Cordination, 2012), 126.

learn how to work hard for their living. In fact this skill teaches them how to live and stand in their on foot, to live self- dependent life. It is also through the land they calculate the time and history of the village and the people as they move along with the cycle of the soil and the environment. The land also provides them the required medicinal herbs produced from the soil and heals their ailments.

For the Lotha Nagas, the concept of the Creator God cannot be fathomed without land as they are inseparably related. The land as such not only sustains but also unites the spirits, humans, living creatures and the Creator God. Thus it becomes a symbol of uniting all life in the cosmos.[406] In the pre-literate Lotha Naga society land is a living entity where the spirit of the Creator God indwells and thus it becomes their scripture. K. Thanzauva, a Mizo tribal theologian also supplemented this land centred spirituality and pointed out that, "In a non-literate society, the land is their scripture through which they read about the spirits and the God and create myths and songs."[407]

As the land is sacred and central to the life of the people, land was never regarded as a disputable property. Acquiring of land by forceful means or dishonest would mean inviting danger and even death, so land was never commercialized. There is a popular dictum among the Lothas which states, "Never swear on the land falsely and possess or else you will die." The principle of land ethics teaches the Lotha Nagas in a way to be truthful and honest people. One cannot subject land to a mere piece of commodity because it is they identity and will be for the generations to come; the land will keep the history of the family, clan and the village. Land is priceless because it is a special gift of God to the people; without land there is no life.

In the light of this resourceful eco-theology of the Lotha Nagas, here I will proceed to the crafting of eco-homiletics. Narrative preaching can be considered as one method of developing eco-homiletics. I do not claim that in no way this is only the valid methodology for eco-homiletics. Other ways and methods can be

---

[406] Wati Longchar , *Returning To Mother Earth…*, 29.

[407] K. Thanzauva, *Theology of Community: Tribal Theology in the Making* (Aizawl: Mizo Theological Conference, 1997), 130.

considered as well. Now, I will enshrine the three process involved in the narrative preaching namely, retrace, repossess and renarrate.

Before explaining the process involve, it is appropriate that I present brief explanation on narrative methodology that I have followed. For doing this, Fred B. Craddock's understanding of narrative form of preaching is adopted.[408] I consider narrative structures of preaching not as a mere narration without any logical arguments or critical assessment. Narrative form in Christian discourses cannot be understood as a means to replace rational arguments or the absence of critical movement. I do not also mean to propose a narrative form which does not need a thorough exegesis and interpretation of the Biblical text. The work of proper exegesis can in no way be substituted by any steps or methods in Christian preaching. I would not propose narrative structure of preaching as mere reading or recitation of a long biblical narrative passage as "though the ancient texts can be thus simply and uncritically transferred from on language, land, culture, century to another."[409] By narrative structure I also do not mean proposing a sermon with a long story or series of multiple stories or illustration. It is beyond doubt that stories or illustration can be an effective part of the sermon. Narrative methodology is about taking into consideration the contextual realities and experiences of the people to the Biblical text.

3.2. Retrace

Retrace is to trace back or to walk back again. In other words 'retrace' can be understood in terms of discovering, following, and going back to its source or beginning. In any contextual issues going back to the root, the background, the history, faith, beliefs, and experiences of a particular context is essential. Preaching must retell the Biblical stories with relevance to the day to day life of the hearers. And in order to bring out this relevance, the study of the close relationship

---

[408] For detail reading see Fred B. Craddock, *Overhearing the Gospel: Preaching and Teaching the Faith to Persons Who Have heard it all Before* (Nashville: Abingdon Press, 1986).

[409] Craddock, *Overhearing the Gospel…*, 136.

between preaching and the human experiences is paramount. The Bible explicitly declares this, the message or Word of God is given to a particular social and cultural context. Retracing helps in deepening the knowledge of the particular context of the social and cultural backgrounds and their realities. Retracing would unearth the realities and experiences of a particular context.

The functional applicability of this process especially for preaching sermons to the Lotha Nagas can be identified in the following discussions. As discussed in the second chapter, the rich traditional heritage of the Lotha Nagas on ecology needs to be revisited for theological reflection. The eco-homiletics of the indigenous Lotha Naga people must be retraced and see how relevant they are today. Re-reading of the Lotha Nagas eco-theology for eco-homiletics is vital. This theory would allow preachers to visit again or to reconsider or to re-experience something. Perhaps retrace does not necessarily mean that we go back to an oral culture and their ways of thoughts and living. As mentioned earlier, human race has so far lived in three stages of communication eras. The first is the oral culture of communication; the second is the emergence of script culture with the invention of the alphabets; the third stage is the electronic era. Communication strategies and methods have changed along with the movement of the time and space. I do not intent here neither to do detail arguments of the relevance of oral communication era to the post-modern world nor develop communication theories from the oral to the electronic era. The purpose here for endorsing this theory is to review and reconsider the rich oral culture rather than adopting their mode of communication. The oral culture[410] particularly stories, myth and legends needs to be retraced. The process of 'retracing' would take the preacher beyond the explicit understanding of the history of the people to firstly unveil the numerous resources within the Lotha Nagas socio-religious and cultural life which perhaps can be used as extra-biblical sources for eco-preaching. Secondly, it would direct the preacher to understand how the myths, stories and legends have functioned and operated in the faith journey of

[410] By oral culture hereafter, the I would mean pre-literate Lotha Nagas indigenous stories, myths and legends.

the pre-literate Lotha Nagas. Thirdly, it would reveal the classless/ communitarian society of the people which was also extended to the other creaturely beings. Fourthly, the cosmo-centric spirituality of the people would be discovered. This process will give the urge and the conviction to the preacher to make a fresh walk on the road of the pre-literate indigenous Lotha Naga social, cultural and religious practices and explore the richness of the oral culture for reviewing and reconsidering for eco-preaching.

The word 'retrace' would mean having a clear understanding of the history, socio-religious and cultural life of the pre-literate Lotha Nagas. In any sermon context of the hearers must be seriously taken care. The different philosophy, the different expression of the cultural and social values, the history of the people, the emotional backgrounds, the faith background and many other things must be consider in the process of sermon preparation. In retracing the core eco-theology of the Lotha Nagas becomes explicitly visible and also asserts its vital applicability for eco-homiletics. The concept of God as the Creator and Owner of land, forest, river, natural resources and the sky which are essential potential elements for eco-homiletics are retraced. On the other hand, retracing engages in bringing back the nature friendly inherent lifestyle of the Lotha Nagas such as the mutual dependence, reverence and respect towards the other creaturely beings. It also strains in the unnoticed elements such as intrinsic worth and sacredness of the natural world practice especially through the taboos and totems.

This process will enable the preacher to relate the applicability of the Lotha Naga eco-theology for eco – homiletics. Talk on ecological themes such as eco-justice, creation's care, stewardship, theocentric ecology, eco-centrism, equality, etc., which are explained earlier no longer become a new thing and a new concern for them. When these issues are addressed through preaching, it becomes inevitably a means of treasuring and valuing the legacy of the forefathers. It will open up new pages for using this as extra-biblical source for supplementing the biblical interpretation. It unveils the resources available for eco-homiletics and thirdly it leads to the realization of the greater need of the tribal eco-theology for making potential impact upon the hearers. Ultimately, it will help the preacher in establishing strong foundation for constructing eco-homiletics.

What happens in this theory is stimulating; it awakens the Lotha Naga eco homiletics to tell their story or speak about their story and experiences. It leads the preacher into a level of listening to the narrative identity of the Lotha Naga eco homiletics. The process of listening will then urge the preacher to search for possibilities of attending to the cry, need and value of their narrative identity.

The narrative identity reveals that the Lotha Naga eco-homiletics has been a neglected subject in spite of the inherent values they possess. It also reveals the injustice caused to them as a result of the state of ignorance one has in exploring the inherent and inexhaustible heritage. This will lead the preacher to realise the real expression of the cry of the Lotha Naga eco-theology for the loss of the cultural identity and rich heritage. The process initiates or expedites the urgency of rediscovering the relevance of Lotha Naga eco-theology for today's global ecological crisis. In other words, it exposes the relevance of the Lotha Naga eco-theology for combating contemporary ecological issues. As a result, preacher will be led to acquire a clear theological understanding of the Lotha Naga eco homiletics and the need to address them in preaching and also develop the narrative plot for re-narration.

The process of retracing would therefore discover the values embedded within the socio-religious and cultural life of the Lotha Nagas and lead to unveil the greater depth of resources for enhancing eco-homiletics. After the process of retracing, the preacher then move beyond from invention to the process of absorption called repossessing.

3.3. Repossess

The word repossess is to possess again or to restore ownership. Thus, to repossess can mean reclaiming the right to own certain properties that was lost which was previously owned without any legal procedures. In any presentation, authenticity of the source determines the genuineness and validity of the argument. This will happen only when one possesses the inherent originality of the resource for encoding. The validating character of repossession is that it enables the retraced properties to be re-located to its original location. Repossession functions to re-locate the readers to the original intended meaning, expressions, values, character and significance of the resources/text which otherwise was once lost or unnoticed. This will enhance the knowledge or interpretation of the reader or preacher to comprehension the meaning of the text/source completely without any internal or external source of help.

Again, the functional applicability of this process especially for preaching sermons to the Lotha Nagas can noticed in the following discussion. In this process the preacher works towards repossessing the substantial elements that is already identified in the process of retracing. It functions in repossessing the rich cultural values which is neglected and unnoticed and brings those to the level of recognition. When repossession takes place, reclaiming and owning the Lotha Naga eco-homiletics will begin to take place over against the structure and practices of negligence of the rich traditional heritage of the Lotha Naga eco-homiletics. This process would points towards making use of the richness of resources available from the pre-literate Lotha Naga society and urges for implementation of this substantial tribal eco-homiletics.

The process will function to retain the worth, value and usefulness of tribal eco-theology. Repossession operates to revise the narrative identity, give deeper knowledge of the culture, and preserve the culture and identity of the Lotha Nagas. It also functions in reclaiming the enormous theological truth embedded within the Lotha Naga eco homiletics. It revives the injustice reality of the past and starts locating the avenues for the possibility of new ending. When repossession happens, it creates a space for the feeling of contentment/satisfaction because of the originality of the resources and supplements the preacher to be more confident and authentic. Repossession also opens the scope and horizon for expanding the Lotha Naga eco-homiletics. When repossession happens it begins to notice the values, ways and avenues of using the Lotha Naga eco-homiletics. Explore more avenues for using these resources for constructing eco-homiletics.

When repossession happens, the resounding resources retraced will be reclaimed, the originality or the inherent cultural identity of the Lotha Nagas. As a result, avenues would be opened for the Lotha Naga tribal eco-homiletics to be considered as extra-biblical resources for eco-homiletics. Eventually, the process will demonstrate the relevance of the tribal eco-theology in the contemporary ecological movement. The theory of repossession would further take the preacher into the stage of interaction and interpretation called re-narration.

3.4. Re-narration

Re-narration is reconstructing and reformulating. In Re-narration two major thing takes place; firstly, the Lotha Naga eco-homiletics will experience liberation from their bondage through negligence and ignorance. Re-narration can process the Lotha Naga myths, stories, folklores etc., to function as an integral part of deriving and performing as substantial illustration or as supplementation to the preacher's arguments. Secondly, the theological truth repossessed from the Lotha Naga eco-homiletics will interact with the Biblical eco-theology to draw relevance and derive the possibility of achieving new ending. For interaction, it is essential to identify certain elements from the Lotha Naga eco-homiletics and also from the Biblical eco-theology particularly from Psalm 104. In the interaction, the role of Creator God who is responsible for the existence, sustenance and renewal of the creation become apparent. In other words theo-centrism becomes distinctly visible. Both attribute that creations are sacred because it is made in the wonder wisdom of the divine Creator where the creations are endowed to produce life sustaining food for the fellow creaturely beings. The core idea of interconnectedness among the creaturely beings which underlines the basic affirmation of environmentalists and scholars is one of the most visible resounding expressions in both the eco-theologies. The cosmo-centric spirituality of the Lotha Nagas is explicitly reflected in the Psalm 104. The communitarian life style of the Lotha Nagas where there is equality and mutual understanding between the entire creation – earth, human and nature is also artistically revealed in the Psalm 104. As discussed in chapter two, land plays a very important role in the socio-cultural and religious life of the Lotha Nagas. For them land is their life, identity, history, friend, mother and the greatest gift of God. The spirit of the Creator God indwells within the earth and produces life sustaining resources for their survival. The Psalm also paints this similar picture of the earth. It depicts that the Spirit of God is present in the earth by providing blessing, fertility and also life. The Psalm went beyond the curse of God in Genesis 3:14-19 and reverse that curse with blessings. In Genesis 3:14, the serpent is cursed but in Psalm 104:26 the serpent Leviathan is created to sport in the sea; the land is cursed in Gen. 3:17 but in psalm 104:30, the land is renewed; In Genesis 3:17-18, land produces thorns and thistles while humanity has to work and sweat to make the land produce food but in Psalm 104:14-15 earth produces food, wine and oil to gladden the humans. Thus, the land/earth forms the central character of the Psalm. As it is discussed earlier, the Psalm 104 speaks of the eco-justice principles of the Earth Bible Project so does the eco-homiletics of the Lotha Nagas. First, the Lotha Naga eco-homiletics underscores the intrinsic worth of the earth due to the presence of the Creator God in and within the earth. Secondly, the Lotha Naga eco-homiletics talks of interconnected and interrelatedness through the communitarian life and kinship. Thirdly, the communitarian life and kinship of the Lotha Nagas eco-homiletics recognises the purpose and place of every creation in the universe. Fourthly, the Lotha Nagas land ethics vividly expresses about the principle of mutual custodianship. Fifthly, the Lotha Naga eco-homiletics speaks of the voice and resistance of the earth through the cultural practice of taboos and totems.

In the process of this interaction, identifying the theological expression in both the theologies and developing the theological basis is crucial. The theological expressions can be interpreted in the light of the Scriptures. When the theological expression is interpreted in the light of the Scripture, deeper meaning and truth will emerged.

During the interaction, the similarities and relationship between the Biblical eco-theology and Lotha Naga eco-homiletics will be materialized. When this materialization is done, then the Lotha Naga eco-homiletics which is much neglected elements will be taken into consideration seriously as extra-biblical source. Then the Churches will begin to take note of ecological concerns in the pulpit ministry. When the church starts giving importance to eco-homiletics, eco-liberation would be materialised as preachers will grapples with the issue of justice, inequality, discrimination and oppression. The issues are then further processed for theological reflection and made relevant to the context for creating the possibility of 'new ending'[411] where eco-liberation then would be fully materialised. The earth's community would attain liberation from the oppressive forces as the preacher challenges the evil practices of the society. As a result new and harmonious community would emerge for the entire earth's community. Here, the retraced and repossessed Lotha Nagas stories, myths, taboos, totems etc. can be considered for drawing as illustration and supplementation to the biblical exegetical work for strengthening the argument of the preacher.

3.4.1. The Functionality or the Operational Mode of Re-narration

Narrative preacher can adopt the narrative model of the prophet Nathan in encountering King David in 2 Samuel 12:1-15. In the beginning develop the story using the different mode and theory explained earlier and in the interpretation reassigns the cast of characters to the listeners. Preacher task is to convince the hearers with the truth of the Bible and bring to the state of guilt, "I have sinned against the Lord" (cf. 2 Sam.12:13).

The preacher's main aim here is to identify the liberative element present in the given passages/text. How the text talks about liberation of the oppressed? In what way has the text gives hope? What is the theology of the text? The interpretation part of the eco-preaching has to be processed referring to the discussion on the Biblical perspectives on ecology in chapter one. The Bible is absolutely clear that God the creator care for the welfare and well-being of the entire creation. The Creator God is on the site of the oppressed community as such any part of injustice, oppression and exploitation upon the creaturely beings is treated with outmost condemned. The will and purpose of God is to have peace and

[411] I have borrowed the word 'new ending' from Alfred Stephen in his book 'Homiletics from the underside: The art of contextual preaching.' The new ending would mean achieving liberation from the oppressive forces.

harmony among the creaturely beings and allow them to experience a liberated life away from any forms of oppression and dominance. Here, preacher has to take the role of the prophets and speak on behalf of the oppressed section of the society. In the face of all the corrupt social issues in the contemporary world, Christian preaching cannot be limited to individual holy living, spiritual matters and personal salvation. Preaching has to address the injustice and oppressive forces which is the cause of the suffering in the world. Perhaps today, the natural world of God's creation is being oppressed and exploited by human selfish motives. They can be identified along with the poorer and weaker section of the society. Preacher can interpret or give the meaning of the story taking the prophetic nature of speech; unveiling the truth of the biblical passage with boldness and courage. Prophetic nature of preaching is contextual as well as eschatological in the sense that it takes into consideration the liberation of the oppressed community and gives hope to the community.

In the interpretation of the text, employing the language of resistance – of prophetic assertion becomes critically important. For this prophetic proclamation Walter Brueggemann, an American Protestant, Old Testament scholar has directed preachers towards the use of the Biblical language, which perhaps is prophetic in nature. In one of his outstanding books, *Finally comes the Poet: Daring speech for proclamation* Brueggemann calls for poetic speech against the prose world in preaching. By prose he refers to the world where the truth of the gospel is greatly reduced and by poetic he does not mean rhyme, rhythm, or meter but using the language that unveil the truth of the Bible with boldness or in other words using the biblical language which is prophetic. For him preaching is not moral instruction, problem solving, doctrinal instruction, good advice or soothing good humor. But the true proclamation is unveiling the great truth of the Bible prophetically. In addressing any social issues, preachers need not criticise, rebuke or scold but only present the text to the hearers and allow the text to address the real situation. The Biblical language is prophetic in nature and such language needs to be employed in the hermeneutics of eco-liberation preaching as well.

At this point the methodological directives for preaching ecology proposed by Alfred Stephen become significantly paramount. Homiletic plot can be deduced firstly from the Scriptural directives which reveal the Biblical realities on relation, accountability and revelation of the creation of God. Secondly, homiletic plot can be derived from the social or existential directives which address issues on liberation, justice and responsibility of the human community. In the methodology of Scriptural directives, preacher manoeuvres purely from the biblical outlook positioning oneself and reading the text from the ecological perspectives. I understand this directive as a way of stating the biblical realities as absolute to draw relevance for the contemporary ecological issues. The methodology of social/existential directive addresses the contextual reality/ies which in fact is/are contributing to the ecological crisis of our time. In this methodological process, contextual issues are taken to the scripture for interpretation. In the interpretation, it is very appropriate to apply the hermeneutics of Convergence which has already been discussed in the third chapter on the contextual theory of Alfred Stephen. Preacher takes the ecological issue of the context only as a preface towards mediating in the Scripture. Analyse them in the light of the biblical text and search for possibilities of a new and different way of living as community. Interpretation must concentrate on the fusion of the biblical text and the contextual realities, yet the Scripture should control the movements in the homiletic process. In both the methodological directives, the important area of assignment for eco-homiletics is to identify the homiletic plot and develop the sermon. Homiletic plot can be derived through reading of the biblical passage and creative reflecting. For instance, the following homiletic plot can be identified in Psalm 104.

All the creations are equally dependent on God and as such creation including humans cannot be exalted or deemed above the other. God participates and exhibits His direct relationship with the entire creation.

i) The psalmist displays that there is absolutely God's justice in the divine governance and provisions.
ii) All the creations are inter-related and inter-dependent. Mutuality in existence and lifestyle is manifested.

iii) The egalitarian concept is clearly evident. Creations are seen as partners and co-creatures.
iv) No individuals or groups including the humans are sanctioned to exercise any force of dominion over the others. Justice was the essence of the earth community.
v) Creations are the manifestation of God's wisdom and God delights and rejoices in His creative art of wisdom.
vi) The psalmist teaches that all lives and growth in the cosmos comes from God through the 'Spirit.'
vii) The psalmist invites the readers to celebrate and praise God for the divine creation.

After identifying the homiletic plot, preacher concentrates on the homiletic plots and analyse them in the light of the Biblical eco-theology. Any Biblical interpretation on ecology cannot neglect the six eco-justice principle proposed by the Earth Bible Project team as this principle also deeply correlates the eco-theology of the Lotha Nagas:[412]

i) The Principle of Intrinsic Worth: The Universe, Earth and all its components have intrinsic worth/value.
ii) The Principle of Interconnectedness: Earth is a community of interconnected living things that are mutually dependent on each other for life and survival.
iii) The Principle of Voice: Earth is a subject capable of raising its voice in celebration and against injustice.
iv) The Principle of Purpose: The universe, Earth and all its components are part of a dynamic cosmic design within which each piece has a place in the overall goal of that design.
v) The Principle of Mutual Custodianship: Earth is a balanced and diverse domain in which responsible custodians can function as partners, rather than rules, to sustain a balanced and diverse Earth community.

---

[412] Norman C. Habel ed.,*The Earth Story in the Psalms and the Prophets* (London: Sheffield Academic Press, 2001), 22. For elaborative discussion of these principles see see Earth Bible team, 2000, 38-53.

vi) The Principle of Resistance: Earth and its components not only suffer from injustices at the hands of humans, but actively resist them in their struggle for justice.

Therefore, as the preacher searches for proclaiming the possibilities of new community living, the Scripture can be interpreted reflecting also on the ecojustice principles of the earth Bible project. For preaching on social issues such as ecology, preacher has to identify the issue/s and take the contextual realities to the Biblical text for interpretation. For instance deforestation is one of the ecological issues in the global community. Preacher need to go deeply into the root cause of deforestation in the context. Why there is deforestation? What are the cultural forces or factors behind deforestation? Identify these answers and analyse them in the light of the biblical text especially on ecological narrative passages. For the proclamation of the new ways of harmonious living, the main theological basis of interpretation needs to be on kenotic Christology and cosmic Christology which has been discussed in the first chapter under eco-Christology. Interpretation needs to take the tone of the self-emptying and suffering of Christ for the whole creation. So, also Christ redemption was for the whole creation and not only for the particular human race. In the redemptive work of Christ every segments of the creation is liberated from oppression, exploitation and captivity (cf. Lk 4:18-19). The groaning of every creation (cf.Rom. 8:22) including human beings has been set free through the redemptive act of Christ. Such deeper theological interpretation would construct strong theological basic for eco-liberation preaching.

3.4.1.1. The Role of Imagination and Creativity in Narrative Preaching

In this re-narrative process, preachers can execute the theories of imagination especially to create and recreate, construct and reconstruct the story. For instance, a small child can never understand the story fully that is narrated to her/him by their parents unless the parents re-narrates the story within the psychological calibre of the child - language, images, symbols, tone etc. When the correct and appropriate means are employed and re-narrated then the child's attention will be grasped and she/he can understand the story fully; only then the story can become a story for the child. This is exactly true to narrative sermon; language, images, pictures, symbols plays a vital role in effective communication in narrative preaching. The language, images, pictures, symbols and tone employed for narrative sermon in the Western Christian preaching may not be effectively relevant for India context. One of the great challenges for the preachers is to make the world of the Bible relevant to the contemporary human experience. In other words preachers stand in between the biblical world and the contemporary human experience. Therefore, in this re-narration part of story sermon construction, much attention has to be given to the role of communicative imaginations. Operation of imagination theory in narrative preaching do definitely takes the preacher to the state of mental rehearsal and it certainly involves certain degree of thinking. I would distinguish clearly the word imagination from reason even if both involve cognitive ability. Imagination is one of the modern trends of preaching in the study and practice of homiletics. Imagination is processed through thinking (mental images) and the primary source for imagination is the mind. Human imagination is limited by our realm of beliefs, understanding and knowledge. As such a preacher is required to keep on updating these realms of beliefs, understanding and knowledge.

Preachers need to use the cognitive faculty to read the Bible and interpret - discerning and shaping particular image for preaching so as to unveil the mysterious depth of biblical reality. Imagination is interested in poetic and artistic characteristic of homiletics; as such the imaginative approach is less interested in the older rhetorical theories of homiletics and more inclined towards an imaginative theology. Implementation of creative theories and critical imagination in the interpretation of the Scripture becomes critical in imagination. Images and symbols are the means used in the imaginative homiletics to probe the mysterious meaning behind the biblical passages and other mentioned sources for preaching.

The Bible is so vibrant and filled with pictorial imagination. God Himself is a creative Creator. This very fact calls forth preachers for imagination and creativity in the science of transmitting the written Word through oral and other means of communication to the people. Imagination is seeing and creation something within the framework of mind. It is developing certain ideas in one's mind. Creativity is the result of that imagination. When imagination is processed into art, it is creativity. Narrative preaching involves a magnitude of imagination and creativity. The challenge of a preacher is to take any biblical literary genre and construct, reconstruct and imaginatively create a story for the hearers. When the task of imagination is neglected in a narrative preaching, sermons exhibit poor quality appeal to the hearers. This is one of the dangers for every preacher. As Aristotle rhetoric indicates and as already discussed in the last chapter, content of a sermon has to be processed with proper shape and arrangement. The aesthetic part of sermonic shape has vital importance. Imagination enables the storyteller to graft the story in such a way that it captivates the minds of the listeners and store the message into their memories.

Therefore, for developing sermon on ecology, preachers after reading/mediating on certain portion of the biblical text need not go immediately to the biblical commentaries but imagine the story of the text first because every biblical text has a story in it or behind it. Imagination can even go beyond what the text has not revealed or told about a person, place, situation etc. Then the narrative sermon on ecology can be processed to shape by picturing the text with certain images and symbols.

3.4.1.1.1. Linguistic Imagination

This imagination mode can operate within the limits of the listeners' vocabularies/words/languages adaptabilities and abilities, thus emphasising on ushering the use of common/relevant words to the listeners of a particular context.

Language is an oral phenomenon. Perhaps human beings communicate in multiple ways and means and it is beyond doubt that non-oral communication does have rich communication effect yet language is paramount. Human beings do things within language. The Biblical literature clearly shows us the significance of language in the Tower of Babel (Gen 11:1-9). Human do relates with one another within language; we express our love, concern, anger through our language. Humans perhaps do think with language. As David Buttrik asserted, "...we do not think in words. Nevertheless, we could not think without having language."[413] Preachers are to employ vocabulary of everyday conversation of the congregation. Using of too many big theological words and jargon may be a boring sermon for the common listeners. The complex language can be substituted by simple and common vocabulary of the congregation; re-narrate the biblical text into a more conventional understanding. Language is the vehicle through which one expresses thoughts. Renewing the use of language is vital here. For choosing the language of preaching, David Buttrick has put forth three substantial questions – "Is the language theological apt? Does the language form in congregational consciousness? Does the language serve the statement of a particular move?"[414] These questions are worth reflecting as preacher step into processing the narrative story sermon. Linguistic imagination needs to take into consideration the important issue of language in any communication. Preachers need to imagine within the linguistic standard of the listeners. For instance, the metaphor of a camel going through the eye of a needle can be replaced by more relevant words where the metaphor can be drawn from the day to day life experience of the people. Take another instance, when a story sermon on Noah's art is narrated, preachers ought to employ such language which would prompt the listeners to hear the rain on the roof in the world of their conscious. That's what exactly I am talking about here in the linguistic imagination.

---

[413] David Buttrick, *Homiletics: Moves and Structure* (Philadelphia: Fortress Press, 1988), 174.

[414] Buttrick, *Homiletics...*, 193.

Conclusion

Environmental issues today have become one of the most serious global concerns, in spite of the tremendous efforts from the global leaders including the ecumenical community for making the earth a pleasant habitable place. In fact the global ecological crisis is increasing each year. The house hold of God is bleeding and groaning for deliverance. The fresh air we breathe is already polluted, the water we use now contains high amount of toxins, chemicals and other dangerous bacteria, the green grass lands are mostly being replaced by the dumping of waste products and the tropical forests which are much in need for human survival and rainfall were destroying. Today, the cedars of Lebanon that is planted (Psalm 104:16) are no more, the artefacts of God where the Creator continues to rejoices in renewing, the 'good' creation of God (cf. Gen. 1:31) are distorted, endangered, suffering and disappearing from the face of the earth. Human community must continue to check their anthropogenic evils such as rapid growth of human population, industrialization, urbanization, rapid economic growth, greed for power, rapid nuclear test and development, etc.

Historical survey reveals that the Christian ecological consciousness goes back to the 3rd century of the early church fathers such as the Cappadocian fathers (c.a. 330-395) and St. Augustine (354-430). However, the urgency of addressing the ecological crisis among the ecumenical fraternity became increasingly visible only in the 20th century. And as a result of this urgency to combat the ecological crisis by the global community investigation suggest and discovered that the causes of this ecological crisis begins with the human's behaviour, actions and attitude towards the other creaturely beings on the earth. The Bible is very definite and clear that God is the Creator of every tiny segment that exists in the universe. The Bible advocates the intrinsic value of every creation and the ownership of the Creator God over all the creations. This Biblical truth was explicitly noticed in the ecological themes especially from the Old Testament such as justice, stewardship, Sabbath etc. Furthermore, the New Testament affirms these claims through the life and redemptive work of Jesus Christ. Christ redemptive work upon all the creation was discerned through the relation between ecology and Christology, ecology and eschatology etc.

Even in the face of alarming ecological crises, there is a ray of hope. The Biblical eco-theology ushers a resounding resources which can serves as a means to contribute to a life of healthy eco-balanced life. It is vital to inculcate a theological approach from the perspective of the cosmo-centric spirituality and develop hermeneutics that is shaped by ecological concerns. In this process preaching can be one of the means of spreading awareness and urging the people to participate in the struggles of the global community on environmental concerns. Undoubtedly there are differences between human beings and the other creaturely beings. But, this difference should neither be taken for exploitation nor should it create barriers. On the other hand, certainly human beings could never be elevated to greater and unique beings than the other creaturely beings. However, the difference noticed and present must be acknowledged, respected and regarded as mutual others.

What will happen by 2030 or 2040 cannot be ascertain even if one can predict. But, what is definite and clear is that there is some problem in the human behaviour and attitude. As the world move and struggle towards a future eco- just society, it is demanding and also a promising reality with which human generation has to come in terms if we are to make the planet earth habitable for the coming generation. This will happen when technology must look forward to serve the people, controls human made pollution and reduce the human's work of assault on the earth's resources; it will happen when the Bible is articulately read from the earth's perspective; it will happen when the human and non-human rights are respected and valued.

The Church must continue to proclaim and nurture her members to come to the realization about the facts on ecology and justice in the light of the Biblical ecological themes. The Church must continue to equip her members theologically, spiritually and practically about the issue of ecology of our times.

The church must implant such prophetic passion and work towards eco-just society. It is extremely urgent for the Churches to make strong, concrete and consistent spiritual and moral commitment to the emerging ecological crisis of our time.The elaborate argument on ecology put forth in the book does not totally neglect the needs of the human generation but it calls for reviewing one's attitude, selfish actions, and greed. The need of the situation demands adopting a just and equitable ways of living in the *oikos*; learning to live in humility and harmony with the other earthly creations. In other words, there is a challenge for developing ecological spirituality and hermeneutics that is shaped by ecological concerns. Therefore, preaching is challenged all the more to creatively formulate homiletic methodologies to adequately address this existential issue through the pulpit ministry.

I now would like to conclude the book by giving a concrete definition of the core essence preaching and why preaching must address the contextual reality such as the environmental problems?

In my understanding and conviction, preaching can be defined as 'the communication of the divine truth i.e., the Word of God through human language.' The divine truth is the uncompromising, unchanging and eternal truth, which is the good news; it's the forgiveness of sins, the redemption and salvation ushered to the world through Jesus Christ.

For Karl Barth "Preaching is Word of God which he himself speaks claiming for the purpose of exposition of a biblical text in free human words that are relevant to contemporaries by those who are called to do this in the church that is obedient to its commission.

Preaching is the attempt enjoined upon the church to serve God's own Word, through one who is called there to, by expounding a biblical text in human words and making it relevant to contemporaries in intimation of what they have to hear from God himself."[415]

Alfred Stephen affirms that "Preaching is 'Word of God' in that it participates in God's purpose; initiated by Christ in that it dialogically interacts with the existential reality of the hearers and reflects on the dialogical interaction of humans in their effort to make sense of and find meaning in living together as a harmonious community of (with) God; and supported by the Spirit within the community in the world."[416]

The above definitions suggest and confirmed that preaching is predominantly the 'Word of God.' I would further agree with Alfred Stephen when he said that "preaching becomes word of God when it fulfils the redemptive and liberative purpose of God, leading the hearers to the redemption from the sin and causing the liberation of people from the human made social bondage and oppression."[417] Preaching has two fold missiological foundations namely the redemptive aspect and the liberative aspect. These two missiological purpose of God in preaching needs to be understood in line with the purpose of God for the entire creation which was revealed in and through Jesus Christ. Redemptive aspect focuses on the forgiveness of sin and salvation. In other word, the emphasis of preaching is on the call to conversion to the power of the saving grace of Jesus Christ brought about through the death and resurrection. The liberative aspect emphasise on the state of liberation every creation longs for even if the situation and intensity differs. In the context of economic poverty, social discrimination, ideological oppression, and unjust social order, the Biblical message is reread and identifies the liberative elements or message for the people. This process in fact would enable the Biblical message become more meaningful to those who experience suffering and affliction and preaching ultimately becomes

---

[415] Barth, Karl, *Homiletics*, Translated by Geoffrey W. Bromiley and Donald E. Danielsn (Louisville: Westminster John Knox Press, 1991), 44.

[416] Stephen, *Homiletics: Handbook for Teachers...*, 11.

[417] Stephen, *Homiletics: Handbook for...*, 13.

meaningful to the existential realities of the hearers.[418] Therefore, preaching must include both the redemptive and the liberative aspect so that preaching becomes the 'Word of God' revealed in and through Jesus Christ.

The post-modern ecumenical community must continue to support and participate in the environmental movement of our times. The Church must strive to inform and also form the people to be more committed to the participation on eco-justice, peace and integral growth of the earth's community.

---

[418] Stephen, *Homiletics: Handbook for...*, 17.

Bibliography

Books

Agarwal, Kirti. *Population Ecology*. Delhi: Pacific Publication, 2010.

Allen Jr., O. Wesley. *The Homiletics of All Believers: A Conversational Approach to Proclamation*. Louisville: Westminster John Knox Press, 2005.

Allen, Ronald J. "Theology Undergirding Narrative Preaching." *What's the Shape of Narrative Preaching*. Eds., David Schlafer and Michael Graves. St. Louis: Chalice Press, 2008.

Allen, Ronald J. Barbara Shires Blaisdell and Scott Black Johnson. *Theology for Preaching: Authority, Truth and Knowledge of God in a Postmodern Ethos*. Nashville: Abingdon Press, 1997.

Aristotle. *On Rhetoric: A Theory Of Civil Discourse.* Translated by George A. Kennedy, 2nd edition. New York: Oxford University Press, 2007.

Barth, Karl. *Homiletics*. Translated by Geoffrey W. Bromiley and Donald E. Danielsn. Louisville: Westminster John Knox Press, 1991.

Batumalai. S. *An Introduction to Asian Theology.* Delhi: ISPCK, 1991.

Bauckham, Richard. *The Bible and Ecology: Rediscovering the Community of Creation*. Texas: Baylor University Press, 2010.

Bergmann, Sigurd. *Creation Set Free: The Spirit as Liberator of Nature*. Translated by Douglas Stott. Grand Rapids: William B. Eerdmans Publishing Company, 2005.

Boff, Leonardo. "The Dalai Lama on Religion." *Meetings Rivers: Reflections On Culture, Religion And Ecology*. Ed. Siddhartha. Bangalore: A Meeting Rivers Publication, 2014.

___________. *Cry of the Earth, Cry of the Poor*. New York: Orbis Books, 1997.

___________. *Ecology and Liberation: A New Paradigm*. New York: Orbis Books, 1995.

Bonhoeffer, Dietrich. *Christology*. Introduced by Edwin H. Robertson and translated by John Bowden. London: Collins, 1966.

Bookchin, Murray. *The Philosophy of Social Ecology: Essay On Dialectical Naturalism.* New Delhi: Rawat Publications, 1996.

Bramwell, Anna. *Ecology in the 20th Century a History*. London: Yale University Press, 1992.

Bredin, Mark. *The Ecology of the New Testament: Creation, Re-creation and the Environment*. Colorado Spring: Biblica Publishing, 2010.

Broadus, John A. *Lectures on the History of Preaching*. New York: A. C. Armstrong & Son, 1893.

Brown, William P. Ed. *The Oxford Handbook of the Psalms*. New York: Oxford University Press, 2014.

___________. *The Seven Pillars of Creation: The Bible, Science, and the Ecology of Wonder*. New York: Oxford University Press, 2010.

Bruggemann, W. *Genesis*. Atlanta: John Knox Press, 1980.

Bulgakov, S. *The Bride and the Lamb* .Grand Rapids: Eerdmans Press, 2002.

Buttrick, David. *Homiletics: Moves and Structures*. London: SCM Press Ltd, 1987.

Buttrick, George Arthur et. al. *The Interpreter's Bible*. Vol. IV. Nashville: Abingdon Press, 1955.

Campbell, Charles L. *Preaching Jesus: New Directions for Homiletics in Hans Frei's Postliberal Theology*. Grand Rapids: Eerdmans, 1997.

Campbell, Karlyn Kohrs. *The Rhetorical Act*. Belmont: Wadsworth Publishing, 1996.

Cardock, Fred B. *AS One Without Authority*. St. Louis: Chalice Press, 1971.

Coffin, William Sloane. *A Passion for the Possible: A Message to U.S. Churches*. Louisville: Westminster/John Knox Press, 1993.

Collin, P. H. *Dictionary of Environment & Ecology*, Fifth Edition. London: Bloomsbury Publishing Plc, 2004.

Cunliffe-Jones Hubert and Benjamin Drewery eds. *A History of Christian Doctrine*. Edinburgh: T&T Clark Ltd.,1978.

Craddock, Fred B. "Is There Still Room for Rhetoric?" *Preaching on the Brink*: The Future of Homiletics. Ed., Martha J. Simmons. Nashville: Abingdon Press, 1996.

Crawley, Winston. *World Christianity, 1970-2000*: *Toward a New Millennium*. California: William Carey Library, 2001.

Dargan, Edwin Charles. *A History of Preaching*. Vol. I: *From the Apostolic Fathers to the Great reformers A.D. 70-1572*. Grand Rapids 6: Baker Book House, 1954.

____________. *A History of Preaching*. Vol. II: *From the Close of the Reformation Period To the End of the Ninteenth Century 1572-1900*. Grand Rapids: Baker Book House, 1970.

Deane – Drummond, Celia. *Eco – Theology*. London: Darton, Longman and Todd Ltd, 2008.

____________. A *Handbook in Theology and Ecology*. London: SCM Press Ltd, 1996.

____________. *The Ethics of Nature*. Oxford: Blackwell Publishing, 2004.

____________. *Christ and Evolution*: *Wonder and Wisdom*. Minneapolis: Fortress Press, 2009.

Duchrow, Ulrich and Gerhard Liedke, *Shalom: Biblical Perspectives On Creation, Justice & Peace*. Geneva: WCC Publications, 1989.

Duduit, Michael ed. *Handbook of Contemporary Preaching*. Nashville: Broadman & Holman Publishers,1992.

Dunn, James. "The Pentecostals." *A Lion Handbook: The History of Christianity*, Tim Dowley. Et.al. England: Lion Publishing, 1977.

Eaton, Heather. *Introducing Ecofeminist Theology*. London: Continuum, 2005.

Ebeling, Gerhard. *God and Word*. Translated by James W. Leitch. Philadelphia: Fortress Press, 1967.

Edwards, Denis. *Ecology at the Heart of Faith*: *The Change of Heart that leads to a New Way of living on Earth*. Maryknoll: Orbis Books, 2008.

Edwards, Denis and M. Worthing eds. *Biodiversity and Ecology as Interdisciplinary Challenge*. Adelaide: ATF, 2004.

Elsdon, Ron. *Greenhouse Theology: Biblical Perspectives on Caring for Creation*. England: MONARCH, 1992.

Eslinger, Richard L. *Narrative & Imagination: Preaching The Worlds That Shape Us*. Minneapolis: Fortress Press, 1995.

Figueroa, Robert Melchior. "Environmental Justice and Environmental Racism." *The Encyclopedia of Religion and Nature*. Bron R. Taylor et al. London: Thoemmes Continuum, 2005.

Fisher, G. P. *A History of Christian Doctrine*. Ed., Hubert Cunliffe-Jones and Benjamin Drewery. Edinburgh: T&T Clark Ltd., 1978.

Frei, Hans W. *The Eclipse of Biblical Narrative: A Study in Eighteenth and Nineteenth Century Hermeneutics*. New Haven: Yale University Press, 1974.

___________. The *Identity of Jesus Christ: The Hermeneutical Bases of Dogmatic Theology*. Philadelphia: Fortress Press, 1975.

Gadgil Madhav and Ramachandra Guha. *Ecology and Equity*: *The Use and Abuse of Nature in Contemporary India*. New Delhi: Penguin Books, 1995.

Garvie, Alfred Ernest. *The Christian Preacher*. New York: Charles Scribner's Sons, 1921.

Gibson, William E. ed. *Eco-Justice-The Unfinished Journey*. Albany: State University of New York Press, 2004.

Gonzalez, Justo L. *Church History*: An Essential Guide. Nashville: Abingdon Press, 1996.

Goodman, Martin. "The emergence of Christianity." *A World History of Christianity*. Ed., Adrian Hastings. Grand Rapids: William B. Eerdmans Publishing Company, 2000.

Gosling, David L. *Religion and Ecology in India and Southeast Asia*. London: Routledge, 2001.

Gottlieb, Roger S. Ed. *The Oxford Handbook of Religion and Ecology*. New York: Oxford University Press, 2006.

Granberg-Michaelson, Wesley. *Redeeming the Creation, the Rio Earth Summit: Challenges for the Churches*. Geneva: WCC Publications, 1992.

Graves, C. *The Holy Spirit in the Theology of Sergius Bulgakov*. Geneva: WCC, 1972.

Habel, Norman C. Ed. *The Earth Story in the Psalms and the Prophets*. London: Sheffield Academic Press, 2001.

Hajer, Maarten A. *The Politics of Environmental Discourse: Ecological Modernization and the Policy Process*. Oxford: Clarendon Press, 2000.

Hastings, Adrian. "150-550." A *World History of Christianity*. Ed., Adrian Hastings. Grand Rapids: William B. Eerdmans Publishing Company, 2000.

Heick, Otto W. *A History of Christian Thought*. Vol. I. Philadelphia: Fortress Press, 1965.

___________. *A History of Christian Thought*. Vol. II. Philadelphia: Fortress Press, 1996.

Hessel, Dieter T. Ed. *Theology for Earth Community: A Field Guide*. Maryknoll: Orbis Books, 1996.

Hill, Jonathan. *The History of Christian Thought*. England: A Lion Book, 2003.

Hogan, Lucy Lind & Robert Reid. *Connecting with the Congregation: Rhetoric and the Art of Preaching*. Nashville: Abingdon Press, 1999.

Holbert, John C. *Preaching Creation: The Environment and the Pulpit*. Oregon: CASCADE Books, 2011.

Holland, DeWitte T. *The Preaching Tradition: A Brief History*. Ed., William D. Thompson. Nashville: Abingdon, 1980.

Illathuparampil Matthew and Vincent Kundukulam eds. *The Contemporary Theologians: Context and Contributions*. Bangalore: Asian Trading Corporation, 2006.

Irvin, Dale T. & Sunquist, Scott W. *History of the World Christian Movement: Volume I, Earliest Christianity to 1453*. New York: Orbis Books, 2001.

Isaiah, G. *Preach the Word: The basics of Homiletics*. Tiruvalla: Christava Sahitya Samithi, 2005.

James, E. O. *Creation and Cosmology: A Historical and Comparative Inquiry*. Leiden: E. J. Brill, 1969.

Jensen, Richard A. *Thinking in Story: Preaching in a Post-literate Age*. Ohio: CSS Publishing Co., Inc., 1993.

John, V. J. *The Ecological Vision of Jesus. Thiruvalla: CSS-BTTBSA, 2002.*

Joseph, M. J. *The Eco-Vision of the Earth Community (Biblical and Theological Perspectives)*. Bangalore: BTESSC/SATHRI, 2008.

Kay, James F. *Preaching and Theology*. St. Louis: Chalice Press, 2007.

Kent, John H. S. "Christian Theology in the Eighteenth to the twentieth centuries." *A History of Christian Doctrine*. Ed., Hubert Cunliffe-Jones and Benjamin Drewery. Edinburgh: T&T Clark Ltd., 1978.

Ker, John. *Lectures on the History of Preaching*. Ed., A. R. Macewen. London: Hodder & Stoughton, 1987.

Knowles, David. "The Middle Ages 604-1350." *A History of Christian Doctrine*. Ed., Hubert Cunliffe-Jones and Benjamin Drewery. Edinburgh: T&T Clark Ltd., 1978.

Knox, R. Buick. "The History of doctrine in the Seventeenth Century." *A History of Christian Doctrine*. Ed., Hubert Cunliffe-Jones and Benjamin Drewery. Ediburgh: T&T Clark Ltd., 1978.

Kochupurackal, Sebastain. *Eco-Mission: A Paradigm Shift in Missiology*. Bangalore: Asian Trading Corporation, 2007.

Larsson, Per. "Your will be done on earth…" *Ecological Theology for Asia: An Ecumenical Textbook for Theological Schools*. Hong Kong: Clear-Cut Publishing & Printing Co., 2004.

Lasetso, Razouselie., Marlene Ch. Marak & Yangkahao Vashum, eds. *Tribal Ecology: A Search For Ecological Values From The Cultures And Practices Of The Tribes Of North East India*. Tribal Study Series, No. 20. Jorhat: ETC Programme Cordination, 2012.

Lindbeck, George A. *The Nature of Doctrine: Religion and Theology in a Postliberal Age*. Philadelphia: The Westminster Press, 1984.

Long, Thomas G. *Preaching and the Literary Forms of the Bible*. Philadelphia: Fortress Press, 1989.

Longchar, A. Wati. *Returning to Mother Earth: Theology, Christian Witness and Theological Education, an Indigenous Perspective*. Kolkata: PTCA/SCEPTRE, 2012.

___________ ed. *Green Theology*. Kolkata: SCEPTRE, 2014.

Lovelock, James. *The Revenge of Gaia: Why the Earth is Fighting Back - and How We Can Still Save Humanity*. England: Penguin Books, 2006.

Lowry, Eugene L. *The Homiletical Plot: The Sermon as Narrative Art Form*. Louisville: Westminster John Knox Press, 2001.

___________. *The Sermon: Dancing the Edge of Mystery*. Nashville: Abingdon Press, 1997.

MacCulloch, Diarmaid. *Groundwork of Christian History*. London: Epworth Press, 1987.

Mark, Bredin. *The Ecology of the New Testament: Creation, Recreation, and the Environment.* Colorado: Biblica, 2010.

Martin-Schramm, James B. and Stivers, Robert L. *Christian Environmental Ethics: A Case Method Approach.* Maryknoll: Orbis Books, 2003.

McClure, John S. *Preaching Words: 144 Key Terms in Homiletics.* Louisville: Westminister John Knox Press, 2007.

__________. *The Otherwise Preaching: A Postmodern Ethics for Homiletics.* St. Louis: Chalice Press, 2001.

Meye, Robert P. "Invitation to Wonder: Toward a Theology of Nature." *Tending the Garden: Essay on the Gospel and the Earth.* Ed., Wesley Granberg - Michaelson. Grand Rapids: William B. Eerdmans Publishing Company, 1990.

Moltman, Jürgen. *The Future of Creation.* London: SCM Press Ltd, 1979.

__________. *The Coming of God*: Christian Eschatology. London: SCM Press Ltd, 1996.

__________. *The Way of Jesus Christ*: Christology in Messianic Dimensions. Minneapolis: Fortress Press, 1993.

__________. *Theology of Hope.* London: SCM Press Ltd, 1967.

__________. *God in Creation: An Ecological Doctrine of Creation.* Translated by Margaret Kohl. London: SCM Press Ltd, 1985.

Murray, Robert. *The Cosmic Covenant.* London: Sheed and Ward, 1992.

NRSV, The Green Bible: Understanding the Bible's Powerful Message for the Earth. New York: HarpersCollins Publishers, 2008.

Osborne, Grant R. *The Hermeneutical Spiral: A Comprehensive Introduction to the Biblical Interpretation.* Illinois: InterVarsity Press, 1991.

Old, Hughes Oliphant. *The Reading and Preaching of the Scriptures in the Worship of the Christian Church.* Vol. 1. *The Biblical Period.* Grand Rapids: William B. Eerdmans Publishing Company, 1998.

____________. *The Reading and Preaching of the Scriptures in the Worship of the Christian Church.*Vol. 5 Our Own Time. Grand Rapids: William B. Eerdmans Publishing Company, 2010.

____________. *The Reading and Preaching of the Scriptures in the Worship of the Christian Church.*Vol. 7 Our Own Time. Grand Rapids: William B. Eerdmans Publishing Company, 2010.

Pettegree, Andrew. "Reformation and Counter-Reformation." *A World History of Christianity*. Ed., Adrian Hastings. Grand Rapids: William B. Eerdmans Publishing Company, 1999.

Raj A., Daniel Anand., Olaganathan S, and Duraipandi P. *Perceived Impact of Climate Change in Agriculture: From a Livelihood Perspective*. Madurai: Palmyrah Workers Development Society, 2012.

Rasmussen, Larry L. *Earth Community, Earth Ethics*. Maryknoll: Orbis Books, 1996.

Rongsen, M. *Development and Ecology*. Delhi: ISPCK, 1999.

Royal, Robert. *The Virgin and the Dynamos: Use and Abuse of Religion in Environmental Debate*. Michigan: Ethic and Public Policy Center & W. B. Eerdmans, 1999.

Sarkar, R. L. *The Bible, Ecology and Environment*. Delhi: ISPCK, 2000.

Sarkar, Saral. *Eco-Socialism or Eco-Capitalism? A Critical Analysis of Humanity's Fundamental Choices*. London: Zed Books, 1999.

Sengupta, Ramprasad. *Ecology and Economics: An Approaches to Sustainable Development*. New Delhi: Oxford University Press, 2009.

Sessions, George. "Deep Ecology as Worldview." *World Views and Ecology: Religion, Philosophy and the Environment*. Ed., Mary Evelyn Tucker and John A. Grim. Maryknoll: Orbis Books, 1994.

Smith, Christian. *Preaching as Weeping, Confession and Resistance: Radical Responses to Radical Evil.* Louisville: Westminster/John Knox Press, 1992.

Stephen, Alfred. *Homiletics from the Underside: The Art of Contextual Preaching* . Madurai: Ecumenical Centre for Homiletic Orientation Forum for Ecological Spirituality and Sustainable Turnover, 2014.

____________. *Homiletics: Handbook for Teachers and Learners of Preaching.* Mokokchung: TDCC&ECHO-FOREST, 2017.

Taylor, Bron R. et. al. *The Encyclopedia of Religion and Nature.* London: Thoemmes Continuum, 2005.

Thanzauva, K. *Theology of Community: Tribal Theology in the Making.* Aizawl: Mizo Theological Conference, 1997.

The Green Bible, NRSV. New York: HarperCollins Publishers, 2008.

Tisdale, Leonora Tubbs. *Preaching as Local Theology and Folk Art.* Minneapolis: Fortress Press, 1997.

Trainor, Michael. "Celebrating Diversity: The Hymn to Christ in a letter from Ancient Colossae (Col. 1:15-20)," *Biodiversity and Ecology as Interdisciplinary Challenge.* Ed., Denis Edwards and M. Worthing. Adelaide: ATF, 2004.

Trivedi, R.R. and Gurdeep Raj, eds. *Environmental Ecology.* New Delhi: Akashdeep Publishing House, 1992.

Walker-Jones, Arthur. *The Green Psalter: Resources for an Ecological Spirituality.* Minneapolis: Fortress Press, 2009.

Wallace, Mark I. *Fragments of the Spirit: Nature, Violence and The Renewal of Creation*. Harrisburg: Trinity Press International, 2002.

Ware, Kallistos. "A Note on Theology in the Christian East: The Eighteenth to Twentieth Centuries." *A History of Christian Doctrine.* Ed., Hubert Cunliffe-Jones and Benjamin Drewery. Edinburgh: T&T Clark Ltd., 1978.

____________. "Christian Theology in the East 600-1453." *A History of Christian Doctrine.* Ed., Hubert Cunliffe-Jones and Benjamin Drewery .Edinburgh: T&T Clark Ltd., 1978.

Wilkinson, Loren et. at., *Earth Keeping: Christian Stewardship of Natural Resources.* Grand Rapids: William B. Eerdmans Publishing Company, 1980.

Willimon, William H. and Richard Lischer, eds. *Concise Encyclopedia of Preaching*. Louisville: Westminster John Knox Press, 1995.

Wilson, Paul Scott. *Preaching and Homiletical Theory*. Missouri: Chalice Press, 2004.

Wilson, Paul Scott et. al. *The New Interpreter's Handbook of Preaching*. Nashville: Abingdon Press, 2008.

Wright Nancy G. and Donald Kill. *Ecological Healing: A Christian Vision*. Maryknoll: Orbis Books, 1993.

Wood, A. Skevington. "Awakening." *A Lion Handbook: The History of Christianity*. et. al.,Tim Dowley. England: Lion Publishing, 1977.

Young, Richard A. *Healing the Earth: A Theocentric Perspective on Environmental Problems and their Solutions*. Nashville: Broadman & Holman Publishers, 1994.

Zachariah, George. *Gospel in a Groaning World: Climate Injustice and Public Witness*.Tiruvalla: Christian Sahitya Samithi & NCCI, 2012.

Journals

Gregersen, Niels Henrik. "The Cross of Christ in an Evolutionary World." *Dialogue: A Journal of Theology*, 40/3 (2001): 203-205.

Rossi, V. "Christian Ecology is Cosmic Christology." *Epiphany*, 8 (1988): 53-55

Stephen, Alfred. "Preaching Ecology: Methodological Considerations." *Arasaradi Journal of Theological Reflection*. XXIV/1 & 2 (January – December, 2011): 89-93.

Commentaty

Vaughan, Curtis. "Colossians." *The Expositor's Bible Commentary*. Vol. 11. Frank E. Gaebelein et. al. Grand Rapids: Zondervan Publishing House, 1978. 179-185.

Newspapers

The Hindu (Madurai), November 13, 2014.

The Hindu (Madurai), April 7, 2015.

Online Resources

"About Global Hunger." http://www.bread.org›About Hunger. (November 13, 2015).

"Air Pollution." http://www.en.wikipedia.org/wiki/Pollution. (November 16, 2015).

"Birth *and Death Rates.*" http:/www.ecology.com/birth-death-rates/ (November 13, 2015)

"Current global food production trajectory won't meet 2050 needs." *http://*www.sciencedaily.com/releases/2013/06/130619195135.htm (November 13, 2015).

"Deforestation," http://www.livescience.com/27692-deforestation.html. (November 18, 2015).

"Deforestation," http://www.en.wikipedia.org/wiki/Deforestation. (November 18, 2015).

"Deforestation Statistics." http://www.worldpreservationfoundation.org/blog/news/deforestation-statistics. (November 18, 2015).

"Pollution of the Ganges." http://www.en.wikipedia.org/wiki/Pollution_of_the_Ganges. (November 16, 2015)

"Pollution." http://www.en.wikipedia.org/wiki/Pollution (November 16, 2015).

"World Population." http://www.en.wikipedia.org/wiki/Population_growth (November 16, 2015).

Bordeianu, Radu. "Maximus And Ecology: The Relevance of Maximus the Confessor's Theology of Creation for the Present Ecological Crisis." http://www.duq.edu/documents/theology/_pdf/faculty.../art-mordeianu-max.pd. (December 05, 2015).

Hayes, Randy. "The Root Causes of Social and Ecological Crisis." http://www.ecowatch.com/2011/11/.../the-root-causes-of-social-and-ecological-crisis. (December 09, 2015).

Heat wave kills more than 1,100 in India – CNN.com," http://www.cnn.com/2015/05/25/asia/india-heatwave-deaths/ (November 20, 2015).

http://www.newworldencyclopedia.org/entry/Theodicy. (December 06, 2015)

Shah Anup. "Today, around 21,000 Children Died Around the World," http://www.globalissues.org›Issues›Articles (November 16, 2015).

Shah, Anup. "Environmental Issues." http://www.globalissues.org/issue/168/environmental-issues. (November 16, 2015).

US Climate Change Science Program, The Effects of Climate Change on Agriculture, Land Resources, Water Resources, and Biodiversity, http://www.climatescience.gov/Library/sap/sap4-3/public-review-draft/sap4-3prd-all.pdf. (November 7, 2015).

"Water Pollution." http://www.en.wikipedia.org/wiki/Pollution. (November 16, 2015).

Water Encyclopaedia, "Global Warming ad Glaciers." http://www.waterencyclopedia.com/Ge-Hy/Global-Warming-and-Glaciers.html#ixzz3lKaYytxB. (November 18, 2015).

White, Jr., Lynn. "The Historical Roots of Our Ecological Crisis." http://www.siena.edu/ellard/historical_roots_of_our_ecologic.htm. (November 13, 2015).